PRAISE FOR DYLAN HOWARD AND COLIN McLAREN AND *DIANA: CASE SOLVED*

"Dylan Howard is the rare combination of cutting-edge journalist, true crime commentator and relentless investigator. Howard passionately brings comprehensive and groundbreaking analysis to the most compelling mysteries of our time."

—*Dr. Phil McGraw, host of TV's #1 daytime talk show,* Dr. Phil

"Princess Diana's untimely death was one that brought great sadness to the world. I lived through her life, and the reporting on her tragic death leaving behind two young sons, which was absolutely heartbreaking. Reading *Diana: Case Solved* has been riveting. There is so much in this book that I never knew before about Diana the woman, the mother, and the princess. Each page literally introduced me to something new that I was hearing and reading for the first time. I could not put this book down. A must read for anyone who wants to learn more about the icon Princess Diana was, and is, to so many around the world."

— *Sean Hannity, radio host, news commentator, and the most-watched television host in cable news*

"Dylan Howard is one of the finest journalists writing today. His depth and breadth of experience are second to none; he follows every intricate angle of a story and exposes the truth. As a former detective, I know firsthand the skills that make an exceptional investigator, and Dylan has them in spades."

—*Bo Dietl, former NYPD homicide detective with over 1,400 felony arrests*

"A tabloid prodigy."

—*Jeffrey Toobin, CNN and* The New Yorker

"I first met Diana at Balmoral Castle, Scotland, in August 1980 during my service with Her Majesty The Queen. In 1987, I became Diana's butler and for the next ten years was considered to be her closest confidant. She famously called me her 'rock' and 'the only man she ever trusted.' I was delighted to participate in this book and its companion podcast, as I believe that history should be told by those who witnessed it."

—*Paul Burrell, Diana's former butler and friend*

"The king of Hollywood scoops."

—Adweek

"When Dylan Howard focuses his attention to investigating a case, you can be sure he will uncover sensational new information that we, as readers, viewers or listeners, will find astonishing. Enlighten yourself with his findings about what *really* happened to Princess Diana on that fateful night."

—*Dr. Drew Pinsky*

"The go-to guy for authoritative showbiz news and analysis on cable and over-the air television."

— *Los Angeles Press Club*

DIANA:
CASE SOLVED

DIANA: CASE SOLVED

The Definitive Account That Proves What Really Happened

DYLAN HOWARD & COLIN McLAREN

Skyhorse Publishing

Skyhorse Publishing books may be purchased in bulk at special discounts for sales promotion, corporate gifts, fund-raising, or educational purposes. Special editions can also be created to specifications. For details, contact the Special Sales Department, Skyhorse Publishing, 307 West 36th Street, 11th Floor, New York, NY 10018 or info@skyhorsepublishing.com.

Skyhorse® and Skyhorse Publishing® are registered trademarks of Skyhorse Publishing, Inc.®, a Delaware corporation.

Visit our website at www.skyhorsepublishing.com.

10 9 8 7 6 5 4 3 2 1

Library of Congress Cataloging-in-Publication Data is available on file.

Cover design by 5mediadesign
Cover photo credit: Getty Images

ISBN: 978-1-5107-5503-1

Printed in the United States of America

DEDICATION

To the tireless investigative reporting team of outstanding men and women who helped with Herculean deeds of journalism and research. James Robertson, Aaron Tinney, Andy Tillett, Patricia Gonzalez, Tom Freestone, Billie Spear, and Doug Montero—you're all the best in the business.

Special acknowledgment goes to Ken. E. More, my writing partner, and a man who should be frustrated with this author, but never is (at least, that's what he leads me to believe).

Finally, to those, like Colin McLaren, who believe the truth is out there and still worth searching for, and that the role of journalists is akin to that of the detective in shining a light on the darkest of crimes or the worst written pages of history.

—Dylan Howard

AUTHORS' NOTE

Diana, Princess of Wales.

She was a beauty, icon, mother to the future King of England, and the world's most photographed woman, tragically killed in a car crash on the night of August 31, 1997, speeding through Paris, pursued by a pack of paparazzi. Twenty-two years later, the events surrounding the crash are still shrouded in questions and conspiracy theories abound.

On that fateful Parisian night, at the time, both of these authors were living in the state of Victoria, Australia: Colin, then forty-two, was a police detective sergeant and task force team leader having worked on many of Australia's worst murders. For three years he went undercover and decimated the Calabrian Mafia in the biggest covert sting in Australian history. His work would take him on to an independent investigation into the assassination of the thirty-fifth president of the United States, John F. Kennedy, and yield startling results.

Dylan, back in 1997, then a tender fifteen-year-old, having grown up as an aspiring journalist, was transfixed at the constant media coverage of Diana and the British royals. He would go on to work in Hollywood as one of the most feared journalists in town, having brought down the careers of Mel Gibson, Charlie Sheen, Hulk Hogan, and Paula Deen via explosive stories of misdeeds. Dylan's sense for scandal and the truth saw him rise to become the undisputed most powerful gossip editor in the world—and second-in-command to David J. Pecker, chairman and chief executive officer at publishing powerhouse American Media Inc. As one of the most powerful gossip editors in the world, overseeing a vast network of consumer driven magazines, including *Us Weekly*, *OK!*, *Star*, *In Touch*, *Life & Style*, *Closer*, *The National Enquirer* and its U.K. edition, *Globe*, the *National Examiner*, and RadarOnline.com

Unbeknownst to each other at the time, these two authors would meet for the first time in 2019—during France's worst heat wave ever—to collaborate on *Diana: Case Closed*. We were two Australian exports to the wider world with one common goal in mind: to combine our years of experience reviewing the evidence in the case of Diana's death and, together, smash wide open the conspiracy of silence behind what really happened inside that Parisian tunnel.

The result is *Diana: Case Solved*—a groundbreaking investigation and conclusion into one of the century's most gripping conspiracies.

Together, after traveling to Paris a combined five times, we bring to an end a mystery that has long baffled the world. To create this unflinching account, we have assembled a global team of investigators—handpicked, high-profile, and utterly meticulous men and women (including retired crime-scene detectives, forensic pathologists, and royal insiders)—to dissect evidence, alibis, and motives; track down new witnesses; hear Diana's own voice on secret, long-lost recordings; and interview key players and those who knew the *real* Diana best.

At the end of this remarkable project, we arrive at some startling new conclusions into the tragic end of the woman they called "the people's princess."

***

From her first introduction to public life as the painfully shy teenage fiancée of the heir to the British throne, Prince Charles, through a desperately unhappy marriage, struggles with bulimia, depression, suicide attempts, and multiple affairs, to finally blossoming into one of the world's most beautiful and influential women, Diana, Princess of Wales, spent her entire adult life under the media spotlight.

Some believe it was precisely this unprecedented global obsession with Diana's every move that resulted in her death, as the Mercedes S280 in which she was a passenger sped through the Paris streets pursued by a pack of paparazzi desperate for a multimillion-dollar snap of her and (supposed) lover Dodi. Then their car spun fatally out of control, slamming into a tunnel alongside the Seine River.

But many others believe her death was not an accident.

During the course of our real-time investigation, we have meticulously untangled the strange circumstances and conflicting theories surrounding her death—from the wildest conspiracies concerning an eerie pact between senior royals, security services, and global arms dealers, to the official line that chauffeur Henri Paul was a drunk who was irresponsibly speeding. We interviewed new witnesses who saw the crash and its immediate aftermath . . . and, crucially, unearth the one man who knows for sure what happened—and who, for twenty-two years, has been ordered to remain silent. He was the keeper of the world's biggest secret of them all.

In *Diana: Case Solved*, we'll conduct our own crime-scene analysis, applying principles and procedures the French ignored, laying out the evidence the official inquiry missed. We will reveal photographs showing two telling, parallel skid marks at the tunnel entrance adjacent to a merge lane for slower-moving traffic wanting to merge onto the faster Cours Albert roadway. How were they caused? And by whom? And why didn't the French cops see them?

We will prove the Mercedes S280 sedan carrying the world's most famous woman could have *only* become airborne after hitting a second car and leaving the road surface—and staying airborne for a distance of 85 feet.

What you are about to read is the eye-opening reality of a secretive, buttoned-up, ultra-elite, and intimidating world of law enforcement—a world with literally its own rules—where protecting the good name of a nation takes precedence over all . . . even a beloved princess.

We will also provide the shocking details of how—from the very start—Diana didn't fit into the Windsors' way of doing things, how she was mocked, scorned and resented by her in-laws, and how even her own husband came to consider her little more than an irritation.

We will lay bare the alarming depths to which Diana was driven by her treatment at the hands of senior royals and the stark, repeated betrayals of her husband. And we'll discover how she learned to fight back.

Diana: Case Solved will uncover in unprecedented detail just how convenient Diana's death was to the establishment. We will learn of the secret diaries and recordings she made, logging the Windsors' most intimate secrets and hidden scandals as a desperate kind of insurance policy.

We will uncover how the royals were not the only powerful enemies Diana made; her pioneering campaigns against AIDS and land mines drew admiration from the public, but enmity from powerful institutions like the international arms industry, the British and American governments, MI6, and the CIA.

This is not simply a retelling of recorded history and a rehashing of existing conspiracy theories.

Through our dogged investigative reporting, plus insight and analysis from experts and insiders, *Diana: Case Solved* will, for the first time, paint a complete picture of why the most famous woman in the world came to meet her tragic end . . . and how it *really* happened.

Dylan Howard & Colin McLaren

"This particular phase in my life is the most dangerous. My husband is planning 'an accident' in my car, brake failure and serious head injury in order to make the path clear for him to marry."

Letter written by Diana, late 1996

"Voilà, c'est pour ça je les laisse penser ce qu'ils veulent."
("That's why I let them think what they want.")

Le Van Thanh,
driver of the mysterious white Fiat Uno, summer 2019

CHAPTER ONE

Had she lived, Princess Diana would have toasted her fifty-eighth birthday on July 1, 2019. If she hadn't succumbed to the catastrophic internal injuries suffered in her 1997 crash, the world's most photographed woman would have hosted a glamorous party to celebrate heading toward her big 6-0.

Flute of champagne in hand and wearing her Hermès 24, Faubourg perfume, she'd have been clad in a gown designed to cover up the pink scar that ribboned down her chest—a raised pink remnant of having her chest cracked open by surgeons so her heart could be massaged back to life.

She would have laughed with A-list guests, bonded with her sons' wives, Kate and Meghan, and used the latest iPhone to video her four grandkids playing.

It's the kind of alternative reality that the millions who adored and idolized Diana can't help but dwell on—twenty-two years after she died, literally broken-hearted, on a bloody surgical table at the Pitié-Salpêtrière Hospital. A rip in the left pulmonary vein of Diana's heart was the fatal injury that ended her short and tormented life, leaving her declared dead by exhausted medics at 4 a.m. on August 31, 1997.

She survived her black Mercedes S280, registration 688 LTV 75, hurtling into the thirteenth pillar of Paris's Pont de l'Alma tunnel at a devastating 121 mph.

But she suffered two heart attacks and, on the way to the hospital, was in such distress that she yanked out drips pumping drugs eighty times more powerful than morphine into her veins while mumbling indecipherable last words.

***

Many of the millions who wish "England's rose" was still alive have spent decades haunted by the unsettling mysteries that shroud her life and death.

For many, there is the feeling that there must be something more to the events of that night. That the official story cannot truly be the whole story, and what happened to Diana has the feeling of something deeper and more harrowing.

In this unprecedented investigation, and through groundbreaking forensic testimony, we confirm that these feelings are indeed correct—so correct that the findings of *Diana: Case Solved* will renew calls for a fresh inquiry into the car crash that left three people dead and the entire world reeling.

More specifically, we expose an almost unbelievable list of interconnected players who, in their own ways, had a hand in Diana's demise. And we show that the truly remarkable thing about late August 1997 was that Diana survived until that date in the first place. Because if many in the circles of power had had their way, she would have been dead long before that.

To help establish the real story of August 30 and 31, 1997, I partnered with Colin McLaren, famed for his work on the assassination of John F. Kennedy (disproving Lee Harvey Oswald's "lone-gunman" involvement) and facing down the underbelly of Australian crime and the Mafia.

Most recently, I had presented a case in *Fatal Voyage: The Mysterious Death of Natalie Wood*—a podcast series that broke new ground on one of Hollywood's most enduring murder mysteries, one involving showbiz icons Robert Wagner and Christopher Walken. All was not as police made you believe. I was humbled that Colin, with his decades of law enforcement experience, found my investigation into how Natalie, the A-list Hollywood actress, vanished from a yacht following a brutal argument on November 29, 1981, so compelling that he wanted to join me on another crusade.

***

When Diana was pronounced dead at 4 a.m. on August 31, 1997, Colin began investigating the case and undertook his own independent investigations, uncovering startling new facts on the streets of Paris where Diana met her fate.

Luckily for us, we still live in a world where a determined, honest investigator—willing to go to places where others fear to venture and to ask the questions others won't—has the ability to make the kind of powerful, meaningful discoveries that finally shed light on the mysterious dark places that have captivated the world for years. That is exactly what we did, traveling to Paris and London in June 2019, our last trip to the City of Light, to finalize research on *Diana: Case Solved*.

As we go chapter by chapter, you'll read the dual narratives about what we established and how we found it, particularly in Colin's own inimitable voice.

Here, then, is the definitive inside story of Diana's death, life, and superhuman heartbreaks, told in her own words and by those who knew her most intimately. This book reveals the hidden aspects of Diana's life, from her first introduction to the world as a painfully shy nineteen-year-old—a character trait that was later overcome during her groundbreaking charity work that positively impacted the lives of some of the world's most vulnerable people—to the ill-fated royal slide into addiction. In the end, she found herself corrupted and twisted by those who walk the corridors of power.

What's more, *Diana: Case Solved* prints Diana's shocking final conversations that reveal her most personal thoughts at the end of her life . . . and what they reveal about the mystery of her fate.

Diana died convinced "the firm" was plotting to have her murdered.

Heartbreakingly, she also went to her death knowing her last love, Dodi, was cheating on her with an American model. She died with multiple actors, agencies, and even nations working against her. (Perhaps alone, perhaps not.)

Come along, then—if you dare—into a world of money, sex, and power, and see how one woman's elevation into the glamorous universe of royal, celebrity, and unimaginable wealth became a meat grinder that destroyed the young woman who was truly the darling of the world.

CHAPTER TWO

Prince Harry appeared to wipe away tears as he and his bride, the American-born *Suits* actress Meghan Markle, along with the six hundred guests packed into St. George's Chapel on the grounds of Windsor Castle on May 19, 2018, sang the last bars of "Guide Me, O Thou Great Redeemer."

The hymn was his mother's favorite, and thirty-three-year-old Harry chose to include it as part of the ceremony as a tribute to Diana, twenty-two years after it was sung at her funeral in Westminster Abbey in 1997. It was thought he cried at his wedding to Meghan purely because of the emotions stirred up by hearing the hymn again.

But we can—now, here—reveal he welled up because he was recalling his mother's warning to her sons' future brides to not be "eaten" by the British monarchy and their Mafia-like secret wealth streams and strict stranglehold over their members, according to a palace aide.

"Harry and William knew their mum died tortured by the treatment she received at the hands of the royal family, and the last thing Harry wants is for Meghan to endure the same thing," the source said.

Thirty-six years, nine months, and twenty days before Harry said "I do" to Meghan in an unconventionally nonroyal ceremony that would have made his mum proud, Lady Diana walked up the aisle of the ancient St. Paul's Cathedral in London and became Princess Diana. It had all the hallmarks of a fairy-tale wedding—but the problems were there almost from the start.

"Diana had no experience and was thrust into that world as a nineteen-year-old," remembered Ken Wharfe, the man who served as her Scotland Yard police protection officer.

Richard Kay was royal correspondent for the *Daily Mail* newspaper at that time—and gained a unique insight into the royal marriage.

"Diana, I think, was in love, madly in love with Charles," he said. He added:

> But for her, the scales fell from her eyes fairly quickly when she realized that he was very much set in his ways and he wasn't going to change.
>
> It was an unhappy marriage. They were ill-suited. They barely knew each other when they married. They'd only met on a dozen occasions before they got engaged. In the early days of their relationship, she had to call him, "Sir." I mean all these things seem utterly laughable, but we're only talking about twenty-five years or so ago.
>
> The other thing you got to remember, she had married a man who was twelve years older than herself who had vastly different interests. Diana was an extremely young woman when she got married. She never had the kind of normal relationships that young couples have before they marry.
>
> I feel there's sympathy on both sides. It's hard not to have sympathy for Prince Charles. He's married this beautiful young woman. He felt under huge pressure to marry her, not just from the public, but also from his own father. He made a terrible mistake. The real courageous thing he should have done was to have called it off. But he couldn't do that and he didn't do that and he's had to live with the consequences ever since.

Diana had found herself in a gilded cage. Her dashing prince had turned out to be a rather set-in-his-ways older man with whom she shared almost nothing in common. Worse, she was not only living with him, but with a whole palace full of similarly stuck-in-the-mud people, too.

Recalled Ken Warfe:

> She was unhappy, and a young woman unable to deal with the fact of being a princess, without any help from anybody within Buckingham

> Palace. There was no manual of how to be a princess, there were no training courses; she was thrust into this situation and literally had to get on with it.
>
> There must have been moments that must have been horrific for her. People had imagined that Buckingham Palace, Kensington Palace is alive with fire-eaters, jugglers, musicians, but it isn't.
>
> It's a very lonely place . . . it's a pretty lonely existence and I'm sure there's a lot went through Diana's mind that said, "What am I going to do? What's happening to me? Where am I going to go? Where will I end up?"
>
> But one thing you are giving up is actually your freedom, your right to do what you want when you want, but that's the price you pay—or they pay—for being royal.

To millions, Diana was living a dream-come-true life—but behind the palace walls, her loneliness was becoming all-consuming. Half the royal family, it seemed, resented her, and the other half actively disliked her.

In November 1981, it was announced that Diana was pregnant. Less than a year after she married Charles, she bore him a son, Prince William. Two years after that, she gave birth again, to Prince Harry. Charles had done his duty; the succession was assured. Now that Diana had provided the so-called "heir and a spare," her usefulness was effectively over. What followed were to be the darkest days of Diana's life.

Noted Richard Kay, "She did turn to psychics and alternative healers. They in a way sort of filled the void, vacuum, of her empty social life. She didn't have that many friends and the people who helped her deal with the stresses and strains in her life. It's kind of sad really, when you think this beautiful young woman who was adored by the world should have no real close friends. It told you a lot about her and it told you a lot about her situation."

In despair, Diana turned her unhappiness on herself: she developed eating disorders, starving herself, forcing herself to throw up . . . and, in one incident, even endangering the life of her then-unborn baby.

So, what might have been? How would the royal family—and, indeed, the world—have been different if Diana had been able to be physically present and unburdened of the crown at the weddings of her sons? What updated advice might she have given their brides-to-be?

We will never know the answers to these questions with any precision. We are forced to conjecture. Yet, in a way, the circumstances of Diana's death speak volumes. Perhaps they speak more loudly than we think.

To understand what might have happened at Diana's end, we have to go back to the beginning of the mystery for most people. We have to go back to the news of the horrible accident itself that snuffed out the lives of three people.

There is no better guide to take us than Detective McLaren, whose experience with the case is unmatched—at least by any investigator who has talked to the press honestly and openly.

Here, Colin begins by taking us intimately close to his very first encounter with the mystery of the princess and her passing. The horrible emotions Colin felt upon learning of Diana's death are, for many of us, all too relatable. Yet did Colin's arch-investigator's eye see things that the rest of us did not see—or could not bring ourselves to see?

***

DETECTIVE'S NOTEBOOK

DATELINE: Sunday, August 31, 1997, Melbourne, Australia

The rain spat on the tin roof of my partially converted warehouse abode as I languished alone in bed. The night before and far too many boutique beers had me feeling foggier than a Scottish moor, and my bedraggled body had aches in places I didn't think possible. A combination of renovation and celebration had me reeling. Peeping my head over the duvet, I assessed the waiting morning, the last of what had been a bleak winter in Melbourne, Australia. What little daylight crept through the sheet I'd tacked over the window offered nothing to inspire, so I rolled over for another five minutes.

I was under the weather after a late function the previous night with work colleagues, for I was a detective with the fifteen-thousand-strong Victoria police department. I'd lived a life of detectives and squads, major crimes, kidnappings, drug traffickers, undercover work, violence, and way too many homicides. Last night had been a pat on the back with fifty handshakes and too many investigators recalling crime scenes in between mouthfuls of tapas.

The trip down memory lane had transported me back to my early days, cutting my teeth on Melbourne's underworld and embracing the camaraderie, as cops do. I'd had a good career, worked some of the country's worst crimes, and locked away my fair share of rabble. It was what I knew, what I did—and I'd been good at it, so they said, between beers: investigating and analyzing, unraveling the charcoal mysteries of wrongdoings, working my way up the promotional ladder by hard slog. Finally, I'd been handpicked to head up a national probe into the Mafia and the bombing of the National Crime Authority, a defiant act by the Mafia. By now I stood proud of the number of times I had served as the team leader of task forces, a tally that was greater than that of any detective nationwide.

I mustered my strength, propped myself up on a mountain of pillows, and surveyed the room. Stacked up, as if waiting my rising, were lengths of timber, plasterboard, trestles, piles of glass bricks, and kilometers of electrical flex conduits. So, I padded to the bathroom, suffered a bracing shower, and donned my overalls. After working up a sweat hammering the last of the main structural items into place, I parked myself on an upturned milk crate and flicked the remote control to my television.

Much-liked morning television anchorman Jim Waley flashed to the forefront looking earnest and reading an announcement. News footage followed of an underpass and a twisted Mercedes-Benz being hoisted onto a flatbed tow truck. An image of Princess Diana was superimposed. I watched, bemused, as the flatbed tow truck bounced along cobblestone streets.

I moved closer to the screen, flicked the remote volume up, and listened openmouthed to the words that accompanied the images. A tragedy of extraordinary proportions, Jim announced, had just transpired in the other hemisphere. I focused on the television images and began to recognize telltale signs of one of the world's most important diplomatic cities. The flatbed tow truck kept bouncing along, as the Mercedes-Benz it carried disappeared into the French darkness.

Lady Diana Spencer had been holidaying in Paris, I recalled, trying to make the link. Recent paparazzi snaps of her in a fetching swimsuit had been splashed all over the weekly women's magazines. Like many others, I admired Diana immensely. And as a man, I thought she was a doll, and a champion of causes close to my own heart. I paced, unsettled, as the studio backdrop reappeared and the announcer continued. Two of her male companions in the twisted and mangled Mercedes wreckage were dead; a third, a mess. Diana, the only female, had been pulled out barely alive and was now fighting desperately for her life.

Somehow my hangover didn't seem all that important anymore.

My brain ticked over, struggling to process what I had seen. I made myself a strong macchiato as I surfed other stations for bulletins but found nothing new. I carried my small bedroom television into the main room to join its larger cousin. With both television sets tuned to different channels, I picked up my bag of nails and attempted to refocus on the tasks at hand. But any further work done was lackadaisical at best; for the most part I couldn't take my eyes off what the cameras were showing.

Sometime that afternoon came the news that Princess Diana had lost her fight. It was then that a seed was sown in my mind, as the television spent time showing reflective footage of her tumultuous life. As a parent, I shuddered at the dreadful shock this would deliver to her two young sons. As a detective, I started to wonder, to think.

I stayed up for the rest of the night watching the telecast, trying to make sense of the now-death of Princess Diana. Images of a nondescript support pillar in a nondescript tunnel on the Place de l'Alma where the Mercedes had come to rest were being televised from every conceivable angle. Television reporters were camped on the asphalt nearby theorizing everything from a multiple-car collision to a possible terrorist attack; even the sounds of shots were debated. This crime scene was busier than a discounted retail sale and I feared that it was rapidly falling into a state of virtual ruination. The French gendarmes were treating it as they would have any other traffic accident—nothing more, nothing less. No sooner had rescue workers removed the dead and injured than street sweepers got busy with their hunched backs and piled up vital clues, only to dispatch them to the municipal dump. Within hours the thoroughfare was back to being a major carriageway with thousands of commuters an hour driving over the surface, driving over evidence. I wondered what was going through the minds of the officers who attended the scene to allow such contamination. Who was in charge? Who made the decision to clear the debris? Broom-swinging workers and emergency service trucks don't just arrive at 4 a.m. I shook my head, time and again.

One thing I knew was that a crime scene should be treated like a new baby, with great care, a fine touch, and meticulous concentration. At the Victoria police department's detective training school, I lectured trainee detectives on how to approach a crime scene, how to take charge, and how to work through the clues. There are tried-and-true procedures to follow, principles to be applied when working a scene; there rarely is a second chance. Any detective worth his salt knows the perils of trying to garner conclusions from a scene that's been tampered with, stepped on, swept away, lost, or replaced. I'd taken pride in teaching what to do and what not to do at a crime scene, and the French were giving a global show-and-tell of how to fuck it up. Frustrated, I switched off both televisions, carried the smaller back to the bedroom, and turned in. I pulled the bedcovers up over my head to counter the horror I had watched and attempted a few hours' sleep.

Next morning I made a conscious decision to absent myself from the miseries of the world. But inherent curiosity won over; I gave in and turned on the box. A silent vigil of mourners stood where only twenty-four hours ago there had been a cacophony of noisy media, cameras, and emergency crews. Gardens of bouquets bloomed around the support pillar, forever to be known as number thirteen, only to be scattered by fast-moving passing cars. Above this exact spot, on the overhead roadway atop the tunnel, a shrine was set up by teary pilgrims who had come from far and near to mourn a dead Lady. On the news, crosscuts to the princess's home in London showed tearful citizens gently laying small bunches of handpicked roses among large floral wreaths, colorful notes, and cards of sorrow and despair. Night in both cities failed to succumb to darkness, bathed as they were in a glow of candles honoring one of the world's brightest lights now extinguished. I couldn't help but be impressed by such compassion, sadness, decency.

Over subsequent days I kept waiting for the gendarmes to get down to the business of investigating. But as each successive day came and went with the crime scene still unvisited by the investigating magistrate, the chances of finding any conclusive answers continued to diminish exponentially with the number of vehicles that passed through the tunnel. No one seemed to search for answers to this tragedy. The French seemed to just ignore it. And with the major exhibit, the crippled Mercedes, having been jolted a distance of twenty kilometers through the streets of Paris without a thought for what might have dislodged along its path, I speculated on whether anything could still be found intact, if someone qualified and forensically experienced were to go looking.

I mused on this idea and then picked up the phone and began to dial my travel agent to cost an airfare to Paris. With the best deal available spelt out and my hand reaching for my Visa card, I stopped short and took stock of what I was contemplating. Somehow I had found myself in the process of planning a trip to France. I placed my ticket on hold and put the phone down. I paced the walls of my apartment checking my sanity, wondering if I was a fool or just a frustrated detective in need of one more hit, one more crime scene. I resolved to give it a couple of days and, if nothing improved, if the French detectives didn't turn out with their measuring tapes, their cameras, and their notebooks, then I would.

Each morning I would drive to the largest newsdealer in town, McGills Newsagency, and purchase a copy of every international paper they had for sale. I was lucky; they carried a fine range of respectable press, including the *London Times*, *Telegraph*, and the *New York Times,* among others. They were journals I could rely on for the accuracy of their content.

By midweek I had amassed a small library of newspapers that I had laid out on the floor of my lounge room. Trestles had been dismantled and pushed aside to gain more floor space and plasterboard scraps had become tables. My entire day was devoted to poring over the latest copy, making notes, studying the printed image, and channel surfing the news services. The world's foremost correspondents kept feeding me tidbits, acting as my briefing paper, keeping me abreast of the latest developments. I had put my head fat in the middle of this riddle and, truth be told, I was enjoying every minute. I ached for more.

Having gotten a good handle on the collision and deaths, I started to ponder what had actually occurred. At the least, it was a most serious road accident; at worst, a multiple homicide. On every level this inquiry screamed to be approached with the utmost professionalism. With a proliferation of consulates and embassies, one would expect Paris to boast a police force poised to deal promptly and proficiently with a situation resulting in misfortune to a visiting dignitary, government head, or official guest. The world was watching, more intently than for any other televised event in history. This level of global scrutiny should have had a police department rallying, pulling out all stops to showcase their detecting skills. My initial outrage at the inaction of the French constabulary was mellowing into an unsettled reality.

I scanned my sea of newspapers, fine-tuning my mind's eye. Stepping, metaphorically speaking, back into the tunnel, I revisited pillar thirteen as it would have appeared that night. I put myself in the shoes of the investigators on site to consider what they confronted. The first in attendance at the crash would have been uniformed officers whose principal duty was to render assistance to the injured and call for ambulances. The magnitude of this particular incident would certainly have directed a second call to police headquarters, requesting the attendance of more cops and investigators. As in any major city in the world, a team of skilled detectives, well-versed in issues of diplomacy and protocol, would have been working late shift. It goes without saying that when these officers reached the entrance to the tunnel they would have sensed a challenge. In those initial few seconds, when you approach something really dire, you take a deep breath. You breathe it in and let it out as you walk forward to take charge.

A large crowd had already gathered, and the first police at the scene confirmed two persons were dead and two others gravely injured. Dauntingly, one of the injured occupants had been identified as the princess of Wales, and one of her dead companions was Dodi, the only son of Egyptian billionaire Mohamed Al-Fayed, the owner of Harrods of London and the Ritz-Carlton Hotel in Paris.

Flashbulbs dazzled as half a dozen paparazzi frantically snapped shutter triggers while standing over still trapped victims. Verbal and physical confrontations had erupted with onlookers as photographers jostling for vantage positions, greedily satisfying their need for sensation, hampered paramedics attempting to free the injured. Motorcycles and cars parked haphazardly nearby made it clear that the paparazzi had been close by when the collision occurred. And at the center of the melee the tortured wreck of a Mercedes-Benz sat, the damage to the crashed vehicle so extensive that every panel including the roof was misshapen.

Even seasoned minds would have been racing as they attempted to get a handle on this scene. Distancing themselves from the surrounding mayhem would be the only way for investigators to consider an approach. Although the incident bore all the initial hallmarks of a high-speed accident, professional objectivity needed to kick in, questions needed to be posed.

What caused this tragedy?

Were other vehicles involved?

Was there negligence or other factors?

Could it have been foul play?

Could mechanical interference be a contributor, or criminal interference? Could this be murder?"

The word "murder" triggered a recollection. I snapped out of my fantasy and began hunting through a pile of newspapers that I had stacked in the laundry to await my paintbrushes.

Toward the bottom of the pile and dated several days before the crash, a feature article wrote that the French police were monitoring threats made by a Turkish terrorist group on Paris. I brought the paper out to join those archived on the floor and paged through my work address book. Following a few well-placed phone calls to a contact in the department of foreign affairs, I was armed with the knowledge that all consulates and diplomats had been on high alert.

Could this then have been an act of terrorism? Had the Turkish group selected the princess of Wales as their target?

I couldn't ignore this proposition, yet the French had seemed to be doing just that. I picked up a well-thumbed newspaper and thumbed again. Anxious to be of help, some witnesses had offered comments of hearing "a noise like a gunshot," others "an explosion" and "a loud bang." Alarm bells began ringing in my head.

These salient points drove it home to me; the tunnel and the Mercedes-Benz should have been treated as a crime scene. Not just another accident scene.

Surely the anti-terrorism squads should have been called in to inspect the scene and undertake preliminary investigations to confirm or eliminate this type of involvement?

Too many questions were being left unanswered. Too many possibilities were being swept aside, being allowed to ebb and fade with the passage of time. I was no longer unsettled, I was worried—and I wasn't alone in my worry for long.

Hundreds of millions of the world's perplexed citizens were finding a collective voice in the media. People everywhere were beginning to ask why such scant attention was being paid to the suspicious death of the world's queen of hearts. As far as I was concerned, the inaction of the cumbersome French magistrate system and its limp attendance at the crime scene was indefensible. Having suffered days of frustration, watching the slapdash investigation, I paid for my airfare, put together a travel bag with tapes, notebooks, pens, and a camera, and headed for the airport. I was booked on an Air France flight, and I only hoped that the French pilots would get their job right. I was back on duty.

Five days after the accident, I sat high above the clouds wedged between a pair of restless teenage backpackers, reading an in-flight magazine. And on the ground in Paris, for the first time, a team of investigating magistrates had finally closed off the traffic along the approach road to Tunnel Two. Like me, they were about to observe what remained of a scene that troubled the world. Inspecting the section of roadway was an eleven-member team, a mix of detectives, uniforms, and the overseeing magistrate. They strolled through the tunnel, hands in pockets, heads cocked and looking very haute couture as photographers lapped up the opportunity to capture the performance on film. The tour, in which not one notebook, pen, or camera was visible, lasted a mere thirty minutes. Then they were gone and the appetites of the media temporarily sated.

The conclusions drawn from the inspection, if indeed there were any given the nature of the very public parade, were not broadcast. The French judicial system directly forbids investigative personnel from making statements to the press. I watched the news footage on the small screen in front of me and observed the actions of one of the team who may have been a forensic officer. He singled out a speck or two of debris that had lodged in the walls, fortuitously missing the cleaners' brooms, and he appeared to take a sample for analysis. Glancing at the reactions of my fellow passengers, hearing their comments and high praise that "the police were on to it and would now sort it all out." I could only shake my head. While the public relations department of the French system appeared to have scored a win, I wondered how many other detectives across the globe were also smarting at the arrogance of such a flash visit to such an important scene.

My relief at being finally free of an aircraft that allowed not only cigarette smoking but also the pungent coils of cigar fumes to waft through the cabin was almost palpable. I stepped from the avant-garde, *Barbarella*-looking Charles de Gaulle airport and hailed a ratty old Renault cab, pleased to drop my luggage into its tiny trunk. Settling into the rear seat, I watched the familiar architecture flash by and took in the fresh aroma of the driver's Gauloises. I rolled down my window and pondered my days ahead.

On each of my previous visits showers had greeted me, so a blue sky was a rarity. I was relieved to hear, in my driver's heavily accented English, that there had been no rain for the past couple of weeks, so like the family hound, I put my head out of the window and sniffed my solace in the moisture-free weather. It was still summer. While I'd be playing catch-up in the area of crime-scene management, the last thing I needed was for any remaining evidence to be washed away by a downpour. So far, so good, I thought.

My driver pushed on through the streams of early morning motorists toward the eighth arrondissement. We were headed for my favorite part of the old town, the Montmartre. I had a hankering to see the tunnel at the Place de l'Alma as soon as I had checked into my hotel, so when we came to a virtual standstill in the peak hour traffic, I suggested that my driver head back that way first. In classic cabbie manner, his reaction to the change of direction was to hit the horn a few times, force his way into a U-turn, swerve expertly across the flow of traffic, and resume a nonchalant cruising speed, ignoring the wild gesticulations of other motorists. Moments later we came to a halt before what appeared to be a standing wake: hundreds of silent people, heads bowed. It was 9 a.m., and already a crowd of internationals stood staring.

The cab rumbled to life again and we cruised on past into the tunnel itself, where my driver slowed at pillar thirteen, draped in dead flowers. We stopped, to the annoyance of the commuting French. Literally invisible beneath the wilted wreaths, most of the rendered surface of the pillar was cracked—scars of the previous week.

On our way again and emerging at the far end of the tunnel, we came to rest on the side of the road. I stepped out and looked back at the overpass to the tunnel and the well-manicured rose garden along the approach. Not the types to lose themselves to overt flashes of grief, Parisians buzzed by, hurrying to work, faces straight ahead. The contrast between international grief and local hustle and bustle was as apparent as black and white, hot and cold. As I walked closer, the foreign faces that glanced up toward me said it all: heartache. The outpouring of respect was unforgettable. I could have been at Lourdes or the Wailing Wall instead of downtown Paris. I bowed my head also and stepped carefully around the floral tributes, then back to my taxi. It was time to find my hotel.

I don't think I've come to Paris and not stayed at the Hôtel Chopin. At 10 Boulevard Montmartre, it's tucked away at the very end of a magnificent eighteenth-century arcade on the edge of the ninth arrondissement. Boasting fifty rooms over four levels, it's only ten minutes' walk from the Paris Opera and the famed Galeries Lafayette and is surrounded by picturesque boutiques selling chocolates, handmade toys, cinema memorabilia, and ladies' haute couture. Laying down my Visa card on the reservations counter, I took in the ambience of the foyer. The decor was the very image of the 1920s with its heavy influence of patterned fabrics and rickety furniture. I turned back to Charles, the manager of what would be my home for the next couple of weeks. The cheery fellow, pleased by the lengthy booking, made sure I had one of his largest and brightest two-star rooms, and with a view of a dozen downpipes. I climbed the stairs, dropped my bags, pulled open the heavy brocade drapes and unpacked my world in budget heaven. My room had a comfortable queen-sized bed, a television set with a mess of channels, a direct-dial telephone, and a large desk waiting to be filled. Apart from my trusty traveling shoulder bag, I also carried a mind that wouldn't rest. As comfy as my room was, I couldn't wait to head back to the Pont de l'Alma, so I packed a small kit and hightailed it back to the scene.

As I walked through the streets, I mulled over my approach. Arriving in early September, there were two major disadvantages to be overcome: firstly, the lack of resources; and secondly, the inevitable contamination of the scene. In investigative terms, I was horribly underdressed for the occasion. With insufficient equipment, no backup, no authority, and less command of the French language than a four-year-old child, I'd be running on bluff. I feared that virtually all the evidence would have been swept away and my presence would look more ridiculous than probative. The only pleasure I had was in knowing that I wasn't far behind the official team. While the French magistrate had only spent moments in the tunnel, I planned to call the scene home for as long as it took. I picked up my stride and listened to the hum of Paris.

Moments later, I was in the thick of it, back to the watchful stares of the gathered mourners. I stepped gingerly to one side. As I adjusted my backpack and fidgeted for a pen, a familiar yet very unwanted feeling returned, like that sensation in dreams when you find yourself naked in the main street of town. So it is to be a detective at a crime scene, under the spotlight with the whole world watching via a telephoto lens. I paused at the curbside knowing that the moment I stepped onto the roadway and began taking measurements and photographs that all eyes would focus on me. And there were literally hundreds of pairs.

CHAPTER THREE

To understand what might have happened at Diana's end, we have to go back to the beginning. We have to see what she was, who she became . . . and who was angered by it.

With the whole world watching, the shy young schoolteacher married her handsome prince on July 29, 1981, but this would not be her happily ever after. The relationship was plagued by secrets and infidelity from the start.

To understand Diana, we must understand the deep loneliness of Diana's time at the palace, from her isolation from Charles to the icy royal snobbery served up to her as an outsider. We must also appreciate her bouts of depression, bulimia, and self-harming, and how after she produced the required "heir and a spare" sons, William and Harry, her usefulness was effectively over. As Charles and Camilla Parker Bowles—who was nicknamed "The Rottweiler" by Diana—resumed their affair, Diana also sought comfort in the arms of other men . . . with sometimes tragic consequences, as in the case of bodyguard-lover Barry Mannakee, who, in 1987, shortly after their affair was discovered, died in a mysterious car crash.

Outside the palace walls, however, the press provided the attention she so desperately craved and soon Diana's every move became front-page news. The rogue princess was born—and as the paparazzi grew more insatiable, Charles's resentment of her popularity increased.

***

The woman they called the "people's princess" and the "queen of hearts" was lauded with extraordinary affection. But the final year of Diana's life was far more complicated; behind the headlines and photos, the Princess had cultivated enemies that could have cost her life. Yet, for most of the public, these enemies were invisible and unknown. The legions of admirers knew only Diana, and could not fathom that anyone would or could want to harm such a loving and dedicated woman.

As Diana's biographer Tina Brown put it in an exclusive interview, "Diana had charisma. . . . She had this great accessibility in which she always made everyone she spoke to feel as if she were only connecting with them."

Put another way, people took Diana personally. She meant something to them. It went beyond being relatable; there was empathy and sympathy. She was painfully shy and had been thrust into the limelight of the world's stage. There had been royals before—and would be royals after—but Diana was the first true superstar. What must this burden have been like? Many shuddered to imagine the burden on the poor girl's shoulders. They felt protective of her.

And Diana touched millions in this way. Her adoring public hung on every word that she said, every item that she wore, every time she changed her hairstyle. Even her facial expressions in newsreels were powerfully meaningful to many. Explains Tina Brown:

> You could tell what she thought from the flush of her face and her big, huge, luminous blue eyes that welled with emotion when she looked at you, and made you feel completely connected. She had this great accessibility in which she always meant everybody she spoke to feel as if she was connecting only to them. That was who she was. That combination of her stature, her incredibly refined beauty, that wonderful peachy skin that was just flawless. Then, this great accessibility and kindness where she was able to connect with people in this very human way. In a rope line, she would get down on her knees and bend down and talk to the children as if she was their mom, and she would have great personal conversations with people and made them feel very special.

Indeed, it didn't take a rocket scientist to understand that Diana's beauty far surpassed those of other royals. She was literally stunning, sometimes rendering those who met her utterly speechless. Her grin could disarm the powerful and make people forget themselves utterly. On television it was one thing; but in person and up close, it was truly a kind of magic.

Yet the magic died forever in the early hours of August 31, 1997. Diana's light was snuffed out forever, and in highly suspicious circumstances.

***

Among many other things, Diana's death had the effect of freezing her in time. She would never grow wrinkled or old, or suffer any of the indignities that come with age. Her failing and foibles would be, mostly, concealed. She would not make a slip of the tongue or rash statement in anger that might betray a secret. She would stay as she was—as she had been in people's minds—forever.

As Ingrid Seward, royal expert and editor of *Majesty* magazine, said:

> It was like a Greek tragedy, the whole of her life. . . . Diana was so many different people whirled into one that she was endlessly fascinating. She was one thing to me, and she would've been one thing to somebody else, and it depended on her mood of the day. Because her life ended in such a terrible tragedy, she will be like Marilyn Monroe. She will be an icon forever. . . . Because certain people in certain parts of the world are determined to believe that there was a conspiracy theory, the rumblings will always go on.

But to tell the story in this book, we are forced to tell the story of another Diana. The one behind closed doors. The one whose life was—to put it indelicately—a complete mess. Diana doubted herself. She was self-conscious about her own body, and feared that those who admired her were insincere. Further, she believed she had alienated herself from the very people she desired to be closest to, including husband Charles, Prince of Wales (the heir apparent to the British throne), whose wandering eye—and hands—would stab Diana in the heart.

Interviewed exclusively for this book, Diana's butler of many years, Paul Burrell, expounded on the alienation Diana felt.

> I think the royal family take the view that things happen. The queen knows. She's never interfered in any of her children's relationships. Her attitude is they make their beds, they lie on them, and they have to get on with it.
>
> These things aren't spoken about. They happen but they happen in private and very quietly.
>
> I stood beside the queen for a long time. I know how she performs, and I know what her attitude would be. The queen would say to Diana, "It's your husband. You have to sort out this situation. It's nothing to do with me."
>
> She does not interfere until it upsets the apple cart, until it comes to a situation where it involves the constitution of the monarchy—or the country.

***

The one area where Diana really came into her own was in her tireless devotion to charity work. Millions benefited in real, tangible ways from her crusades against land mines and the spread of HIV. And Diana always insisted that she should not be a figurehead only. She insisted on being in the trenches, sometimes literally.

As Burrell noted, "I remember the Red Cross once said to her, 'We would like you to become an executive member of the board,' and she said, 'No, that's not what I want. I want to be on the factory floor. I don't want to be in the boardroom.'"

And truly, Diana moved mountains in the course of her charity work. But not everyone in power was pleased by the particular causes she championed. And some felt that such work might not be the proper place for a princess at all.

Observed Tina Brown:

> There were people who felt that this is not what a royal person should be doing. She was constantly changing the rules and breaking the

> rules, and I would argue they were upset. [They felt] the rules that should not have been broken. Of course, since Diana, we have seen so many celebrities try to leverage their own fame in the same way that Diana did . . . but no one has had the same kind of global effect that Diana had.

Put bluntly, Diana's charity work—the most rewarding and straightforward part of her life—eventually became yet another place where she ruffled feathers and made enemies.

Powerful enemies.

According to Paul Burrell:

> There were factions around the world who said that Diana was meddling in something she didn't understand because the land mine campaign was worth billions to certain countries, and the manufacturer of these land mines, and she was getting into very hot political and diplomatic water.

Land mines. HIV. These were highly sensitive areas with huge sums of money tied up on them. And Diana was successful at what she set out to do. This made her dangerous to the brokers of power.

But if Diana was making enemies in the powerful international arms trade, she was also angering those at the very top of the British establishment. When her feud with Prince Charles spilled from the private to the public arena, Diana became an embarrassment . . . and a liability.

Adds Paul Burrell:

> Immediately, there was Team Prince of Wales and Team Diana. I was happily—by now—on Team Diana, and I thought I was on the winning side. I thought I was on the side that mattered most, but a lady-in-waiting whispered in my ear, "Oh, don't you realize? Diana will be gone and forgotten within a couple of years, so you're backing the loser. Remember

> who pays your wages. Remember where the money comes from. Remember who's going to be king."
>
> All of that was being drilled into me as I gave my allegiance to Diana. Soon Diana was being undermined, seriously undermined, by Charles's people. There was a movement.

For any person in a royal family, going through marital difficulties would come with the added strains of being in the public eye.

But to say Diana was merely "in the public eye" would be a gross understatement. She was the most photographed woman in the world, probably the most photographed in all of human history. Media outlets were building an empire on her. She had created an entirely new level of interest in and adulation for the royal family. Even the most hardened journalists and photographer realized that something uncannily special was going on.

Darryn Lyons owned one of the largest international photo agencies in the world and photographed Diana personally many times. Testifying as to the eerie power of the princess, he said:

> Really, the hairs on the back of your neck stood up when the princess of Wales was in your presence. . . . It was just an extraordinary experience. . . . She was truly hypnotic for a photographer, and truly an extraordinary experience to photograph.
>
> It was a penny for her thoughts, the world around her. Although, the penny turned into a multimillion-dollar business of photographing her every movement, of every minute of every day. I think she was the first of the great royal supermodels as well.

Yet crucial to understanding her life and death is to understand that Diana was not only under the surveillance of photographers looking to get the next great cover shot. She was under almost constant surveillance by the secret services. She received the kind of security attention usually reserved for the leader of a nation. We know for certain that agencies such as the CIA kept files on her, but those spy agencies have always refused to make any of their collected information public.

***

DETECTIVE'S NOTEBOOK

DATELINE: Early September 1997, days after the horror

A detective's workplace, his crime scene, is often in a very public location. And there is something about the yellow and black striped crime-scene tape that draws spectators to its edges, like bees to honey. So under the watchful nods of inquisitive heads, the one with right of access to the inner sanctum, the detective, untrained as he is for celebrity, becomes just that. It's his workplace. And, whether he likes it or not, it's his stage, and the audience is happy for standing-room-only tickets. Their eyes study his every move, taking note of his note-taking. They watch and gape, roll out their own theories and point fingers. It's a strange phenomenon when you're just trying to do your job, a fusion of self-importance, self-consciousness, and a burning need to unravel a puzzle. A dead body is the ultimate of all puzzles. Detectives embrace the game, relish the challenge, and hold dear the methodology that needs to be employed to come up with the answers. I know I did, each and every time I stepped into "my" crime scene, "my" workplace.

But this was a very different scene. It could possibly be described as the most televised crime scene in history, and I was about to step into it and take ownership. At the Pont de l'Alma I found no crime-scene tape; in fact, there never was any. I was going to need a keener eye than ever before, as this crime scene was all but gone. What was still there was a bigger crowd than I'd ever witnessed. I felt alone and a tad ill at ease. In a normal crime-scene environment, there were usually at least half a dozen others assisting, helping to block out the audience and making it easier for everyone to get on with the task. I mingled a little longer, getting a sense of being there, touching on a mood. Finally, I hitched up my pack, stepped onto the outbound carriageway, and strolled purposefully toward the tunnel, to the scene of the accident.

I spent the first hour letting my eyes do all the work. My brain was on overload from the flood of information I had soaked up during the 24/7-television

The Place de l'Alma, above the tunnel, scene of the accident. The actual tunnel is under an eternal flame shown in the center foreground. *Shutterstock*

coverage since the incident occurred. I must have read every written word on the subject at least a few times over. The mountain of discarded newspaper stories that I had left on my warehouse floor would wrap fish and chips well into the new millennium. I had as good a grasp on the job as I could get; now I stood and tried to imagine it. Protected by a concrete divider, I ambled along the center of the carriageway and watched traffic approach the tunnel, enter, and whizz past on both sides. Designed to move the flow quickly and efficiently without the hindrance of traffic lights or pedestrians, the dual carriageway was more a freeway than an inner-city street. Almost without exception, the cars approaching from the direction that Princess Diana's Mercedes would have traversed were moving at speeds above 50 mph despite clearly visible 50 kph (30 mph) road signs along both sides of the carriageway. This was the first of many absurdities that I would discover in Paris.

My eyes followed the path of a small Citroën. I noted that just prior to the tunnel entrance the roadway dipped away sharply and veered to the left at the same time. It was a stretch of asphalt that called out for care and a slowing of speed; a pair of dark skid marks attested to someone's miscalculation, yet the Citroën and the other Parisians that followed seemed to hum along undeterred. As it disappeared into the tunnel, I glanced upward at the structure of the approach. Years of pollution, rain, snow, and exhaust emissions had weathered the dividing walls. They were heavily coated with a layer of brown filth that masked in entirety the rendered concrete surface. However, even after the passage of days, when confronted by the visibly deep scrapes in this surface it was still obvious that something had recently hit at great force; something entirely consistent in this investigator's mind, with a mass of metal containing four adults and weighing a total of nearly two tons. I strolled farther along the road and disappeared into the tunnel. My first up-close look at pillar thirteen showed, despite its trampled and squashed floral adornments, the indisputable scars of where the Mercedes had come to rest. The surface was seriously fractured.

Back in the daylight and growing accustomed to the stares of mourners, I decided it was time to start sketching. Out came my notebook and measuring tape and off to work I went. The first few hours were dedicated to determining dozens of distances, aspects, and lines between the points of impact. At regular intervals some of the less reticent onlookers would approach, curious to ascertain what I was doing. Was I a French detective? Conscious of their genuine concern, I answered inquiries as best as I could while remaining aware of making as much progress as possible before nightfall. It was as I stopped for one of these chats during the course of the afternoon that I became aware of the glances of a small crew of municipal workers on the opposite roadway, the city approach. I looked up on several occasions afterward, admiring the diligence of a gardener working on a run of roses. Occasionally we nodded. By 5 p.m. he was gone with the two others, and I was also looking for an end to my workday.

I rested my eyes with the view of his roses. Following the taper of the flower bed downward, I admired the well-manicured grassy shoulder and looked over the majestic square-cut concrete capping. An identical capping existed on my side of the roadway, running along the top of a 118-foot-long retaining wall ranging in height from zero to 6½ feet as the road fell away. The garden on my side was in need of work; mourners had trampled most of the planting. Glancing back toward the Pont de le Concorde, I realized that I was standing in a direct line with the approaching traffic. Should a vehicle fail to veer left or misjudge the turn, it would collide with me and then the retaining wall. As the cars continued to whizz by, the square capping caught my eye again. I stopped short, initially startled by my observation, a feature that had not been reported by any media.

Along the uppermost length of the capping was a well-defined fresh tire marking. The principle of "every contact leaves its trace" sprung to mind. The wheel of a vehicle had obviously made contact with that capping and at great force, leaving its telltale thick black residue, a distance of two meters long. I moved closer. The black rubber against the white surface of the capping looked like a horrific scar; the stretch of minute bristles of rubber still adhered to the concrete surface. Obviously, the official magistrate's team missed this. Let's not forget, had they found it, and pored over it, the many TV cameras would have highlighted their discovery.

The white capping above the retaining wall at the foot of the rose garden showing a large tire scrape on the side surface with black rubber residue. *Colin McLaren*

I rubbed my hand very lightly over the length of about a meter and felt the tiny rubber residue tickle my palm. Some of the fragments fell to the road surface as I touched them. It was very fresh, very recent. The oddity of such a bold tire mark over a meter above the road surface held my attention. For a vehicle to leave a mark at this height, it would have had to be airborne. There was simply no other explanation. Regardless of the obvious, I tried to think of other ways that tire residue could adhere to the vertical surface of the capping. There were none. This was one of those investigative moments that detectives love: simple induction and then, deduction. The Mercedes had clearly reached an enormous speed on its approach path. I imagined the car ricocheting from the capping, from where I was standing. I turned to look into the tunnel and found myself staring directly at pillar thirteen.

Two 23-foot-long parallel skid marks on the right-hand side adjacent to the merge lane before the road drops away on the approach to the tunnel. *Colin McLaren*

Close-up of the skid marks showing tire tread and fluctuations in the tread consistent with the vehicle suffering a minor impact with another vehicle. *Colin McLaren*

As pleased as I was to discover the marking, I was equally disappointed to conclude that my speculation was correct. There was no evidence—such as a scalpel marking for a controlled sample—that a sample had been collected for examination by the French forensics team. It was perfectly "in situ," as detectives say, found as it had happened. Time and weather conditions would in due course brush the residue from the wall surface to be washed away down the stormwater drains, but for now the tire markings were a deep rich black in color. I took many photographs and a tiny sample of the rubber residue for later analysis, and left the rest untouched. I chalked one up to the independent investigator and turned back to my crime scene looking towards the city for signs of excessive speed, or anything else that would help me to understand why the car had become airborne.

There on the roadway in the distance, in a neat line between the tire residue on the capping and the center of the road, was a pair of dark skid marks. I'd noticed them earlier at the point just before the road starts to dip, but had failed to make the connection. I envisaged a driver hurtling along, desperately attempting to pull up his vehicle before losing control. I walked to the center of the roadway and stood between the marks and observed two precise parallel markings, each of seven meters. I measured them. I also took a range of measurements to estimate the distance between the tires using the center of the skid mark as the start and finish of each measurement. They were consistently 4.52 feet apart. The rubber appeared relatively fresh and darkest toward the center of the markings. There was a wavering or fluctuation, or bubble-like bulge in the front section of the tread closest to the tunnel. I looked back to the retaining wall and then into the tunnel. I stood there off and on as passing cars allowed. It was becoming easier to understand how three deaths had come about.

Many detectives, when they think they have the answer to a particular puzzle, play the negative. I took on that exercise, playing devil's advocate trying to discount my theory to prove myself wrong. I threw in half a dozen hypothetical notions. I tried to separate the two sets of markings. Skid marks might not result in an airborne vehicle, but for a vehicle to literally fly into a retaining wall at such a height, some lead-up markings would surely be expected. There were no other tread marks of any sort in the vicinity.

The two sets of markings that I had discovered appeared to my seasoned eye to be of similar ages, both still black, both fresh, so I linked the two features.

I imagined a vehicle other than the princess's chauffeured car leaving 23-foot skid marks at the same scene. I imagined that same vehicle's tires leaving their residue on the side of the capping near the rose gardens and then not cannoning into pillar thirteen. But who and how and what were they doing up there airborne themselves, and where could they have come to rest if not at pillar thirteen? There had been no mention of another major crash at this site. And for the residue to be still fresh, it would have to have been shortly before the Mercedes' last voyage. I simply couldn't find credence in another vehicle becoming airborne in the same location after the August 31 collision, especially as that location had been crowded with bystanders, municipal workers, police, and the omnipresent media since then.

The more I imagined the possibilities, the stronger my original hypothesis seemed. I was now convinced that the Mercedes had braked sharply (evident from the skid marks) then became airborne (where the tires kissed the side of the capping) with the result that the (by this stage) out-of-control projectile finally slammed into pillar thirteen within the tunnel.

Night started to fall, and I realized that I hadn't eaten all day. I went looking for a meal. I had much to contemplate.

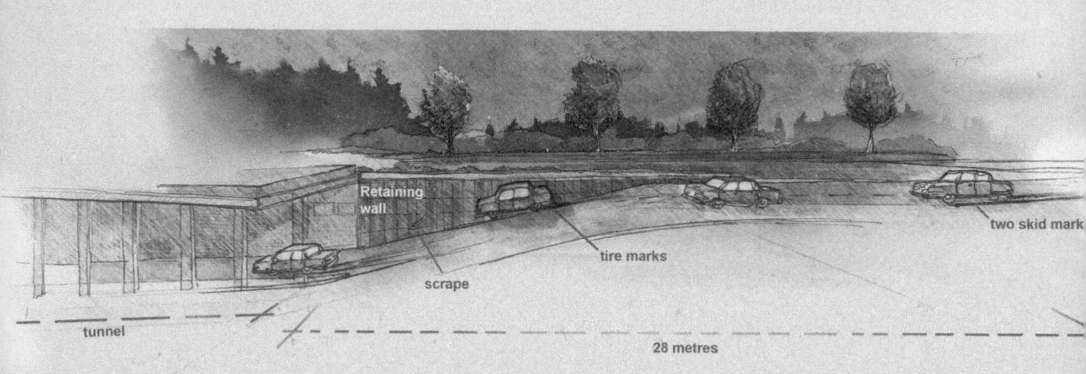

An artist's impression of the path taken by Diana's Mercedes after passing the merge lane, clipping the retaining wall and careering toward the thirteenth pillar in the tunnel. *Dylan Howard*

CHAPTER FOUR

Diana was many things to many people. For many members of her adoring public, she was a naive waif who'd been cast into dangerous waters. She was a victim. She was beset on all sides.

This was true.

It was also just what Diana wanted people to think.

For you see, Diana truly was a woman in great peril. She was mistreated by her powerful husband, and had in-laws who did not particularly like her (and the way she stole the spotlight). She was acutely, and correctly, aware of the powerful forces she had angered through her targeted charity work. And she knew that her own romantic liaisons were transgressive in a way that would not be long tolerated.

But Diana had learned something. As the woman arguably subject to more press attention than anyone else in the world, Diana had come to understand the power of the printed word. (And the photograph. And the video clip.) Diana's manipulation of the press started gently, but quickly grew in intensity.

Diana had seen what kind of a weapon the press could be. What a powerful force it could create. And—in a move that further angered those who disliked Diana—she began using it to protect herself from her enemies.

Diana began keeping diaries and recordings of both her personal experiences and the royal family's secrets. She was perfectly positioned to access the innermost privacies. And when she saw that it would help insulate her from harm—or dissuade someone else from coming after her—she was only too willing to leak this material herself.

By the time Andrew Morton's sensational, tell-all book *Diana: Her True Story* was published in 1992, the Windsors were already embittered against

Diana—forever, in perpetuity, no takebacks—with Prince Philip especially furious. Diana had spoken to Morton about her marriage, about her bulimia, about her frustrations with the royal family, and about Camilla. No other royal family member had ever done such a thing. There had been royal transgressions, certainly. There had been abdications. There had been forbidden romances. But no royal had ever told tales out of school to the press itself.

This was a deep and profound shock.

As the marriage between Diana and Charles very publicly unraveled, Diana also gave a sensational tell-all interview with BBC journalist Martin Bashir.

Tina Brown synthesized the problems this created:

> She elected to do go on television, on BBC of all channels, which has always been big supporters of the royal family, and give this wildly explosive interview to Martin Bashir where she really did looking tragic with makeup that she'd applied very skillfully, with a pebble face and dark eyes and looking like a haunted woman, talked about the agony of being in love with a man who wasn't in love with you, and who had always been unfaithful with Camilla. She said, of course, there are three of us in this marriage, which became a hugely quoted phrase all over the world. How she thought that Charles wasn't appropriate to be king and how the royal family were out of touch. This was explosive stuff. In another century, she would've been sent to the Tower of London, and then executed for talking like that about the monarch.

This proved to be the final straw. It was more than manipulation of the press; it was a declaration of war. Charles would not have it, and the couple divorced in 1996.

Refusing to simply disappear (as the Windsors fervently hoped she would do), Diana instead chose to use her fame to "double down" on her charity work, most especially her work with AIDS awareness and campaigning against land mines. As we have seen, these causes in particular also made Diana a good number of new enemies.

And now the paparazzi was insatiable. Despite the royal divorce—or perhaps because of it—photos of Diana could be worth a fortune, and they had photographers hounding Diana day and night, watching her every move in the hopes of securing a bumper payday.

The ensuing chaos was unsafe.

An astonishing fact for many, Diana's Royal Protection security had actually been dismissed after her divorce from Charles. While security still followed Diana, it did not belong to the crown.

By the summer of 1997, things were coming to a head. The media circus surrounding Diana had reached a fever pitch. Diana had never been more popular with the public, yet had never had more enemies in the establishment. Prince Philip loathed her. The other senior royals were terrified of what she knew about them. British Defense Minister Earl Howe described her as "a loose cannon." US Secretary of State Madeleine Albright called her a "considerable embarrassment."

She was under covert surveillance by MI6 and the CIA, and, perhaps most dangerously, her campaign to ban land mines was threatening the multibillion-dollar business of powerful—and ruthless—international arms dealers.

Yet Diana knew enough to use this to insulate herself. Iconic photos were taken of Diana, in the field, working to fight the use of land mines. In January 1997, she walked into a live minefield in Angola to take a personal lesson in how to dismantle explosives. She was often seen beside young amputees, the victims of the horrible scourge she sought to eradicate. In one memorable picture, Diana stands in full body armor, near a sign that says "danger," in a live minefield. There are many iconic pictures of the princess, but for many of her fans, this one ranks near the very top.

And Diana made sure the press that followed her and reported on her actions saw that it was not just for photo ops that she traveled to these places. Diana also took the time to sit and talk with victims of mines, and to educate herself on the most effective tactics to combat their spread.

Diana also educated herself and spoke out on matters related to policy implementation. This further angered many in government—members of parliament accused her of working outside the system to contravene government policy—yet it also solidified her concern as genuine and real.

And she did not let up her intensity. Just twenty days before the fateful night in Paris when her life ended, Diana had been in Bosnia, seeing what could be done about the land mine problem there.

The news coverage had been spectacular.

***

DETECTIVE'S NOTEBOOK

DATELINE: The next day. Early September 1997

Day two began as day one, pacing out the scene with measuring tape in one hand and notebook in the other. More eyes watching me, more mourners in tears. I did my best to ignore the audience and opened a fresh page of my trusty moleskin. For clarity and to help better document and understand the accident, I chose to divide the scene into two key areas.

***

I called the approach path "Area One." I scrawled a sketch indicating a distance of 1,050 feet from the nearest set of traffic lights on the approach to the tunnel entrance. The first 558 feet was a straight, flat road surface, the last 492 feet (which commenced at the skid marks) I drew with a notation of a 13-foot curved descent (into the tunnel, which I named "Area Two").

An interesting feature of Area One came to my attention as I roughed in the garden beds. As my scope broadened from the immediate road to the larger area, I noted that there was a merge lane that flowed into the highway adjacent to the skid marks. I tossed my notebook and pencil into my pack and strode over for a closer inspection.

Paralleling the highway and flanking a run of office blocks and apartment buildings was a one-way carriageway officially known as Cours Albert. The merge section was at the mouth of this very narrow roadway. I walked back to the main road and stood between the skid marks facing the merge lane, wondering why the driver of Princess Diana's Mercedes had hit the brakes so hard at that exact point. I turned my head to the direction opposite the merge lane and noticed

Area One, the approach to the tunnel with the merge lane at the end of Cours Albert visible on the left. The facades of diplomatic embassies are visible beyond the trees. *Colin McLaren*

fresh scrape marks on the retaining wall that I now faced, the retaining wall opposite the rose bushes. Clearly the Mercedes couldn't have made those marks. On the road surface below the marks, tiny fragments were glistening in the afternoon sunlight. I walked across to the left-hand retaining wall. None of the fragments, obviously originating from a broken headlight, were dirty or dust covered. They were fresh.

I stepped back onto the highway and looked down at the skid marks again, taking closer note of the fluctuations in tread toward the tunnel. It was a classic sign that a vehicle had been nudged from the side, but not with sufficient force to knock it from its course (hence the tire residue was continuous in the one direction). I considered the likelihood of a car having crept onto the highway from the merge lane just as the Mercedes careered past. The rumble of an approaching vehicle had me hop quickly back up to the relative safety of the concrete capping. The more I studied the scene the relationship between the skid marks and the merge lane from my new vantage point, the more likely it appeared to me that a second vehicle had entered the highway from that merge lane and had caused the Mercedes to brake suddenly in an unsuccessful attempt to avoid contact.

I watched with interest as cars traveled single file along Cours Albert and took the merge lane to enter the highway. It was a quiet little street really, the type that would most likely only be known and used by locals. I took a stroll to confirm my premise. After an hour of meandering through the network of tiny one-way and dead-end streets, I was convinced that the only vehicles that would use Cours Albert had to have come from the apartment blocks or the office buildings or from the only side street, known as Rue Bayard. Cours Albert was not a shortcut or thoroughfare to any other road. This was a small little backwater area that only people with a genuine purpose would use. It smacked of local knowledge. I wandered back to the crime scene. For the rest of the day I often looked back along the merge lane at the many facades and buildings. It was preying on my mind.

***

Area Two refers to the flat road surface of the tunnel, running in an east-west direction, well-lit with a continuous stretch of wall sconce lighting. In the center of the carriageway are the equally spaced support pillars with number thirteen standing out like a beacon. I shuffled along next to it and attempted a line of sight toward the retaining wall capping that had been bruised by the tire residue. It was a dead straight line. I moved farther along to pillars fourteen, fifteen, sixteen, and onward, but the tire residue disappeared from view. As I meandered back to pillar thirteen, I had little doubt in my mind the path traveled by the late princess's vehicle. I rummaged in my shoulder bag, found my camera, and began the process of photographing the different points of impact and aspects of the scene.

The municipal gardeners watched my work with obvious curiosity. The caretaker of the roses was doing his best to return my side of the roadway to its well-manicured former glory. He offered a "*Bonjour*," so I strolled over and introduced myself.

Claude was a native Frenchman in his mid-forties. He was a big bloke with a drab, full mop of hair. We struck up a conversation in broken French-English, him wiping the fresh soil on his well-worn pair of blue overalls, I slinging the

Nikon back in its leather case. This was the first of many chats we would have over the next week. This was Claude's patch. He was a proud gardener and we became mates of a sort, toiling alongside each other, both with different objectives but the same workplace.

Claude resided on the outskirts of Paris in an upstairs apartment with his family. He boasted that it was he who had planted the roses and nurtured their growth. He was greatly disappointed by the crowds' carelessness and the damage done to them over the previous week. It was going to be quite a job to bring them back to their former beauty. I guessed that it was his apartment lifestyle that had shaped his devotion to his rose garden. Like most Frenchmen, he was a sporting man. Once he knew I wasn't a French detective but an Australian version of the same trade, he offered banter about our opposing rugby teams and the world tennis circuit. He was great company.

On the day of August 31, Claude had been enjoying a rare sojourn, relaxing with his wife. Rising early the next morning for his working day, Claude had been none the wiser of the tragic event until he arrived in his garden to the first stream of pilgrims to the site. He had been on duty most days since. With his comprehensive knowledge of the area, I was keen to have him confirm the history of the markings and scrapings scarring the barriers.

Claude attested that he first noted the damage when he arrived for work the morning after the fateful accident. He indicated toward the two skid marks adjacent to the merge lane. He claimed those were fresh, too, from the day after the accident. I stood him before the minute burrs of rubber that I had discovered on the retaining wall capping. Witnessing firsthand the alarm in his reaction, I became sure that I had found something that others had missed. Claude knew his garden well and offered me independent corroboration that the points of impact that I was documenting were indeed fresh on the day after the princess's death.

I circled the three prominent points of impact recorded in my journal. They stood out like scars, like wounds on a corpse. The first were on the capping of the right-hand retaining wall and contained the tire markings where small rubber residue fibers still adhered to the wall. A second set of tire markings and scarring of the rendered surface of the retaining wall was situated on the opposite

Close-up of the scrape marks made by the Mercedes, showing the contrast with the dirty retaining wall and verified by Claude as "fresh" the morning after the accident. *Colin McLaren*

left-hand side of the carriageway. And of course, the third and last point of impact was at pillar thirteen.

All of a sudden, the accident became easy to understand. The princess's Mercedes-Benz, hurtling along the last stretch of the highway in Area One, had hit the brakes at the merge lane. The fluctuations in the tire markings indicate a minor contact with another vehicle, but not enough to take the Mercedes off course. With the combination of the curved camber and the road surface falling away, the Mercedes had then become airborne, landed briefly on the capping, having almost mounted Claude's rose garden, before ricocheting toward pillar thirteen. Meanwhile, a second vehicle, having grazed the Mercedes on entering the carriageway from the merge lane, staggered across the roadway and collided with the left-hand retaining wall, brushing tire residue before limping away and disappearing, probably after the Mercedes had come to a rest.

I took a seat in my now usual spot on top of the retaining wall capping and spent an hour staring at the impact points and the approach path, mulling over my theory. The rest of the afternoon I devoted to filling my first notebook with further distances and measurements. I charted the entire region, in and out of the tunnel way and the half of a mile back to the Place de la Concorde at the city center. As darkness fell, I found myself hungry again and headed off to eat. Much had been achieved.

It was while I idled over my stack of *tartare frites* that I unearthed some handy affirmation of my theory. I had taken a handful of newspaper clippings to dinner, mostly photographs that I had collected from the articles. To my delight, among them was a snippet from the *Guardian* newspaper of London dated September 1, reporting, "Fresh skid marks . . . visible yesterday on the concrete dividing wall."

I went through the remainder of my stash and found one further article where a reporter mentioned scarring on the retaining wall. In high spirits with the substantiation, I ordered a double helping of chocolate crème anglaise.

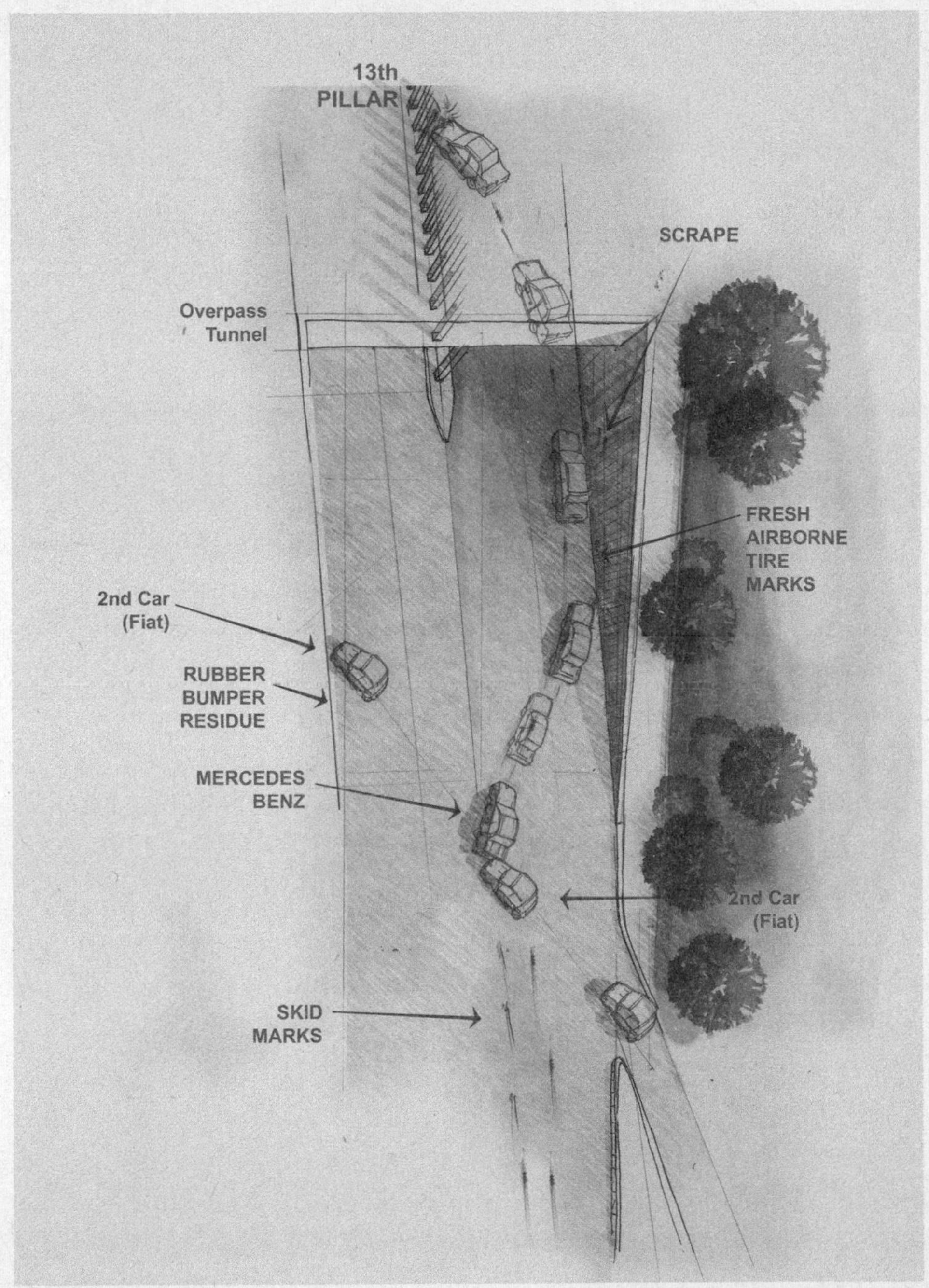

Artist's impression of the path taken by Princess Diana's Mercedes after its minor collision with the Fiat Uno at the merge lane. *Dylan Howard*

CHAPTER FIVE

The words "Happily Ever After" were never in Diana's stars. Romantic happiness was fleeting, at best, in her life, despite a long string of lovers.

Dating the royal carried with it what her inner circle eventually came to call "The Diana Curse." The elite group of men who got entangled with the princess—from aristocrats to a rock star and Academy Award nominee—soon found that falling for the queen of hearts came at a hefty price.

Many of Diana's lovers—several of whom were married or engaged when Diana got her hooks into them—have been struck by scandal, tragedy, and death.

Here, we examine Diana's romantic history, and find out how her lovers' fates were forever altered after their time with the anxious blonde who spent her life desperate to snag "the one."

From this examination, we also come to see how Diana herself was altered by her entanglements and, indeed, how they contributed, step-by-step, to her own undoing.

***

"Our wedding day was the worst of my life."

WHO

Prince Charles

WHEN

First and only husband, 1981–1996

WHAT HAPPENED

This was the man initially idolized, then despised, by Diana.

Diana was an introverted virgin who thought she was fat, spotty, and stupid when they met. She had posters of Charles on her wall at both her divorced parents' homes, seeing him as some sort of James Bond character.

Charles reckoned he was some kind of Renaissance man—a swashbuckling "action star" with a fierce intellect to boot.

A year before he proposed to Diana, the prince of Wales was on the rebound from his affair with Anna "Whiplash" Wallace, whose ferocious temper earned her that nickname. Wallace was a dangerous version of Princess Diana—tall, blonde, and a reckless horsewoman. Charles was sexually obsessed by her and would probably have married her if she hadn't dumped him because of his love for Camilla Parker Bowles.

It was that enduring love that drove Diana to tears a week before her wedding to Charles, who famously once told Diana he refused to be the only British prince without a mistress.

His cruelties continued. Diana spent every day crying during their monthlong stay at the queen's rain-lashed Balmoral estate in Scotland when she found out he had been wearing a pair of cufflinks given to him by Camilla. Instead of spending their honeymoon sleeping with Diana, he lay on bed reading the books of Laurens van der Post, about the author's mystical and religious experiences in Africa. While Charles was steeped in his newfound interest in horticulture and indulged his passion for fishing at Balmoral, Diana had two words for the place: "rainy/boring." And while Diana is a very young bride, Charles was a very old thirty-year-old.

Despite their being worth millions, Diana became appalled in the early days of their marriage by his Scrooge-like frugality. One of his most unappealing habits was refusing to update the decor at his home in Highgrove—and he constantly checked the fridge for signs servants were overeating. To offset her boredom and sexual frustration, Diana went into overdrive with interior designer Dudley Poplak, revamping the interior while forming friendships with celebs to get out of stuffy royal dinners. The frustration grew into rage and poisonous exchanges—Charles telling Diana she was moronic and mocking her bulimia by telling her it was a "waste" for her to eat if food was going to be brought up again.

She went on to blame him for sparking her self-harm and suicide attempt when pregnant with Prince William.

Richard Kay:

> She did fall or threw herself down a flight of stairs at Sandringham, the queen's estate in Norfolk, England, and the Queen Mother found her at the bottom of the stairs. Obviously, they had to call a doctor to make sure the unborn child was all right.
>
> She was desperately unhappy, and she wanted people to know that she was unhappy. She found no one would listen to her. They all thought, "Oh it's just a question of Diana you've just got to adjust. You've just got to pull yourself together and get on with it. You know, a stiff British upper lip. Just pull yourself together. You're in the royal family now."

Ken Warfe:

> Diana herself said to me that yes, she did throw herself down some stairs and . . . I said, "Well, I can't imagine you throwing yourself down—why would you throw yourself down the—?" Well I was just so unhappy that I just wanted people to know." It was a real quest for "look at me." As in, "Nobody's listening to me"
>
> Part of Charles "having his own way" included rekindling his relationship with Camilla Parker Bowles—even as his young, desperately unhappy wife was at her absolute lowest.

"Diana felt the threat of Camilla very early," noted Tina Brown.

"He always felt she was the love of his life. Then, when the marriage began to go wrong, which was pretty early on, the wedding and even the engagement was going wrong. The feelings for Camilla surfaced again."

According to Brown, Diana's suspicions that Charles and Camilla had never truly ended their relationship began before they had even got married.

> During the engagement, she was absolutely devastated when she found in Charles's private secretary's office a package that was destined to go

> to Camilla, which was a bracelet that Charles had brought her engraved with GNF. . . . It was a nickname between them, and she was livid.
>
> Then, on the honeymoon, she was further devastated when Charles appeared at dinner wearing a pair of cufflinks that Camilla had bought for him. Then, she started to overhear phone calls. She started to hear horrid quiet calls between Charles and Camilla, which Charles would be taking from the bathroom because he didn't want her to hear.
>
> She always felt, though, Camilla was in their marriage and that she couldn't somehow get her out. Of course, that feeling grew, and it was almost a self-perpetuating prophecy because she was so deeply jealous and became so deeply paranoid about Camilla, that in a sense, she's in a way almost willed the truth to be as it was, which was that they became reinvolved.

The suspicions proved to be well-founded.

"Camilla, from my time in the mid '80s, was very present," said Warfe. "You know, it's a fact that when Diana would leave Highgrove House on a Sunday afternoon to return to London with her children for school. In a very short period of time thereafter, Camilla arrived at Highgrove House. That was known. That happened. There was nothing secret about the prince of Wales's relationship with Camilla . . . everybody inside Buckingham Palace and Kensington Palace knew exactly what was happening. This was the problem."

Wharfe remembers one incident in particular, when Diana's crushing despair at her husband's betrayal led her to finally confront the woman he was betraying her with: at Camilla's sister Annabel's fortieth birthday party.

> I didn't think, really, that the prince anticipated that Diana would really accept this invitation, knowing full well that Camilla would be there.
>
> I remember driving with them both to Richmond, and very little was said in the car, if anything at all, and we arrived, and I don't actually think the vast majority of the guests were expecting Diana there, either, because once the door opened, it was like . . . the only thing I

> could liken it to was like freeze framing her, a shock in a movie, with absolute horror when they saw that Diana was there.
>
> I'd been there for about forty minutes, forty-five, maybe a bit longer. It could have been an hour. I heard my name being called outside and it was Diana, and Diana said, "Ken, I can't find my husband or Camilla."
>
> Within a short period of time, we found Prince and Camilla sitting on a sofa, away from the other guests. I didn't quite know what Diana was going to do now. I stood there in complete anticipation, not realizing or thinking what she might do. It was a sort of moment of silence from everybody and eventually, Diana, with a great deal of courage and confidence, went across to Camilla and said, "Listen, please don't treat me like an idiot. I know exactly what's going on."
>
> Then Camilla said something which I will never forget. She said, "Well, it's okay for you. You've got two marvelous boys, two wonderful boys." That, I don't think really Diana was able to still understand what she was talking about, because I certainly didn't. The prince was looking very bemused by it all. I tried to excuse myself and Diana said, "No, stay. Just wait there, Ken. Wait there." There were some other exchanges and eventually, they all returned to where the room was, and we returned to the garden at the end of the evening. Nothing was said on the return journey back to Kensington Palace.

Diana's humiliation was complete. Rejected by her husband, scorned by Camilla, ignored by the other royals, desperately alone, and suffering from self-harming issues, she embarked on a series of affairs of her own.

Diana later revealed their marriage was sexless and claimed Charles plotted to kill her and have her committed when she threatened to reveal the secrets of the royal family—including her suspicion Charles was bisexual. And she blamed his lack of love for driving her into the arms of a series of men as their marriage crumbled. But it was Charles who transformed the blushing English virgin into a global campaigner for good causes, leading her to be dubbed "the mouse that roared."

As Charles resumed his affair with Camilla, Diana went on to have her own string of suitors before finally separating from Charles in 1993—something royal courtiers claimed never bothered the callous prince.

Diana's own infidelities included dashing cavalry officer James Hewitt, car salesman James Gilbey, and art dealer Oliver Hoare—who was not only married, but a close friend of Prince Charles.

Finally, it seemed, Diana had had enough of being pushed around. After over a decade of misery and rejection at the hands of the royal family, she vowed to fight back. The rogue princess was born—and she had a weapon in her armory they simply couldn't handle. Charisma.

WHERE HE IS NOW

The seventy-year-old is in line to become king. Father to his two sons to Diana, Harry and William, Charles eventually married his longtime love, Camilla Parker Bowles, in a civil ceremony in 2005.

***

"I think he was bumped off. He was the greatest fellow I have ever had—I was like a little girl in front of him the whole time, desperate for praise, desperate."

WHO

The Father Figure: Sgt. Barry Mannakee

WHEN

Affair, 1985–1986

WHAT HAPPENED

Diana believed her married police bodyguard Barry Mannakee paid the ultimate price for getting involved with her.

He was the first of the men from whom the princess sought comfort from during her unhappy marriage to cheating Prince Charles—and the second man she'd ever bedded. They got together when Diana, then only twenty-three, suffered postpartum depression after the birth of Harry in September 1984. Thirty-seven-year-old Mannakee became her father figure and confidant. Diana became so enamored with the plain-looking Royal Protection Squad officer she told him, "I'm quite willing to give all this up," and often lay in bed with him talking about how she wanted to run away with him.

The affair ended in disaster when, on the eve of Prince Andrew and Sarah Ferguson's wedding in July 1986, Charles's bodyguard Colin Trimming discovered Diana and her married protection officer in a "compromising position."

By September, Mannakee had been transferred to other diplomatic duties.

Diana gushed about him, "I tell you one of the biggest crushes of my life, which I don't find easy to discuss, was when I was twenty-four/twenty-five and I fell deeply in love with somebody who worked in this environment. I should never have played with fire. But I did. And I got burned."

WHERE HE IS NOW

Dead—suspected assassinated. The following May after Mannakee was found getting intimate with Diana, and just two weeks before his fortieth birthday, Mannakee was killed in a motorcycle crash on the outskirts of East London. He was on his Suzuki motorbike when it collided with a teenager's car. While a coroner ruled that the death was a tragic accident, Diana was convinced that he was murdered by the British secret service, who feared she had spilled royal secrets during pillow talk. The princess's next major love, James Hewitt, would claim without a shred of evidence that Mannakee had been murdered by a rogue British intelligence officer. It's perhaps his take on Mannakee's death that led Diana to later say, "It was all found out and he was chucked out. And then he was killed. And I think he was bumped off. But, there we are. I don't . . . we'll never know."

Diana always kept a brown teddy bear in her bedroom after Mannakee's death—a gift from him. Charles is said to have cruelly taunted Diana over Mannakee's death, telling her to go and "cry to the cameras" when she found out he had been killed.

***

"Yes, I adored him. Yes, I was in love with him. But I was very let down."

WHO

The Cad: James Hewitt

WHEN

Affair, 1986–1990

WHAT HAPPENED

A hero in war but not in love, Hewitt broke Diana's heart by cashing in on their relationship by cooperating on a tell-all memoir about their fling written in the style of a trashy Mills & Boon romance.

The former Household Cavalry officer and tank commander began the affair with Diana in 1986 when he was twenty-seven after they met at a cocktail party and Hewitt promised to teach Diana to ride and cure her fear of horses—something Charles hated, and which allowed him to bond with Camilla.

Diana had first laid eyes on Hewitt when he played polo against her husband-to-be Charles less than a week before their wedding in 1991. It was the match from which Diana fled after discovering Charles and Camilla had been sending each other love notes and gifts using their code names Gladys and Fred.

Hewitt told Charles when he scored the winning goal in the match, "There's your wedding present, sir."

A passionate affair of love-nests and visits to Highgrove followed for the next five years until Hewitt left to serve in the Gulf War.

They met in secret at Combermere Barracks in Windsor and according to Hewitt—whose laddish pals boasted he was a well-endowed lothario—they also had trysts at Althorp, the Spencers' ancestral home, as well as in his mother's home in Ebford, Devon.

When Hewitt reported to fight as a tank commander in the first Gulf War in 1991, Diana was frantic about his safety and started using the nickname "Dibbs" for him in the love letters she would post to the battle zone.

Hewitt returned from service safe, but their passion started to wane and Diana worried their affair would be exposed and she would take full blame for the breakdown of her marriage to Charles. She stopped taking his calls, but in 1994 the affair came back to haunt Diana when Hewitt decided to risk the princess's wrath by selling out.

The book he cooperated on with Anna Pasternak, *Princess In Love*, was packed with graphic details of their five-year romance.

Diana later said she was heartbroken the moneygrubbing soldier had sold her down the river. She also had to go through explaining to William and Harry what had happened before they saw it in newspapers.

Diana said:

> He was a great friend of mine at a very difficult, yet another difficult time, and he was always there to support me. And I was absolutely devastated when this book appeared, because I trusted him, and because, again, I worried about the reaction on my children.
>
> And, yes, there was factual evidence in the book, but a lot of it was . . . comes from another world . . . didn't equate to what happened. There was a lot of fantasy in that book, and it was very distressing for me that a friend of mine, who I trusted, made money out of me. I really minded that. And he'd rung me up 10 days before it arrived in the bookshops to tell me that there was nothing to worry about, and I believed him, stupidly. And then when it did arrive, the first thing I did was rush down to talk to my children. And William produced a box of chocolates and said, "Mommy, I think you've been hurt. These are to make you smile again."

But the affair haunts Diana's sons to this day.

Many believe party-loving Hewitt is Harry's real father as the ginger prince bears a striking resemblance to the army officer. Hewitt insists there was "no possibility whatsoever" he was Harry's biological father as the boy was already a toddler when he came on the scene. Yet others believe he is only protesting as he fears he could be snuffed out by the royal family.

WHERE HE IS NOW

Alone, ashamed, ill, and living with his mother. Hated by Diana's sons, Hewitt, now sixty-two, has never recovered from his moneygrubbing kiss and tell. After retiring from the army in 1994, he ran a series of failed business ventures, including a Spanish bar, called the "Polo House" in Marbella, that shut in 2013. He also appeared on reality television shows including 2006's *X Factor: Battle Of The Stars*, in which he sang "Addicted To Love" with Rebecca Loos. The fallen cad now lives in a two-bedroom apartment near Exeter with his elderly mother, Shirley. He cuts a disconsolate figure on the rare occasions he is seen out shopping. He never married, is reported to have suffered a heart attack and stroke in May 2017, and insiders say he carries the shame of selling out Diana everywhere.

***

"I felt very protective about James because he . . . was a very good friend to me, and I couldn't bear that his life was going to be messed up because he had the connection with me."

WHO

The Old Friend: James "Squidgygate" Gilbey

WHEN

Affair, 1989–1990

WHAT HAPPENED

The man who made her lonely palace life tolerable, Diana's next major love since Hewitt was a gin heir who had known Diana since she was seventeen. Even after her engagement to Charles, she used to iron James Gilbey's shirts. Gilbey became obsessed with Diana when they grew closer in 1989, though she never felt the same adoration for him that she had lavished on Hewitt. But like the fling with Hewitt, this affair involved Diana having to rely on trusted friends to provide more safe houses, places where she could spend hours with her latest male admirer, confident of absolute privacy away from the prying eyes of servants. She often used the elegant London home of Mara Berni, owner of her favorite restaurant, San Lorenzo in Beauchamp Place, for her romps with Gilbey.

Her close friend Lucia Flecha de Lima, wife of the Brazilian ambassador, also gave her the run of her home. It was at Mara's house—close to Harrods, bought by Dodi's father for $814 million in 1985—that she would meet the mystics, psychics, and fortune-tellers she would become hooked on consulting. While seeing Gilbey, she was locked into searching for an answers and solutions to her tangled love life. The hours she spent babbling to Gilbey on her mobile phone—which she called "my talking brick"—would prove the downfall of the fling. When Diana poured out her heart to Gilbey, as she often did, she would rage about Charles's affair while oblivious to her own infidelities. In one incriminating call, she went still further, despairing at the hostility she felt from her husband's family "after all I've done for them." In the same call, she warned Gilbey that she could not afford to get pregnant with his child, and he burbled affectionate nonsense, calling her "darling" fifty-three times and "Squidgy" or "Squidge" fourteen more.

Gilbey may never have kissed and told, but the call made him part of Diana's embarrassing history of affairs. Three years after her New Year's Eve 1989 call to Gilbey in which he called her "Squidgy," a tape of the lovestruck conversation emerged. It surfaced at the height of the crisis in Diana and Charles's marriage and became known as the "Squidgygate" scandal. The princess confirmed what happened in her 1995 BBC television interview with Martin Bashir.

Asked if she had made the call, she answered, "Yes, we did. Absolutely, we did." Excerpts of the tape included Diana giggling as she told Gilbey, "I don't want to get pregnant."

"Kiss me," he demands. "Oh God, it's so wonderful, isn't it? This sort of feeling? Don't you like it?"

"I love it, I love it," Diana tells him, getting more frisky when she asked him, "Playing with yourself?"

He informs her, "I haven't played with myself actually—not for a full forty-eight hours."

Diana bursts into laughter and makes kissing noises, telling Gilbey he's "the nicest person in the world."

Diana later claimed the tape was leaked by the royals as part of a plot to shame her. She added:

> It was done to harm me in a serious manner, and that was the first time I'd experienced what it was like to be outside the net, so to speak, and not be in the family.
>
> It was to make the public change their attitude toward me. It was, you know, if we are going to divorce, my husband would hold more cards than I would—it was very much a poker game, chess game.

Diana was certain her husband's establishment friends were responsible for leaking the recording. Yet despite Squidgygate, Charles was losing the popularity war that was being played out between the couple in the media.

At the time of the Squidgygate call, Diana had been talking nonstop of escaping the firm. The scandal—which broke in Britain's press on August 23, 1992—made her even more desperate to escape, and she separated from Charles in December 1992.

Gilbey then broke up with his fiancée, Lady Alethea Savile, who had stood by him in the furor. In 1994, she died of a drug overdose.

WHERE HE IS NOW

Gilbey, sixty-three, remained single for years after Lady Savile's death before marrying interior designer Lavinia Hadsley-Chaplin in 2014 and is stepfather to her five children. He also runs a property company in London. He has never openly spoken of his time with Diana.

***

"I was reputed to have made three hundred telephone calls in a very short space of time which, bearing in mind my lifestyle at that time, made me a very busy lady."

WHO

The Suave Art Dealer: Oliver Hoare

WHEN

Affair, 1990–1993

WHAT HAPPENED

There was an extra frisson for Diana in her liaison with this swarthy dealer in Persian artifacts—he was a close friend of Prince Charles. Oliver Hoare, a father-of-three and sixteen years Diana's senior, was also married. Their affair started weeks after Diana's Squidgygate call to James Gilbey. It also began after the death of Diana's father, Earl Spencer, in March 1992.

Hoare, then forty-six years of age, was a friend of Charles, and he and his wife Diane had been guests at Windsor Castle. He had often hosted Charles during summers at the chateau belonging to Hoare's mother-in-law, in the heart of Provence.

Diana first met him during Ascot week in 1985. The princess was instantly attracted to him. Darkly good-looking, with thick, wavy black hair that he wore long, he was confident around the royal family where others in the room were anxious to please. Diana later confessed to her bodyguard Ken Wharfe she had felt a little shy when, at Windsor, she shook his hand for the first time, and had blushed as she flirted with him. That conversation ended abruptly when Charles and the Queen Mother joined them.

When the Waleses' marriage moved closer to open warfare, Hoare and his wife began to act as intermediaries. Diana got together with him after spending hours admiring his body while they both worked out at London's Chelsea Harbour gym. She questioned him constantly, trying to understand what her husband saw in Camilla—whom she called "the Rottweiler."

Hoare then started to spend hours in her private rooms at Kensington Palace, and soon became a lot more than a friendly shoulder to cry on. The lovers went to extremes to keep their affair private. Shortly after Diana first started seeing the suave Hoare in 1992, she smuggled him into Kensington Palace in the trunk of her car, said Wharfe. Ken also once found him one summer evening the same year cowering naked behind a bay potted plant outside Diana's apartment door, smoking a cigar. Fumes from his Cuban had set off all the smoke alarms in Kensington Palace at 3:30 a.m.

Ken said:

> I headed toward the princess's apartment but before I reached the door I discovered the source of the false alarm. Cowering behind a huge plant in the hallway, clutching a cigar, was Oliver Hoare. Diana, who hated the smell of smoke, must have sent him out of the bedroom. It was not without a twinge of amusement at his expense that I advised him to put it out and go back to bed. He looked almost pathetic as he gathered himself together and left. Next morning, I tried to make a joke of the incident, suggesting that Diana and Hoare had been playing cards together in her room—perhaps strip poker.

In fact, there is room to suspect that Princess Diana got hooked on bondage and outdoor sex thanks to Hoare, who "awakened" her sexual desires after years of misery married to Prince Charles.

The charmer aroused Diana so much she romped with him in the bushes of royal grounds and once visited him wearing nothing but a fur coat and high heels she called her "tart's trotters."

Wharfe once revealed, "She needed him at every conceivable moment. Diana confided to me that he was the first man who had ever aroused her physically. That admission did much to explain the humiliating events that followed."

Another source with intimate knowledge of Diana's sex life said:

> She may have seemed demure, but Diana had a wild side that led a lot of aides to dub her "Dirty Diana." She was a virgin when she married Prince Charles and he did nothing for her sexually. So when the marriage started to crumble, Diana decided to have fun—a lot of it. Her most passionate fling was with Oliver. He was a smooth businessman and she couldn't get enough of him. Years before *Fifty Shades* came out, they were messing about with bondage and had sex in the bushes around Diana's home at Kensington Palace. They went at it like rabbits, and Diana got a real kick out of the danger they could be caught—she cared that little about her marriage to Charles at that stage.

Wharfe claimed that over the course of their yearlong affair Diana fell "completely in love" with Hoare. And she once confessed to her close friend Lady Bowker, she "daydreamed of living in Italy with handsome Hoare."

In fact, Diana talked obsessively about eventually marrying Hoare and moving to Italy to start a second family with him. But there was a major hitch in her escape plan—Hoare's wealthy French aristocrat wife Diane de Waldner Hoare, who ended his romance with the royal in 1993 when she threatened divorce. Born into a family of minor Norfolk landowners, Hoare had worked hard to establish himself as a dealer in Islamic antiquities. He married Diane in 1976 and struck up a friendship with Prince Charles in 1984, becoming a frequent visitor to Highgrove. Before his fling with Diana, he previously cheated on his wife with Ayesha Nadir, the wife of Turkish fugitive tycoon Asil Nadir. When he tried to call off his affair with Diana to save his marriage and the future in the art world he had worked so hard to secure, the royal refused to take no for an answer—and showed further evidence of her mental instability when she became Hoare's stalker.

Hoare's wife complained to police about more than three hundred late-night "nuisance" calls to her home after she told her husband to finish with Diana. The stream of calls included one in which a woman shouted "a stream of abuse." Diane insisted her husband ask police to investigate, and cops were stunned to discover the calls had been made from Diana's cell phone and private number at Kensington Palace. Police ended their inquiries at the request of Hoare, who vowed to speak to Diana when she called again.

When she next rang he allegedly shouted at her to shock her into a confession.

Yet within days the calls were said to have resumed, from phone boxes in Kensington, from the home of Diana's sister Sarah and Kensington Palace. Diana admitted in her famous *Panorama* interview with Martin Bashir in 1995 that she had sometimes called Hoare. She said the calls took place "over a period of six to nine months, a few times, but certainly not in an obsessive manner, no."

But in her bombshell book *The Real Diana*, royal biographer Lady Colin Campbell claimed the princess was "almost unhinged with misery and grief" because she was pregnant and had to have an abortion. She also hinted Hoare got Diana pregnant with her third child, which she secretly aborted after her affair with the art dealer ended—despite dreaming it could be the girl she always wanted. Lady Campbell wrote, "Day and night she'd sit on that telephone calling Oliver's house 30, 40, 50 times."

According to Campbell's account, the princess was desperate to keep a secret baby, saying to friends, "Suppose it's a girl."

The book did not go as far as to name the father of the child.

When Diana and Hoare's relationship was made public in August 1994, he admitted only to having "consoling conversations" with Diana, and the princess, publicly humiliated once again, finally cut the art dealer completely out of her life.

WHERE HE IS NOW

Died on August 23, 2017, aged seventy-three, at his family home in France after moving there when he was diagnosed with cancer.

But his life post-Diana was not plain sailing.

In 2005, he was embroiled in an inquiry into the financial dealings of Qatari sheikh Saud Al Thani. The sheikh was accused of embezzling funds from the country by getting vastly inflated invoices sent for art he was buying for the Qatar state. Hoare maintained his innocence, as did Al Thani, and charges against the sheikh were eventually dropped.

In 2015, Hoare again made headlines when he lost his driving license for seventeen months after being pulled over following a boozy lunch. He is said to have spent his life despising the fact he was forever tied to Diana and preferred to move in aristocratic circles and socialize with his art clients from Middle Eastern royalty without ever speaking of the fling.

***

"He sent me flowers every week . . . for three years"

WHO

The US Billionaire: Theodore "Teddy" Forstmann

WHEN

Affair, 1994–1995

WHAT HAPPENED

There was a time when it looked like New York billionaire Theodore "Teddy" Forstmann might play Aristotle Onassis to Princess Diana's poignantly single Jackie Kennedy—one of the royal's idols.

While not blessed with the good looks of a dashing Major James Hewitt or her other lover, swarthy art dealer Oliver Hoare, he was, like Onassis, rich, clever, and more than able to provide private security and private jets—owning not only a Gulfstream jet, but the company that manufactured them.

Like Barry Mannakee, the financier was an older father figure, more than twenty years her senior and a dealmaking man of the world. In her posthumous biography, *The Diana Chronicles*, Tina Brown insisted that their relationship was still "on the boil"—and one of a few options on the hob—when Diana died.

Teddy met Diana when he sat next to her during a black-tie dinner thrown by the banker and grandee Lord Jacob Rothschild during Wimbledon fortnight in 1994. Fittingly, it was at Spencer House, the eighteenth-century London palace built for the princess's ancestor, the first Earl Spencer.

The pair bonded over their rampant insecurities. Like Diana, Forstmann grew up with huge wealth but constantly bickering parents—his father an alcoholic who terrorized his wife at their estate in Greenwich, Connecticut, and eventually lost all the family money. And Diana loved how the tycoon had two adopted sons of his own, Everest and Siya—South African orphans he met through his work as a trustee of the Nelson Mandela Children's Fund in the 1990s. Forstmann was already well into his fifties and unmarried when his fling with Diana began, although he did have a fiancée, a New York model named Debbie Hagerty with whom he had been for three years.

Debbie admitted she was "furious at Diana," fuming, "For her to pursue my man for a sexual affair made me so angry. It shocked me because Teddy is different from most men with money. He is so kind and so decent I had never thought of him as a cheater."

After the Spencer House meeting, Forstmann sent Diana flowers every week for three years. On an early date they had dinner at the Compleat Angler, in Marlow, Bucks, and he was so mesmerized by her that he nearly set fire to the menu.

He told Brown that Diana "was a great mother and very bad to herself," and that she'd had fantasies of Forstmann running for president of the United States with herself as his wife and First Lady, ensconced in the White House.

When they stayed together at Martha's Vineyard, Forstmann was two-timing his fiancée. He sent her a new Lamborghini as a thirtieth birthday present but she was not impressed when she found out it had been bought while he was with Diana, and dumped him.

Forstmann didn't like the publicity that went with being Diana's love interest, but did remain close to her until the end of her life. Diana used him as a telephonic sounding-board, asking him, as an older wiser man, what to do about her war with the royal family, and about her dislike of Camilla and hatred for Prince Philip. She was seeking advice on "tactics," said Forstmann.

A few months before she died in 1997, she asked him to find her a house on the beach near his in Southampton, Long Island. He found one with a pool on the ocean, but it was vetoed by British security.

Instead of going there, she spent that fateful summer with the Al-Fayeds. If she'd taken his advice she'd still be alive, Forstmann believed.

After Diana, Forstmann's track record with women moved on to a series of other impossibly glamorous women, most notably Elizabeth Hurley and Sir Salman Rushdie's ex-wife, Padma Lakshmi. Lakshmi—the model, cook, and television presenter—later declared her love for Forstmann and was still with him when he died.

WHERE HE IS NOW

Died, seventy-one-years-old, in November 2011 from complications from brain cancer after an inoperable tumor was discovered.

***

"He was a 10 in bed . . . it was pure lust."

WHO

The President's Son: JFK Jr.

WHEN

Alleged One-Night Stand, 1995

WHAT HAPPENED

Diana often spoke of the "pure chemistry" between herself and son of former US President John F. Kennedy, according to her friend and confidant Simone Simmons. The royal is said to have had a night of passion with JFK Jr. in the New York hotel where the assassinated president had once slept with Marilyn Monroe.

The revelation is made in Simmons's book *Diana: The Last Word*, and the author said Diana gave Kennedy Jr. a "ten out of ten" rating for his performance in bed and called their session "pure lust." She claims the princess even fantasized about becoming America's First Lady—just as she had with Teddy Forstmann.

The pair met in 1995 when Diana had been separated from Charles for three years and the queen was urging her son to obtain a divorce. Kennedy, who had had a string of high-profile romances with celebrities, including actress Daryl Hannah and Madonna, was trying to persuade Diana to give him an interview for his magazine, *George*.

She refused, but did agree to meet him in her suite at the plush Carlyle Hotel in

Manhattan, overlooking Central Park. When Kennedy arrived, Diana was said to have been "bowled over" by his charm and his toned body. No surprise—he was once voted the sexiest man alive.

She told Simmons, "We started talking, one thing led to another—and we ended up in bed. It was pure chemistry."

On her return to London, Diana had Kennedy's astrological chart drawn up and concluded they were compatible in some ways but not enough to sustain a relationship, Simmons writes. She said the princess confided that Kennedy made her feel "desirable and womanly."

Simmons added in an interview she found out about Kennedy only by chance. Simmons said, "He came up in a conversation as we spoke about great ladies like Grace Kelly and Jackie Onassis, who she admired. Diana was laughing at how Jackie could have gone from someone as good-looking as JFK to someone frog-like like Aristotle Onassis. Then she sheepishly came out with her John Kennedy story. It left me speechless."

Simmons, who works as an "energy healer," said Diana often dreamed about taking the relationship further, the power a relationship with Kennedy Jr. would give her and how, if everything went to plan, she would become part of America's "royal family."

The pair stayed in touch for a short while but Diana eventually accepted that it was not meant to be. The following year, Kennedy married Carolyn Bessette, a public relations adviser for Calvin Klein.

WHERE HE IS NOW

Dead. Kennedy was killed aged thirty-one in a plane crash in September 1999, almost exactly two years after Diana's death. His wife Carolyn, thirty-three, and her sister, Lauren Bessette, thirty-four, were killed with him when their six-seater plane, piloted by Kennedy, crashed in the Atlantic fog. The group had been on their way from New York to one of Diana's favorite holiday spots, Martha's Vineyard, when the plane made a series of turns and plunged out of the sky.

The cause of the accident has never been established.

***

"Isn't he just drop-dead gorgeous? He's my Mr. Wonderful."

WHO

The Heart Surgeon: Hasnat Khan

WHEN

Relationship (which Diana hoped would end in marriage), 1995–1997

WHAT HAPPENED

They met in September 1995 during the final throes of Diana's marriage to Charles. She saw Khan—aptly a heart surgeon—as the man who would heal her wounds. For Diana, it was love at first sight. She reportedly gushed to friends, "Isn't he drop-dead gorgeous? He's my Mr. Wonderful."

She went on to refer to the serious, quiet, thirty-five-year-old Pakistani heart surgeon as "The One."

He was, in fact, the oldest of four children from an affluent, tight-knit, upper-middle-class family in Jhelum, north of Lahore. Diana met him at the Royal Brompton Hospital, where she had gone to visit the husband of her soother-in-chief, the Irish nurse-cum-acupuncturist Oonagh Shanley-Toffolo. Joseph Toffolo had suffered a massive hemorrhage during a triple-bypass operation.

Dr. Khan, the senior resident working with the distinguished surgeon Professor Sir Magdi Yacoub, was in attendance.

Here, in an edited extract from her book *The Diana Chronicles*, Tina Brown dissects this major relationship:

> Khan, a young Omar Sharif lookalike in a white coat, appealed to Diana's taste for the exotic combined with the caring.
>
> When he arrived with his retinue of assistants while Diana was at Joseph's bedside, the doctor was entirely absorbed in the patient's condition and took little notice of the princess—which, for a woman used to having everyone fawn over her, was almost unbearably sexy. So was the blood on his operating shoes, and so were his caring, expressive eyes.
>
> "Oonagh, isn't he drop-dead gorgeous," Diana hissed after Khan had left the room. So gorgeous, in fact, that the bemused Joseph had Diana fussing over him at his bedside for seventeen days straight.

In no time, the Kensington Palace apartment was fragrant with the scent of burning joss sticks. Diana turned herself into a student of cardiology—her night table groaning under a phonebook-sized copy of *Gray's Anatomy* and piles of surgical reports.

They were above Diana's pay grade, and instead she took to watching UK hospital soap opera *Casualty*, believing it was the easiest way to keep abreast of medical terms and developments.

Her closet also quickly filled with a colorful selection of shalwar kameezes, the silk tunics and trousers worn by Pakistani women. She even considered converting to Islam.

Diana took to meeting with Dr. Khan in his small overnight room at the Royal Brompton Hospital.

She asked if she could watch him perform open-heart surgery.

"Anybody with courage enough to watch a heart operation can come in," Khan told her.

He couldn't keep her away after that.

Awkwardly, in late November 1995, a photographer from the *News of the World* caught Diana at the hospital at midnight. She was due to meet Khan as he came off his shift. Borrowing the photographer's mobile phone, she spoke to the paper's royal correspondent, Clive Goodman (nicknamed "the Eternal Flame" by his colleagues because he never left the office).

She told Goodman it was true, she was at the hospital comforting terminally ill patients. She did it, she told him, up to four hours a night, three times a week.

Goodman bit. The headline in *News Of The World* four days later was "My Secret Nights As An Angel."

The story gave birth to an eerie new image of Diana as a compulsive ambulance chaser and death groupie.

Satirical British magazine *Private Eye* came up with a "Diana-no Card," which said, "I, the undersigned, wish to make it clear that in the event of any injury, mental breakdown, life-threatening disease, or other such personal tragedy, I do not wish under any circumstances to be visited by the Princess of Wales."

As her relationship with Khan grew, Diana confessed to her friend Lady Bowker, widow of the diplomat Sir James Bowker, "I found my peace."

And the doctor didn't want anything from her. She reportedly offered to buy him a new car, and he proudly refused. Khan was not interested in high life or fashionability, and he had a dread of personal publicity. His one-bedroom apartment in Chelsea was a mess, and there was a bit of a paunch under the old T-shirts he wore when he was off duty.

He loved what was best about Diana—her compassionate nature, her desire to embrace humanitarian causes.

Diana intended to turn the former equerry's room in her apartment at Kensington Palace into a basement den for "Natty," as she called Khan, so that he could sit around watching soccer after grueling surgery sessions. On weekends, when her staff was off, she would try her hand at cooking him dinner.

"Marks & Spencer have got these very clever little meals that you just put in the microwave and you put the timer on and press the button and it's done for you!" she marveled to psychic Simone Simmons.

She would sometimes disappear for a whole day to Khan's apartment, where she contentedly vacuumed, did the dishes, and ironed his shirts.

On the night of her thirty-sixth birthday in July 1997, she reportedly went out to meet Khan wearing her best sapphire-and-diamond earrings, a fur coat, and, underneath, nothing. Her butler, Paul Burrell, helped run the affair behind the scenes. If there was a lovers' quarrel, he would deliver a message to a pub where Khan hung out, near the hospital.

Khan was also smuggled into Kensington Palace in the trunk of Diana's car—clutching a KFC bucket for dinner à deux with the princess, who loved the "ordinariness" of the fast food meal.

Diana would also meet Khan in pubs and jazz clubs. One of their favorite spots was London jazz club Ronnie Scott's. Diana would disguise herself in a black wig and glasses, and thrilled to the excitement of standing undetected in a line at Ronnie's.

"I'm queuing!" she squealed into her "talking brick" mobile phone to Simmons. "It's wonderful!"

Things got more serious when Diana started to make trips to Pakistan whenever she could to bone up on Hasnat's heritage. Her new best friend became Jemima Khan, the beautiful daughter of Annabel and Jimmy Goldsmith. At the time Jemima knew Diana, she was a coltish twenty-two-year-old, married to the Pakistani cricket legend Imran Khan. The two women would sit up talking late into the night about how to handle marriage to a traditional-minded Muslim.

Diana then asked her butler Burrell to talk to a priest about the possibility of a secret marriage to Hasnat. The butler had a meeting with Father Tony Parsons at the Roman Catholic Carmelite Church, on Kensington Church Street, where Burrell's son was an altar boy.

Fr. Parsons told him it was impossible to marry a couple without notifying the authorities—let alone without notifying the fiancé, as it turned out. Khan was aghast when he learned of Burrell's consultation and said to Diana, "Do you honestly think you can just bring a priest here and get married?"

But Diana was relentless in her pursuit of marrying the doctor. In February 1996, Diana went to Pakistan with Annabel Goldsmith and her niece, Cosima Somerset, to visit Jemima and Imran in Lahore. The ostensible purpose of the visit was to raise funds for the Shaukat Khanum Memorial Cancer Hospital, founded by Imran in memory of his mother, who had died from the disease.

The real purpose was to flood the zone with images that would wow Hasnat's family and show him she was serious minded and passionate about good causes. Some suspect she latched onto campaigning against land mines simply to impress her new love.

Yet Khan was slipping away. He didn't want to go public. He didn't want to marry her. He couldn't face the onslaught of becoming "Diana's new guy" in every tabloid newspaper. And he recoiled from the prospect of his work at the hospital being invaded by reporters.

But he kept up the relationship as he had grown fond of her boys. He got on well with William and Harry—especially William, who had had a long session getting career advice from him one weekend.

But Khan knew his family would also have made marriage a practical impossibility, despite the fairy tales Diana was dreaming their future held.

Khan was a Pathan, a member of a group of peoples in Pakistan and Afghanistan descended from warriors and notable for their fierce attachment to their cultural traditions. His parents had tried twice, in 1987 and 1992, to marry him off to a suitable Muslim bride with equivalent social standing, and by 1996 they were impatient to try again.

Again, Diana was trying to enter a dysfunctional family that did not really want her.

In an interview with the *Sunday Express*, Hasnat's father, Rashid Khan, offered a bruising assessment of Diana as a bridal prospect for his son. "He is not going to marry her," the elder Khan said.

"We are looking for a bride for him. She must belong to a respectable family. She should be rich, belonging to upper middle class. But if we do not find her in our own tribe, we can try outside it. But preferably she should be at least a Pakistani Moslem girl."

Diana saw the declaration as a challenge, but it was hopeless.

In May 1997, Diana upset Khan by using the cover of a three-day trip to Pakistan to raise funds for Imran Khan's cancer hospital in order to descend without notice on Hasnat's sprawling family in an upscale suburb of Lahore.

They clustered around and took her picture and served her English tea until a simultaneous power and water failure drove them outside to sit in a circle in the garden of their walled compound, making pleasant, if stilted, conversation with the charming stranger from the United Kingdom.

It was a surreal scene, especially when one considers that Diana pictured herself moving in with them as their new daughter-in-law. Diana not only had Khan's family and centuries of tradition against her. Hasnat's pager would go off twenty times a day on his medical rounds; his job would always come first.

Amazingly, for a woman who portrayed herself as one of the world's most empathetic figures, Diana was strangely blind when it came to those of the people closest to her. She wanted to own his future, arrange his life. She wanted to rearrange his surgical schedule so that he could travel with her.

The essayist Clive James wrote in *The New Yorker* about Diana's neediness: "She believed, against all the evidence that there was some kind of enchanted place called 'abroad,' where she could be understood and where she could lead a more normal life."

Her hunt for this utopia was taking her to Pakistan, and even to Northern Ireland, where she believed she could help solve the Troubles. She also dreamed of moving to America where she believed her famous face would get lost in the sea of Hollywood stars and lead to eventual anonymity.

She also dreamed of lifting Hasnat out of the annoying grind and insane hours of the Brompton Hospital into some medical habitat where they could live together in sunny exile with a swimming pool, possibly in Australia or South Africa.

At an international think-tank dinner in Rimini, Italy, she found herself next to Professor Christiaan Barnard, the septuagenarian heart-transplant pioneer.

She lobbied him hard to get Hasnat a position in South Africa and twice gave him dinner at Kensington Palace to discuss Hasnat's future. Proud Dr. Khan went ballistic, when, on finally meeting Barnard, he was asked to submit his résumé.

But the breaking point for Khan perhaps came when a *Sunday Mirror* story on June 29, 1997 alleged he and Diana had become unofficially engaged after the "astonishing family summit that sealed their love" in Pakistan in May.

Khan decided it was over. He arranged to meet Diana in an agreed-upon spot in Hyde Park at 10 p.m. one hot night in the second week of July. Knowing she was to be rejected, Diana reproached him with tears and a furious tirade. She could not really accept that it was over, but Khan was sure it was the end.

In August the Khan family, returning to Lahore, gave Hasnat gifts for the beautiful princess who had visited them. He told them to mail them to her instead. He wouldn't be seeing Diana anymore.

Khan told his family, "If I married her, our marriage would not last for more than a year. We are culturally so different from each other. She is from Venus and I am from Mars. If it ever happened, it would be like a marriage from two different planets."

The end of their discreet two-year relationship sent Diana disastrously into the arms of Dodi. Her close friend Rosa Monckton said Diana was "very much in love with" the shy physician and thought romancing the playboy would make the surgeon so jealous he would plead to get her back.

Another reason Diana chose Dodi was that she had come to realize that, in the multimedia age, downsizing was unfeasible. She may also have subconsciously realized she would have died of boredom living in Khan's humble house waiting for him to return from grueling surgical shifts.

And so Diana—like her role model Jackie Kennedy, who tried to re-create the fortress of the American presidency with the playthings of her second husband, Greek shipping magnate Aristotle Socrates Onassis—fell into the arms of a modern kind of prince who could underwrite the trappings of her celebrity status.

It turned out to be the definition of a fatal attraction.

WHERE HE IS NOW

After Diana's death, Khan, now sixty-one, moved to Lahore and had an arranged marriage in 2006. The couple divorced within eighteen months.

Now back in Britain, Khan said in 2013, "It's been difficult for me to get my head around Diana's death. After she died, things were difficult, very difficult. We all have our own traumas and get on with it. But when it's there in your face year in, year out, it's hard."

He is now listed as a consultant cardiac surgeon at Basildon and Thurrock University Hospitals and is believed to be single.

***

"The amazing thing about Dodi is that he makes me feel so beautiful. No man has ever done that to me."

WHO

The Playboy: Dodi Fayed

WHEN

1997

WHAT HAPPENED

To Diana, forty-two-year-old Dodi Fayed seemed perfectly cast for a romance of retaliation against both her ex-lover Khan and the royals. As her friend Lord

Palumbo put it, "She just wanted to make the people at Balmoral as angry as possible."

Her choice of agent provocateur was everything blue-blooded snobs detested—a new-moneyed Egyptian heir.

Like Diana, Dodi's parents divorced when he was young (age two), with his father Mohamed Al-Fayed winning custody—despite the tycoon almost never being home. Dodi grew into a loner, then a playboy who filled the void left by an empty childhood with cocaine and hangers-on. Diana biographer Tina Brown said, "He loved to cook Middle Eastern dishes with his butler, perfume his apartment with scented lilac candles, listen intently at the feet of movie stars, and do lines of cocaine."

When Dodi was twenty-four, his father set him up in a film company, which meant he could date actresses and call himself an executive producer. He got lucky with his very first project, David Puttnam's Oscar-winning *Chariots of Fire*, in which his father invested $2.6 million. It gave him the right to hang around the set until Puttnam threw him off—for handing out coke to the cast.

His house in Beverly Hills was party central, a magnet for freeloaders, gold diggers, and deal jockeys exploiting his childlike generosity. He threw, on average, four parties a week.

The playboy became a regular at Manhattan's Studio 54, where supermodels, pop stars, and Hollywood legends got high on drugs and often had sex in hidden corners of the sprawling club, according to Mark Fleischman in his 2017 memoir *Inside Studio 54*.

"Dodi loved Quaaludes, good quality coke, and hot women, and he always had plenty of those," wrote Fleischman, who owned the club between 1981 and '84.

The two men became so close that they regularly went scouring illegal gay clubs at 5 a.m. in what was then one of the most dangerous areas of downtown New York.

Dubbed the "dawn patrol," the duo and a posse of celebrity drug-abusers, including singers Liza Minnelli, Rick James, and Joe Cocker, tennis ace Vitas Gerulaitis, and Hollywood giants Tony Curtis, Jack Lemmon, Robin Williams, John Belushi, and Nick Nolte would take limos to impromptu parties in boarded-up buildings.

"Dodi always had the most amazing coke," Fleischman added.

By the time Dodi met Diana, he had only quieted down a bit. He was still a restless, unreliable cocaine addict—with the only survivor of the crash that killed him and Diana, Trevor Rees-Jones, saying he infuriated chauffeurs by turning up late, could barely sit still, and always urged his drivers to speed through streets as he hated sitting in traffic.

In the course of his six-week relationship with Diana, he showered her with a multistranded seed-pearl bracelet, a Jaeger-LeCoultre wristwatch studded with diamonds, a silver photo frame with a romantic inscription, and a gold dress ring with pavé diamonds that was on her finger at the time of the accident.

On the first Al-Fayed vacation at his Saint-Tropez estate in July, with William and Harry in tow, Dodi was still dating his red-hot Calvin Klein model and fiancée Kelly Fisher.

Rees-Jones said, "Diana could do miles better than this guy, for Christ's sake."

Diana and Dodi first went public with their relationship when they showed up together at Lucas Carton restaurant in Paris on July 25, 1997.

Two weeks later they were spotted cuddling on a $32 million yacht off Sardinia. Snaps of Diana and Dodi getting intimate had a devastating effect in the UK. Others believe she was only hoping to make her ex-boyfriend, Dr. Haznet Kahn, and even Charles jealous. Either way, sparks flew between her and Dodi—and Diana dared cameras to document her happiness.

Then fifteen-year-old Prince William burst into tears when they were published and had to be consoled on the phone by his mother as he was dreading the commentary from schoolmates when he returned to Eton for the autumn term. They may also have had the desired effect by enraging the queen—but they sent Diana's ex, Khan, running farther for the hills. Many of Diana's pals believed she set up the pictures, wrongly believing they would make her heart surgeon love so jealous he would sweep back into her life with an engagement ring.

Instead, it was the sort of headline-grabbing display that left Khan breathing a sigh of relief that he had escaped her life-sapping whirlwind of drama and fame.

Days before her ill-fated final holiday with Dodi, Diana had been campaigning against land mines in Bosnia. But the final weeks of her life were spent seeing Mohamed Al-Fayed desperately showing off his toys to Diana as he saw her as his ticket into the British "establishment" he both hated and desperately wanted to be inducted into. However, the restored mansion in Bois de Bologne that once belonged to the Windsors that Mohamed Al-Fayed said he would give to his son and Diana spooked the princess, and she stayed only ten minutes when she visited the estate the day before her death.

As writer Tina Brown said, "It cut too close to the bone for her to linger at a place of royal exile, while her boys were nestling in the bosom of the Windsor family at Balmoral and she was floating, Wallis-Simpson-like, around the pleasure spots of the Mediterranean. The ghosts of the Windsor house tour only contributed to her longing to get the hell out of Paris and go home."

Before she could get back to the UK, she endured a final act of bedlam orchestrated by cocaine addict Dodi—the fatal decision to recruit Henri Paul to drive them away from his father's Ritz Hotel in Paris.

Diana told paparazzi, who watched her and Dodi holidaying during her final summer, they were going to be "surprised with the next thing I'll do"—fueling rumors she was going to marry Dodi. But at the inquest into Diana's death, Rosa Monckton testified that her friend died in love with Khan, saying she was still infatuated with the surgeon at the time of her death. She said Diana was "deeply upset and hurt" when he broke off with her in the summer of 1997, adding, "Diana hoped that they would be able to have a future together. She wanted to marry him."

WHERE HE IS NOW

Dodi was originally interred in Brookwood Cemetery near Woking, Surrey, just before midnight the day he died, in accordance with Muslim tradition. However, he was disinterred and reinterred on the grounds of the Fayed estate in Oxted, Surrey, in October of 1997.

Dodi's father has also famously erected two memorials to his son and Diana at Harrods. The first, unveiled on April 12, 1998, consists of photos of the two behind a pyramid-shaped display that holds a wineglass still smudged with lipstick from Diana's last dinner, as well as a ring Dodi purchased the day before they died believed to be an early engagement ring for Diana, bought before Dodi was going to tell her to choose her own.

The second tribute, unveiled in 2005 and titled "Innocent Victims," is a nine-foot-high bronze statue of the two dancing on a beach, beneath the wings of an albatross. (The statue would ultimately be removed in 2018 by new owners of Harrods in Knightsbridge, where it had previously been located, and returned to Al-Fayed.) The memorials were designed by eighty-year-old Bill Mitchell, a close friend of Dodi's father and the architect for Harrods for more than forty years.

***

In addition to the suitors profiled here, there is evidence for another kind of relationship that Diana may have had "waiting in the wings." Though unbelievable—or even unfathomable—for most people, there is reason to believe the litany of men associated with Diana does not quite end here. This is because, despite being believed to have accepted Dodi's proposal the night she was killed, Diana was already secretly making plans to date two other men as "insurance" against their relationship failing like all her others.

From the *Jonikal* yacht, she was deep in discussions with the Chinese entrepreneur David Tang, who was helping her make plans for a three-day visit to Hong Kong in September. He died at age sixty-three in 2017—days before the twentieth anniversary of Diana's crash.

Diana's new interest in China was also stoked by Gulu Lalvani. The Hong Kong-based electronics entrepreneur, now eighty, was founder of Binatone, a company valued at some $572 million. The Monday before her accident, Diana had made plans from the *Jonikal* to see him on her return to London. At that point, she and Lalvani had been seeing each other a couple of times a week.

It was his appearance in her life that caused Diana's last breach in the spring of 1997 with her mother, who exploded on the phone about her daughter's multiple "relationships with Muslim men." (Lalvani was actually a Punjabi Sikh, but, as far as Diana's mother was concerned, he was still unacceptably brown.)

A blind person could see the patterns here. Married men. Taken men. Men with ties to the military. Men with qualities that would make the royal establishment uncomfortable.

Diana was no respecter of convention. Her choice of men makes this abundantly clear. When she chose, she chose dangerously. Perhaps this was part of the attraction for her. Whatever the case, it is also clear that her actions regarding men indicated that she was not a person who could be controlled. She would have what she wanted—when she wanted—and was clearly willing to make very dangerous choices when necessary to get it.

Back in 1997, Colin continued his investigations, with no clue that he had stumbled in at the very end of a long story when it came to the men in the deceased princess's life . . . and so much more.

***

DETECTIVE'S NOTEBOOK

DATELINE: Third day at crime scene, September 1997

With my recent bout of restlessness, I formulated a plan to get my sleeping habits into a routine. Having programmed my alarm clock for the crack of dawn, I turned in for the night. As daybreak peeped through the curtains, I headed straight to the scene. The three-mile walk seemed to get me going for the day, to shake off the jet lag. I needed to get myself into the scene, into the puzzle again, among the mourners. There were always at least a dozen or more souls keeping the vigil, flowers in hand, no matter the weather or the time of day. It was humbling to witness the outpouring. Grief from so many that, like me, had never even met Princess Diana. I stopped, just as you do when you enter a church or a law court. The dignity that this stretch of road now commanded was unfathomable. I then began to walk. I strolled the approach and the tunnel entrance over and over. I ambled up and down the many surrounding side streets and laneways looking for clues, anything that might provide a new slant on my investigation. I tilted my head upward, noting the many windows that overlooked the scene, apartments with ideal vantage points. Were there any wakeful residents on the night of the accident? Anyone who may have brushed aside their drapes for a breath of fresh air and seen the taillights of a doomed Mercedes?

After a brief breakfast at a nearby brasserie café, it was time for me to burn some shoe leather. Time to get back to basics, the stuff of the traditional detective: knocking on all the doors in the region. I stood at the edge of the river and glanced at what lay ahead, hundreds of windows and far too many doors. I figured there was at least two days' solid work in front of me, and I wondered how on earth I'd get through this impossible task. I decided it would be a carefully constructed blend of front and bluff. The front would be the very gumption of knocking on each and every door and the bluff would be the ultimate test to my past undercover police skills: pretending to be a curious Australian, an amateur sleuth with a healthy interest in unraveling the accident that killed Princess Diana. I paced around by the river rehearsing my covert story, as I used to do a couple of years earlier when I was really undercover, ingratiating myself with crooks, drug dealers, and murderers. But this time around I'd be up against the smarts of the French, no easy targets, I thought.

The first building I tackled was at the mouth of the merge lane. Directly overlooking the accident site, it appeared to be an apartment block for well-to-do Parisians. It was. Starting with the lower levels first, I buzzed the ground-floor security button. The voice of what audibly was a little old lady with absolutely no command of the English language replied through a tiny speaker. We verbally wrestled with our respective tongues before she fell quiet. Moments later a pair of fine metal spectacles with the predicted elderly woman close behind peeped cautiously at me from between a pair of lace curtains. Thinking fast, I began waving my hands, pointing to the roadway and the tunnel, making a motion like holding a steering wheel. I pulled my passport from my trouser pocket and held it up to the window before performing an encore of my pantomime. My little old lady let go of her curtains and disappeared. My heart sank. I paced a few steps back toward the street and tilted my head upward, looking for any signs of life at one of the other overlooking windows. No such luck, this covert gig was looking tough, I thought. How was I ever going to make any progress without a fluency in the native dialect of the locals?

As I pondered the arduousness of the task before me I heard a click and the heavy old-world security door released. Filled with a second wind, I bolted in before my benefactor could reconsider. My eyes adjusted quickly to the dimmer light and I scanned the hall for her front door. The kind old dear was standing on her threshold sporting a neat chignon of gray hair and the faintest of smiles. Over a cup of chamomile tea we play acted our way through an awkward conversation, but one that got results in the end. Maybe this was all going to work out after all?

I managed to communicate that I was from Australia and very saddened by the death of Princess Diana. I was wondering if she had heard the collision or seen the aftermath. A watch, notepad, and some stick figure sketches later and I ascertained that she was asleep at the time of the accident, had woken to the noise of sirens, before seeing the flashing emergency vehicle lights. She observed the progress of those assisting for an hour or so before going back to bed. Basically, she'd seen nothing that could help me. In fact she wasn't even aware that the accident had involved Princess Diana until lunchtime of the fateful day, when she had tuned her radio box to the daily news.

Sadly, she had little more to offer than her charm and her grandmotherly smile. She did, however, walk me through her apartment block and fill me in on who was in residence and, by pointing to her wristwatch, what was the best time to tap on their individual doors. I thanked her and persisted, door after door, through the building and onto the neighboring apartment block.

On each successive door knock one common feature of the apartments became more and more obvious. Despite their proximity to the roadway, it was near impossible for occupants to look down on the tunnel entrance, to get a clear view. Fully mature elm trees lined Cours Albert and the highway. And each of the trees at this time of the year bore a full head of lush green foliage that acted as a canopy and effectively hindered any observation of the roadway from above. Most of the residents pointed this out to me as I spoke to them in their apartments; a few even suggested that I lean from their windows to see for myself. The most I could hope for was someone who had heard the accident. As it turned out there were only a mere handful of those, offering little more than corroboration of the time of the accident. I spoke to as many residents as I could locate in those two grand old buildings over the next days, returning time and time again. I managed to fill my notebook with a run of check marks but no revelations. Despite my lack of success in the information stakes, at least my covert skills were working, I kept at it.

Some 50 yards farther along was the structure I named "apartment block three." Draped in scaffold and completely derelict, this building was undergoing a thorough refurbishment at the time of the accident. Of little interest to my investigation for that reason, the construction site did however provide a buffer between the first two inhabited apartment blocks and three buildings that would prove to be the enigmas of my investigation. The immediate neighbor, the Chamber of Commerce International, bordered the impressive Embassy of Brazil and flanked, in the position furthest from the crime scene, the Embassy of the Republic of Congo. Here we had a run of diplomatic offices sitting side by side, each flying their nation's flags, each within feet of the merge lane and each within feet of the skid marks that scarred the main highway. I strode up and down that short stretch of Cours Albert and surveyed their individual facades until I was tired of looking at them.

My attention was captured by the central structure that was the embassy of Brazil. Three stories high, with twenty or so windows fronting the street, this grand chateau style building at 34 Cours Albert was fortified by a nearly 9-foot-high masonry wall. And capping this was a further 6½ feet of spike-topped wrought iron neatly disguised by a lush hedge of greenery. But it wasn't this serious security or the pair of matching metal gates at each end of the allotment that had me transfixed. It was the fact that what lay behind those gates and behind the watchful eyes of the security cameras mounted high on the walls above, was a substantial driveway. A driveway wide enough for a vehicle, I thought.

Almost on cue, the hefty Brazilian gates swung open and a small vehicle rumbled out, passed me, and slowly dribbled onto the merge lane. I craned my neck trying for a closer look inside. There appeared to be a marshaling area around to the rear of the building through a side archway from whence the car must have originated. The building that occupied the Chamber of Commerce International had no driveway, garage door, or car parking area, nor had the building that housed the Congo Embassy, nor indeed my little old lady's apartment block or its immediate neighbor. I rapidly pushed them all to the back of my mind. There was little doubt that a second car had entered the highway from the merge lane on the night of August 31. And there was little doubt that same car had played an instrumental part in the accident that subsequently occurred claiming the lives of three people. The relationship between this embassy driveway and that merge lane was now seriously teasing the mind of this detective.

With my goal of documenting the area thoroughly, I decided it best nonetheless to sketch the relationship of each building to the mouth of the merge. So, half an hour later, having measured and photographed and made numerous notations, I closed my notebook with the task completed. Glancing upward at the sound of a song of starlings in the trees, I met a metal eye peering back at me, seemingly monitoring my every move. No doubt its lens would have zoomed in on my tape, notebook, and camera. Now overtly conscious that the security guards within would have been swapping comments on my recent antics, readying responses for my inevitable pressing of their intercom, I decided not to be predictable, not to press a buzzer, and stir a rehearsed answer. Instead, I packed away my gear and without a second look back at their fortified home I headed farther along Cours Albert to another string of apartment buildings. Back to tapping on doors, but ones whose occupants I hoped would offer up genuine responses.

Next up was an office building which was the home to France Channel 3. The network's blue cube logo burned brightly on the façade that was also home to the office of the Vietnamese Embassy and an assortment of small businesses. Another run of apartments and I found myself at No. 20, which was a building undergoing significant construction. Here I found what would be the only other vehicular accessible building, but as yet it was unserviceable. I scratched it off my list and turned into Rue Baynard. A one-way street steering traffic away from Cours Albert and pointing it toward the area known as the eighth arrondissement, I surmised it unlikely that a vehicle would have traveled the wrong way down it to use the merge lane. However, I knocked on each door and asked my usual questions regardless.

My third door was answered by a very chatty Englishman who confirmed my findings. He had been in his homeland at the time of the accident, but he was able to clarify that the majority of his neighboring apartments were utilized by foreign governments to house visiting personnel. I coined it the "diplomatic zone." From Rue Baynard I walked along both sides of Rue Jean Goujon, wearing down the skin on the knuckles of my right hand. I noted comments, placed check marks, and talked through the accident with anyone who would give me five minutes. Having completed the entire block, I found myself dismayed at how little people seemed to care about the death of the once-to-be queen of England. Most just voiced what trifles they knew or saw and brushed it aside. In short, I discovered nothing that I didn't already know.

It was now quite late, yet the overpass to the tunnel was still awash with pilgrims. I hunted out a quintessential café on the small square overlooking the Pont de l'Alma, found a seat, and stared at the landscape of dying flowers and fallen tissues. Chez Francis was doing a roaring trade. It was a delightful-looking brasserie, with its street-side seats that afforded the ideal views of the Eiffel Tower. It serviced hundreds of extra clients each day, all in need of the outlook, coffee and croissants, and a toilet break from their mourning.

As I sat, I began to speculate what-ifs. What if a late-night guest had this same seat on that fateful Saturday in August? What if they'd heard the crash, perhaps even run to the tunnel to lend a hand? The waiter who took my order this evening had greeted me in English. His name was Roland, and I seized the opportunity to try out my hypothesis. Yes, he said the brasserie was still open after midnight of that night, however there were only the staff lumbered with cleaning up still in attendance. No diners, I thought, but what about those staff? As luck would have it, Roland was one of that team. However, he was embarrassed to admit, he had paid scant attention to the commotion.

He suggested that I wander back this coming Saturday night and inquire of his guests. Many of the late nighters, he continued, were regulars who called the brasserie their "local." Perhaps some had been among those who had gathered on the overpass roof of the tunnel to witness the removal of the twisted mess of metal, rubber, leather, and human flesh. Those sightseers had to have come from somewhere, I thought. It was certainly possible that a stroll home at the end of an evening out could have been interrupted by the sight or sound of the accident. I surmised correctly that my waiter had not been among the spectators, a fact he confirmed. In a hurry to be home after along day's work, Roland recounted, he had no interest in that sort of thing.

I persevered with my door knocking. By the end of my first week, although I had spoken to well over two hundred people, I had learned relatively little. None had seen anything that could possibly advance the investigation. The task had been draining and long; my only consolation that I had at least checked it off. But now I seemed to have run out of leads. So I took Roland's advice and found myself a central table at his establishment on my first Saturday night in Paris. It's well known among those in law enforcement that to visit a crime scene at the same time and on the same day of the week as the incident can often lead to remarkable insights. People are by and large creatures of habit, and those habits extend to doing the same thing at the same time and often routinely on the same day. So here I was positioned perfectly for just such an occurrence. I must have consumed several liters of mineral water during the course of that evening as successive locals came and went. His regulars were a thoroughly decent group. Disappointingly, after all the chat and bonhomie, I still had nothing by way of a witness. Reluctant to write off the experience as a complete failure, I decided to take the opportunity to pay a visit to the Brazilian embassy. It was still niggling away at me.

It was well after 10 p.m. when I arrived at the front. I took a seat across the way beneath a tree and in the dark of the night. I lingered, watching and waiting. Above the wall of green and steel I could see a few of the upstairs windows were open. The occasional chirp of faint laughter emanating from the windows hinted that a function was underway. I listened to the sounds of a small crowd as below I observed security guards patrolling the grounds with dogs. I stretched my legs several times over the next couple of hours, changing my vantage position and pondering the likelihood of such an event having occurred on another Saturday night in recent history. Just then the big metal security doors opened briefly, let out a car, and then closed again.

A guard was leaning his shoulder on the bars next to the gate, smoking. A lean canine crouched at his heels and cocked its head quizzically at me. I approached the gate. Pleased to find a sympathetic ear to his long hours pacing the small grounds, he and I struck up a brief conversation. I nodded understandingly and offered, "too bad" in appropriate silences. These gatherings went on all the time, he bemoaned and I commiserated. Perhaps he had found a break from the routine with the events of August 31? While he hadn't been on duty that night, the security officer went on to happily inform me that, "yes" they had indeed had a function on the night of the accident. Bingo! I attempted to find out more about the function, only to be given the descriptive "diplomatic." My guard friend for the moment had little else to offer me and I realized I was merely a man in the street he chose to speak briefly to as he sneaked himself a cigarette.

Then it was time to get back to work; he moved off to escort another vehicle safely from the compound and I shuffled off down the street. I would get little more from the man with the mean dog.

By the time the last of the embassy lights were turned out, I had observed a dozen or so vehicles depart the grounds. Two of them were Fiats. I watched thoughtfully as all of the cars traveled the 20 meters to the merge lane and turned onto the main roadway, then through the underpass and into the night, just as I had believed was the case on the night Princess Diana's car came to grief. My shift of sticky-nose surveillance ended with a slow walk home.

I spent the subsequent Saturday night huddled near the merge lane, at the same hour, looking toward the Brazilian embassy and the service lane out the front. As I waited, spying on that unremarkable little road, I couldn't help but lock my eyes onto the security doors of the embassy and track the path of the occasional exiting motorcar. Perhaps they were embassy staff driving home, maybe officials at the end of their busy day, or a guest heading wherever, tired and unsure of the dangers that lay ahead as the merge lane met the main roadway. Eventually I suffered my lone, tired thoughts and headed home myself, back to my hotel room.

CHAPTER SIX

August 31, 1997.

A more ominous date in Diana's life, there never was.

As it does for all of us, death came for Diana. But for the beautiful princess, it came tragically and horribly, and wrapped in unbelievable mystery.

That evening, Diana slipped away to shop briefly on the elegant Avenue des Champs-Élysées. By 9 p.m., she and Dodi were seated at L'Espadon. The moon was out and the stars were shining over Paris. A balmy breeze brushed the leaves of the manicured ficus trees around Diana and Dodi's table. After dinner, the couple decided to drive to the fabulous villa they planned to make their love nest after they married, according to the Fayed family.

"They were going to live in Chateau Windsor—the house where the duke and duchess of Windsor spent their exile after he abdicated as King of England," one insider told this book.

It was in 1986 that Dodi's father bought the historic villa in the Bois de Boulogne for $7 million.

Our insider added:

> Dodi's father bought the house after the duchess died and he spent millions restoring it to the glory it had when the Windsors were the toast of Paris.
>
> He restored antiques, bought expensive rugs in exactly the same design as the old ones—and even had the duchess's underwear drawer restocked. He wanted it to be just like the way it was in the Windsors' day—a museum dedicated to them. Dodi insisted they make their home there after his son confided in him he was to marry Diana. He

> immediately made plans to sell the priceless antiques, rugs, and drapes. Dodi was talking about having several children with Diana and a museum would have been no place to bring them up.

It was just after midnight when the couple left the Ritz.

Dodi set in motion a game of cat-and-mouse with the horde of photographers surrounding the front entrance.

He asked his usual chauffeur to drive away in his limo, which was parked in front of the hotel as a decoy, in the hope the photographers would follow.

Immaculately dressed in spotless white trousers, at around 12:15 a.m., Diana climbed into the passenger seat of the black Mercedes that would hurtle her headlong into death.

Their black Mercedes S280 raced toward the Pont de l'Alma tunnel at top speed. Despite the decoy attempt, paparazzi were still in pursuit, hoping to get a picture every tabloid editor in the world had wanted: Princess Diana and her new boyfriend, Dodi.

Behind the wheel of the luxury car with silver trim was drunk (or drugged) chauffeur Henri Paul, in no condition to handle the hulking 4,900-pound luxury vehicle.

Perhaps blinded by love for each other, Diana and her lover Dodi, beside her in the back of the Mercedes S280 with silver trim, had no idea he was incapacitated beyond belief. The autopsy of the forty-one-year-old former French air captain showed he had a blood alcohol level of 0.19 percent, three times the legal limit in France. Medics warn such a high level can cause staggering and double vision—rendering it almost suicidal to get in a car and drive. A September 1997 analysis of Paul's hair and spinal cord also detected the antidepressant Prozac as well as Tiapridal, which is used to combat alcohol withdrawal. The driver also had a chip on his shoulder, as he'd been off-duty that night, downing Scotch and beer at home. It's feared he had sunk the equivalent of one-and-a-half bottles of wine and was furious he'd been called back to work to drive the world's most famous couple.

Before speeding off with Diana and Dodi, Paul snarled at the pap pack Diana spent her life shielding her eyes from, "You won't catch us!"

A photographer at the scene told our investigation that Paul's actions reminded him of an alcoholic he knew well—his father.

With bodyguard Trevor Rees-Jones (who would miraculously survive the crash with serious injuries yet remember nothing) in the front passenger seat, infuriated Paul shoved the $123,000 car in gear and veered away from the back entrance of the Ritz hotel Diana had used to try and evade snappers. But speeding along the expressway along the Seine River, it was obvious the ruse was useless. The paparazzi at first followed a decoy car, but quickly realized they had been duped and quickly zeroed in on their prey.

Paul drove along the Rue Cambon to the junction with the Rue de Rivoli, then turned right, heading into the Place de la Concorde. After being held at traffic lights there, he continued toward the embankment road of the River Seine, avoiding the more direct route of the Avenue des Champs-Élysées. He then drove along the embankment road, Cours la Reine, and Cours Albert, passing under the Alexandre III tunnel.

It was considered by chauffeurs in Paris as the "professional driver's route" as it allows them to avoid the heavy traffic of the Avenue des Champs-Élysées on Saturday nights. But, according to those same drivers, the obvious route after the Alexandre III tunnel is an exit slip road to the right, leading to the avenue George V or the avenue Marceau.

Paul didn't take the slip road, but continued toward the four-lane, two-way Pont de l'Alma underpass with several pap vehicles having closed in on the Merc.

Despite the underpass having a lip at its east entrance, Paul rocketed to 121 mph as the car hit the opening of the tunnel next to the River Seine, under the Pont de l'Alma Bridge.

His speed as he hit the tunnel's opening lip would have sent the vehicle soaring into the air.

It was probably while airborne that drunk Paul disastrously tried to correct his steering while simultaneously trying to negotiate a looming curve in the road.

His driving was a mess he couldn't fix. The car clipped the tight wall of the 660-foot underpass close to the lip of the tunnel. Paul lost control of the massive Mercedes. It was slung diagonally across the road, before careering into the solid concrete thirteenth pillar that supports the canter of the underpass.

The car rolled over a full 360 degrees, then spun 180 degrees before it slammed into a wall on the opposite side of the road.

Coming to rest on all four wheels—facing the direction from which it had entered the tunnel—the car had been mashed like a squeezed accordion.

Passersby heard an explosion and what one couple described as a "big bang." Then there was quiet—except for the car horn blaring. Paul's body had depressed it when it slumped lifeless onto the steering wheel.

The only other noise at this point was smoke hissing from the battered hulk of the Mercedes.

Then came Diana's moans.

Diana—who had not worn her seat belt—was suffering catastrophic internal bleeding. Her battered body was also battling to cope with the extreme shock of the collision.

She had brutally rotated during the crash, and her rare injuries suggested her heart had been thrown violently forward inside her chest when the car crashed.

Paul, forty-one, and Dodi, forty-two, had been killed instantly.

Diana's six-foot-two bodyguard Trevor Rees-Jones—now fifty years old—shattered all fourteen bones in his face and sustained serious injuries to the torso. Doctors would later insert more than thirty metal plates and screws into his face, which was so mangled they had to use family photographs for reference during surgeries. But Rees-Jones's life was saved by the same simple decision many crash experts believe would have meant Diana would be alive today—wearing a seat belt.

There was hardly any sound for the first two minutes after the crash except for the horn. The noise emanated weakly from both ends of the tunnel—from the east end, which the black Mercedes had sped into moments before it crashed, and from the west end, where the narrow tunnel opened onto a spectacular view of the left bank of the Seine.

On the packed streets above—where the lights of the Eiffel Tower had yet to be shut off for the night—the muffled sound of one car horn might not even be noticed.

But seconds before the crash, American tourists Tom Richardson and Joanna Luz from San Diego heard the accident. When they ran into the tunnel, they saw the car facing back in the direction from which it had come, its roof crushed, its windshield smashed, and its airbags deployed.

In front of the wreck, a paparazzo—the last Diana pap—raised his camera and began to snap.

French firefighter Xavier Gourmelon, fifty-one, was one of the first emergency workers to see the blood-soaked innards of Diana's death car—the front airbags that blasted out when Paul hit the pillar soaked in viscera.

He said Diana was curiously free of blood and clinging onto consciousness and had her eyes open as he carefully pulled her from the smoking wreckage.

Xavier gave her CPR but she suffered a cardiac arrest as she was gently placed on a stretcher. Another firefighter said he heard her mutter "Dodi, Dodi" over and over again before her battered body convulsed during her heart attack.

Xavier said:

> My ten-man team was in two trucks and we were first to arrive. The car was in a mess and we just dealt with it like any road accident. I could see the driver was already dead and there was nothing that could be done for him. Mr. Al-Fayed was in the back and in a bad condition. He had a cardiac arrest in the car and when he was taken out he was declared dead by a paramedic. The bodyguard in the front was conscious, but he was trapped and had very severe facial injuries. The woman, who I later found out was Princess Diana, was on the floor in the back. She was moving very slightly, and I could see she was alive. I held her hand and told her to be calm and keep still. I said I was there to help and reassured her. She said, "My God, what's happened?" I massaged her heart and a few seconds later she started breathing again. As far as I knew when she was in the ambulance, she was alive, and I expected her to live. But I found out later she had died in hospital. It was very upsetting. I know now that there were serious internal injuries, but the whole episode is still very much on my mind. And the memory of that night will stay with me forever.

Sadly, Diana died as she had lived much of her life—in agony.

The princess who had survived the torment of bulimia, self-harm, drug and pill addictions, and a string of broken relationships, was in a huge amount of pain from 12:23 a.m. to 4 a.m. on August 31, 1997, when surgeons finally gave up trying to massage her heart back into action and declared her dead.

A review of Diana's official forty-page autopsy report reveals she sustained "blunt chest and probably head trauma" when the Mercedes carrying her hurtled into that solid concrete pillar.

Astonishingly, the first witnesses and emergency workers on the scene found her sitting on the floor of the car, her eyes open while she mumbled indecipherable phrases.

Yet soon after that, she would close her eyes forevermore.

***

For those close to the princess, that night remains seared in their memories. The princess had been on the cusp of finally finding great happiness—or so it seemed—and now, in one horrible instant, all of that was ripped away from her. As millions around the world turned on their televisions in horror and disbelief, they began asking questions—many of which have still not been answered to any great satisfaction. Exactly what happened? Why did the car crash? Who were the people involved?

And the central question on everyone's mind: Was it an accident. . . or was it something more sinister?

From the very outset, the French police made astonishing errors and misjudgments, but perhaps no action on their part was more egregious than failing to treat the accident like the crime scene it was. The entire area around the tunnel was busy. People came and went on foot. There was great disorganization. No real security was implemented to keep pedestrians from approaching. And nobody seemed to know who was in charge.

After the injured and dead were removed from the Mercedes, a tow truck was reversed into the tunnel with a crane. The Mercedes had not even had time to be adequately photographed by police for clues or evidence. Nonetheless, the car was loaded up and hauled away.

After that, a different government vehicle arrived and began hosing down the street. The entire street was washed clean.

Next, four government workers in bright green and yellow cleaning gear arrived to begin sweeping up the debris.

It looked for all the world as though the French government's primary priority had become ensuring that all evidence of the event that had just occurred was removed as quickly as possible so that morning traffic would not be encumbered.

Almost immediately, important facts began to get out. The driver of the car had been drinking. There had been flashes inside the tunnel. The Mercedes had connected with another car.

Yet—unfortunately and unbelievably—it now seemed that definitive answers would not be easy to come by because the French authorities had been so quick to clean up the accident scene.

***

Diana's final hours can hardly be understood without delving into the world of the man at the wheel of the car that ended her life.

We know the numbers, the tale of the tape. The autopsy and toxicology report on Henri Paul showed that he was blind drunk at the time of the accident. He was at thrice the legal limit for drunk driving. His blood also contained a cocktail of drugs. He was said to be a habitual drunk.

In the minds of many casual observers of the accident, this had been the beginning and the end of the story. A drunken driver is startled by photographers and crashes in a tunnel.

But there is more to the story.

***

On paper, at least, Henri Paul was a model employee. He was employed by the Al-Fayed family and had been for over ten years. In addition to being a driver, he was also a pilot, having received his pilot's license in 1976.

This pilot's license is very important.

All French pilots are required to have an annual pilot's physical in order to retain their license. This annual examination tests for—among other things—evidence of alcohol problems. It includes bloodwork, and a test of liver function.

Henri Paul's most recent pilot's physical happened just three days before the accident. He passed with flying colors. Paul's parents have also insisted that it was not normal for him to drink to excess.

After the accident, associates of Paul testified to French police that Paul did not have any special tolerance for alcohol. They said that he did not normally drink to excess. They also said that when he did drink to excess, it was obvious. In short, he lacked any of the symptoms of a classic alcoholic.

Paul's personal physician told French police that Paul was not alcoholic, but that she was worried he might become so out of despondency over a recent romantic breakup. Accordingly, she was prescribing him Prozac for his depression, and an anti-alcoholism medication called Aotal. In the autopsy, a further prescription drug called Zentel—used to treat worms—was also found in Paul's system. His physician could not explain how it got there and denied prescribing it.

On the night he died, security cameras captured Paul waving casually to photographers as they waited to snap photos of Diana and Dodi. It is not known if this was merely a friendly wave, or if it was a sign of intoxication. Witnesses that night have made varying, inconsistent claims about the amount that they saw Paul drink. One account—which was affirmed by his bar bill that night—shows him consuming only two alcoholic drinks before driving. However, other witnesses and expert analysis investigating the case have put the real number closer to ten drinks. They have also cited witnesses who have affirmed that Paul did appear to be visibly intoxicated when he climbed into the car to drive Diana.

Yet there were other questions about Paul that made our investigative team understand that we needed to take a second and third look.

Henri Paul was a forty-one-year-old professional driver. Yet, when he died, it was revealed that he had the equivalent of approximately $340,000 in multiple bank accounts. How? How did this happen, and who was paying him?

Drivers, even drivers of the very wealthy, do not normally amass this kind of money. Many alleged that Paul had earned this money by working covertly for security services. By spying. But for what or whom, it remains to be seen.

Yet there were those who defended Paul's wealth, and insisted he'd come by it legitimately. Paul's coworkers attested that sometimes Paul received four-figure tips from the cadre of international royalty he drove. Further, there was evidence that Paul had apparently used his money to begin buying rental properties, and that income from collecting rents could be a source of the money that authorities found squirreled away.

Yet for too many, the story simply does not add up.

Henri Paul was responsible for the safe travel of the most photographed, most famous woman in the world. Yet his blood was a mess of alcohol, Prozac, and anti-alcohol pharmaceuticals. The romantic breakup that had necessitated the Prozac also suggests that his mental state may have been impaired in other ways. In short, a cocktail of depression and booze added up to Diana's driver being a wholly unfit man who seems to have taken no reasonable security measures to safeguard Diana. His behavior, his drug taking, his boozing, and his irresponsibility is the perfect example for what a security officer should not do when undertaking close personal protection of a dignitary.

But Paul's selfish and reckless actions also seem to have been influenced by his attraction to the celebrity of the whole sordid affair. Paul was a man who wanted to attach himself to the glamour and excitement that surrounded Princess Diana. For you see, he was not only intoxicated by alcohol and drugs, but by the chance to pal around with the very person he should have been shielding, not fascinated with.

How did Paul come to be driving Diana that night? Is drunken driving the chief culprit in explaining Diana's accident, or is something more sinister at play?

***

DETECTIVE'S NOTEBOOK

DATELINE: One week into the crime-scene investigation, September 1997

What will history make of Henri Paul? Will he be remembered forever as the man who killed the queen of hearts? Will his name become as infamous as that of Lee Harvey Oswald or John Hinckley Jr. and be assured of its place as the answer to a future Trivial Pursuit question? Or will he be forgotten, his name simply fade away like the rubber tire residue at the Pont de l'Alma tunnel entrance?

In time, I turned my attentions to Paul, the ill-fated driver of the doomed Mercedes-Benz. In among the mountain of media clippings that I had amassed, there was a decent-sized pile pertaining to the Mercedes driver's supposed intoxication that night. The media was adamant that Henri Paul was as pie-eyed as the proverbial parrot, and all that I had picked up to date seemed to suggest the same. Of course, there was the predictable media release from the Fayed conglomerate's Ritz-Carlton Hotel, stating adamantly that their chauffeur was not intoxicated. Released in early September, it read, "Henri Paul did not have any appearance of being over excited or being drunk as a pig." Odd words, I thought as I read the comment. Then as if the organization was desperate to make its point, their security manager added, "He was sober, he didn't smell of alcohol, his gait was steady, and they had no suggestion or indication that he was anything other than completely sober." What's more, a senior executive affirmed that Henri Paul "was an exemplary employee."

It was now the wrong side of September and there were media leaks and local gossip apropos Henri's drinking habits surfacing daily. Newspaper reports quoted inflated blood alcohol readings and the man's reputation was sliding rapidly down the slippery slope. The initial blood alcohol test administered as a requirement of the autopsy procedure after Henri's death produced a reading of 0.175%. This had been followed by a second comparison test that indicated 0.187%. Either way, blood alcohol evidence had Henri Paul thoroughly smashed. By the law of vicarious liability, culpability for any misfortune that may occur while he was on duty in this condition would unquestionably land on his shoulders, and (normally) on the shoulders of his employer. I was beginning to sense a more self-serving motive behind the Ritz-Carlton's championing of their hapless employee.

To offer the benefit of the doubt to all concerned, I felt it my duty to soak up a few whiskey sours in the Ritz. It was time for me to talk with Henri's friends and workmates and ascertain as much as possible about the sobriety of the driver who not only killed himself but also the hottest targets of the paparazzi. I donned my best outfit and uncharacteristically I caught a taxi, gesturing for him to let me out just shy of the four vanilla-colored canopies that signaled the entrance. Nodding to the doorman on duty, I pushed on the imposing revolving doors and stepped back one hundred years into the vision of its creator, César Ritz. I was almost bowled over by the hotel's magnificence, wondering at how the wealthy spent their time. Keeping on the move, knowing the moment I looked befuddled I would more than likely be called out, I cursed not having packed a Zegna double-breasted cashmere suit, a pair of Berluti Russian calfskin brogues, and a splash of Paul Smith "London" aftershave. Then I could have faced the grand old pub without fear.

However, I strolled purposefully over the polished marble and hand-spun rugs and gathered up a newspaper, flinging it under my arm. In keeping with my nouveau persona I inquired confidently of a bellhop, "Where's the Hemingway Bar, lad?" He pointed me deeper into the building to a nook decked out in original timber paneling and old-world charm. My first win, hopefully an omen of things to come! I pulled up a stool and sat with a lonely cocktail waiter. Itching to divorce his glass-polishing napkin, he was also keen for some small talk as he shook the best and most expensive whiskey sour of my life. Two drinks later and he delivered up the mandatory mixed nuts along with the comment that Henri Paul was a serious drinker who often snuck into the bar to take "a shot or two" while on duty. And yes, Henri Paul had been drinking there on the night of his fateful drive.

My next stop was the quaint restaurant-cum-cocktail bar known as Bar Vendôme, off the hotel garden. I beelined for the bar under the watchful eye of the maître d', who was of the belief that I was seeking a table for an early dinner but opting for a drink first. I had made a mental note of a story reported by London's *Evening Standard* that "Henri Paul bumped into people as he left the bar" just hours prior to the tragedy. When the moment was right, I steered my conversation with the bartender in this direction adding that I had heard that Henri Paul had consumed two shots of pastis (a French aperitif similar in strength to whiskey). He quipped that the story was a "fabrication by the media" as he twirled a sprig of lemon rind on my upcoming third whiskey sour. Then he handed me a real gem. Henri, he confided, was a regular drinker at his swanky establishment, mostly after dinner, after hours. I declined his offer to put my drink on my room tab, paid cash instead, and wandered out, knowing that I had won that battle nicely.

It was now shortly after 9 p.m. I headed for the guest foyer, where, surrounded by Louis XV antiques, I lost myself in my newspaper. I needed to kill some time until the night staff clocked on. With the way my luck was playing out, I was growing confident of my chances of snaring a chat with one of the floor security hounds. The sophisticates were beginning to arrive, and I toyed with a little mental game of "how much did that outfit cost you, buddy?" I didn't come up with anything in my cop's price bracket.

As the lights were dimmed for the parading of the serious fashionistas, I snuck out a side door and bent the ear of one of the hotel's bouncers. We stood on Rue Cambon chatting about this and that. His chest almost puffed out with self-importance that one of the guests was interested in his routine and, in no time, he lost himself to a spate of gossip, about a dead man he had once worked with. Of the opinion that Henri Paul was a bit of a heavy drinker, he was quick to add that he liked him. I was able to squeeze in three significant questions:

> Was Henri an alcoholic?
>
> To which he replied, "Maybe."
>
> Did Henri drink in the bars?
>
> His answer, "Yes."
>
> In the Hemingway bar?
>
> He stated, "Yes."

By this stage, feeling a little puffed out myself, I elected to hit the night air and take a brisk walk to recharge my batteries before doing the rounds of the eclectic collection of clubs in the precinct. I strolled across the lobby and trod the plush red carpet once more before saying goodbye to the Ritz, knowing that I was unlikely to ever return.

As I ambled along the cobblestone pavements, I processed that which my last few drinks had taught me. A clear-cut portrait was forming in my mind of a chauffeur with an alcohol addiction. I coupled this with the widely reported story that Henri Paul was a frequent user of the prescription drugs Prozac and Triapdal, and feared the result of the equation, a lethal cocktail. Diana and Dodi were indeed flirting with death when they stepped into the rear of the Mercedes with Henri Paul behind the wheel. I flicked a look at my notebook and the list I had named "Henri's drinking holes." The well-known Harry's Bar was only a block and a half away, at 5 Rue Daunou. This would be my next stop.

As far as single-malt whiskey is concerned, this old-world bar is an institution. Offering sixty different types of my preferred beverage, Harry's has been around as long as the Ritz, and has played host to the drinking set of Paris since day one. I was greeted with the overused cliché proudly informing me that Ernest Hemingway once drank there. I mean how many bars worldwide could that man have patronized, really? My inquiry, it seemed, had come down to two drunks, both frequenting the same watering hole!

It had been widely speculated by the world media that Henri Paul had been drinking in Harry's Bar on the night of his final shift. I sniffed out the manager before my first drink had found its coaster and went straight for the jugular, posing my nosy questions. He seemed a fairly decent man, despite the usual pomp and ceremony that accompanies owners of such establishments. Verifying beyond doubt that Henri Paul was a regular drinker there, he was equally adamant that he had not been there on the night of August 31, although he had been seen there the day earlier. I could think of no credible reason to stop for a taste of a second whiskey as tempting as their splendid array was, so I moved on to the Champmesle four blocks away. The walk, I thought, would once again do me good.

A narrow-fronted little bar, the type that dotted many of the backstreets of Paris, the Champmesle was the closest geographically to where Henri Paul lived, in his nondescript tiny apartment above a shop. It was so small that a mere ten patrons was all that would be necessary to send the barmen into a flap. He was in a flap on the night of my visit. The joint was jumping, and the sounds of cool jazz saturated the night air. I squeezed a tiny section of space at the counter, ordered a longneck beer, and waited for the right time to mention Henri Paul. An unsettling bout of unwanted eye-to-eye contact from a male patron had me realize that the hole-in-the-wall bar was the second home to the neighborhood gays. I shuffled off to stand at the door. A well-groomed couple struck up a chat so as not to see me waste my beer, so I took the risk of mentioning the name of one of their locals, Henri. Our subsequent conversation cost me an extra three beers; however, by its end, I had proof positive that Henri Paul had consumed a "couple of drinks" there only hours before the crash. The patrons introduced me to the manager, who recalled Henri Paul to be a lonely and depressed man, one of the many, he said, that frequented his bar. He also remembered Henri Paul was on a break from work, having a quiet drink on his way home. The drink was interrupted as he was recalled to duty, and offered, what was sadly remembered as his final farewell.

As I slunk back to my soft hotel bed, I speculated how I would have coped if now called upon to chauffeur Diana at high speed through the streets of Paris late at night while being pursued by a horde of paparazzi. While the thought initially put a smile on my face, I still worked through the essence of the question. I had certainly had way too many whiskey sours to take the risk of driving, but as I had just discovered, prior to the commencement of Henri's last journey, he had not only met me drink for drink but had also been on duty for the previous sixteen hours with virtually no structured break or downtime of any consequence.

I carried this thought with me as I turned out the bedside lamp and rolled over to attempt some much-needed shuteye. Trouble was, there was another thought there also, one that kept pushing its way to the forefront of my consciousness. It was more a snippet of information really, but one that I had heard repeated a few times over during the past evening. Perhaps just workplace gossip, on face value I knew it required investigation. I promised it my keenest attention the following day, pushed it back to the far corner of my mind and closed my eyes.

Knowing there was little I could accomplish along this path in the morning hours, I enjoyed a lengthy lie-in. Showered and shaved, I wandered down to a late breakfast and enjoyed the company of the staff, who were becoming mates by now. I was careful not to divulge what I was really up to, although I had long ago come to know that chambermaids rarely miss a lot. They are a lot sharper than most guests give them credit for; I had learned that much when I was an active detective in Australia.

After idle attempts at chat, I went back to the task that had bothered me the night before. I pondered the best path of discovery. The Benoit restaurant was my quarry—mid-afternoon, between services, my ideal hour of attack.

The story I was following was one that had floated for the duration of the previous evening. A few of the Ritz boys were of the belief that Dodi had purchased an engagement ring. The Benoit was allegedly his chosen location for proposing marriage to Diana on the night of their deaths. When I analyzed the snippets that

I had heard, I rationalized that there were just as many comments from Henri's colleagues that had not heard the rumor as there were those that had, but I needed to find out for myself.

A cab fare from the Ritz, off swanky Rue de Rivoli at 20 Rue St. Martin, I located this gorgeous Michelin star establishment, the home of one of the world's great chefs: Alain Ducasse. With its crispy white tablecloths, fine monogrammed china, and ornate timber paneled partitions between tables, I could instantly accept it as a very romantic location for a proposal. The restaurant was almost empty of lunchtime diners, as I had hoped. The last of the first-class travel set leaving as I entered, black Amex cards being restacked in fat wallets. I decided to take the direct approach and confront the maître d', armed with my best Australian smile. Initially offering a warm handshake in return, the big man's gaze froze over when I explained the purpose for my presence in his dining room. He had adopted his best French maître d' manner: cool, raised eyebrows, and with the accompanying short step backwards. I think my winning line was that I was a police detective in my homeland. He seemed to rationalize that I was a safer bet than a newspaper reporter. I asked the question I had brought with me:

"Were Dianna and Dodi booked into the restaurant on the night of August 30?"

He needed no time to think and replied naturally, and to the affirmative, adding that with such a booking there was no necessity to check his register. He offered that it was his belief that the couple had planned to get engaged that evening, although he could not recall exactly why he held such a belief. He reflected on his last comment for a moment or two before continuing, explaining that Dodi had spoken to him personally about the booking. He walked me over to the table that Dodi had requested, a quiet setting in a corner, away from the windows of the luxurious restaurant alongside the *salon privé*. He added that the couple had never arrived for their table and the booking was canceled, for reasons unknown to the maître d' . . . a love story that ended not long after it had begun: a starry-eyed tragedy that would fascinate forever. We both stared at the empty table for rather too long and then the somewhat stuffy, yet thoroughly decent man offered me a complimentary glass of mineral water and I was away.

On my way back to my hotel room I stopped at a coffeehouse and sat for a spell reminiscing on my time in Paris, allowing the discoveries and disappointments to wash over me. I sat on my coffee until I was forced to order a fresh one as the first cup had soured, as also by then had my mood. My thoughts were lost to a silly man, Henri Paul, and the heartache that he had caused the two sons of Princess Diana, her family, and all the friends and people that cared so deeply for the sometimes troubled, yet magnificently resilient, woman. I found the entire saga almost surreal, as if it had been invented, but I knew to the contrary. It was horribly real. I found a token of solace in the progress of my investigation to date. There was no smoking gun, no terrorism and no espionage, just a drunken driver and a ring that never found a finger.

Ultimately, while Henri Paul may well have fussed over his chauffeuring duties for the princess and her companion, remaining on call, responding to their late-night jaunt, he did a dismal job of evading the paparazzi. In fact, the façade he presented of dodging the photographic pests was just that—a façade. A close study of CCTV footage of the area showed Henri Paul frequently fraternizing with the paparazzi in the hours that lead up to the hurried departure from the Ritz. In fact, the familiarity with which they jousted strongly suggested that he was keeping them abreast of any planned movements. The final footage of Henri Paul outside the hotel clearly shows him signaling to a well-known photographer, just prior to Princess Diana exiting via a rear door.

So, a lonely alcoholic security buffoon, an inconsequential Ritz employee, became lost in a miserable moment of self-importance planning to lead the waiting paparazzi on a merry chase. One that ultimately ensured his name would never be forgotten. And as far as Dodi was concerned, he must surely have been cognizant of the drunken state of his chosen driver. Such quantity of alcohol consumption would not only manifest itself in the chauffeur's swagger, but his breath would have reeked. Under no circumstances should Dodi have allowed Henri Paul to take possession of the car keys that night. Yet, like a lovestruck Romeo, Dodi appeared to have been blind to the potential disaster that would face his love and companions.

Nor should the man more specifically charged with the security of Diana, Trevor Rees-Jones, be absolved from blame. As the only person to survive the horrific smash, he must surely live daily with regrets of his inaction.

As a footnote, in an extraordinary gesture of goodwill, the priest at Henri's burial service recounted to the congregation a letter from the mother of the princess of Wales. It read, “We have neither anger nor reproach. We suffer for Henri’s family. Of all the families concerned their suffering must be the worst.”

The burial of the drunken monkey was overseen by approximately one hundred paparazzi and press photographers, keen to document the latest episode in the saga, before speeding off to deposit their proofs and cash their paychecks.

CHAPTER SEVEN

When Colin McLaren took it upon himself to journey to the site of Diana's death to look for answers back in 1997, he had only the most general sense of the secrets being concealed.

In his own words, Colin has explained how the mystery began to reveal itself—though the answers he sought were still light years away. He wasn't the only one. A confused and grieving public began to pine for answers about what had contributed to the poor princess's death, and conspiracy theories began to emerge.

Meanwhile, those closest to Diana were also aware that she genuinely feared for her life. The conspiracies were given even more credence when butler Paul Burrell came forward with a shocking message from beyond the grave.

To quote Paul Burrell:

> The princess had been persecuted, undermined, misrepresented, misinterpreted all her life, and she was frightened during the last few years of her life. She thought she was being followed. She thought all her phone calls were being tapped. She sat at her desk often late at night and wrote me notes. This letter goes on for ten pages, and part of it reads, "This is the most difficult part of my life. I fear that Charles is going to organize an accident in my car. I am going to die of head injuries and be killed in order that he can marry Camilla."
>
> I read the princess's hand on her own stationery saying that, she prophesized her own death. She prophesized how she would die. She wasn't paranoid. She was an intelligent, young woman who was informed. So, what does that mean? Does that mean she was mad, or

> does it mean that she knew she was going to die? I don't know. I just think it's rather odd that she was here one minute and gone the next.

Paul Burrell's revelations prompted Diana's divorce lawyer, Lord Mishcon, to also come forward.

In October 1996, the princess had shared her deadly serious beliefs with her lawyers, Lord Mishcon, Maggie Rae, and Sandra Davies. They urged her to put her concerns in writing. She wrote:

> This particular phase in my life is the most dangerous. My husband is planning "an accident" in my car, brake failure and serious head injury in order to make the path clear for him to marry.

The document was taken directly to Scotland Yard, where it would stay under lock and key.

Author and magazine editor Ingrid Seward also had a gut response that it might have been more than an accident. As she explains:

> When she died in the crash . . . I thought it might be somebody trying to get at Mohamed Al-Fayed because he had a lot of very powerful enemies, rather than Diana. I never thought that someone would try and kill Diana.
>
> I just thought in order to get to the father, you get to the son. It was a very, very, very high-profile romance, so if someone wanted to get to Al-Fayed, they could've tried to kill his son in what looked like an accident. . . . That was the thing that flashed into my mind.

Many observers shared Seward's suspicions. Some believed that the powers in control of Diana's life were not ready to accept that Diana might end up married to an Egyptian—particularly, to an Egyptian with a father whom they found very distasteful.

Others held that the final straw sealing Diana's fate was likely the "baby bump"—whether real or imagined—that had been observed and captured by photographers working in the south of France. Marrying Dodi would be one thing, but having a child conceived out of wedlock would be another.

Rumors ran rampant as the public imagined forces conspiring to "take care of" this situation.

Yet, slowly—and perhaps despite the best efforts of the powerful—information *did* begin to bubble to the surface concerning what had happened to Diana's car on the night in question.

French police discovered white paint on Diana's black Mercedes, indicating a second vehicle had collided with it. The paint was unique to the Fiat Uno, one of the most popular cars in Europe at the time. The search involved thousands of cars.

When Colin McLaren arrived in Paris, it was into this strange mix of confusion, cover-up, and government incompetence that he waded.

Nonetheless, he was determined to do all that he could to find the truth.

***

DETECTIVE'S NOTEBOOK

DATELINE: Mid-September 1997

Now aware that Henri Paul was the architect of the death ride into the tunnel, I attempted to parse the many descriptions of what sort of car he was driving. Some reports called it an armored car, some said a high-end 600 series limousine with bulletproof windows, on it went. I eventually came to the conclusion that Paul drove a Mercedes that fateful night, and that it had more of a history than most press accounts let on. The vehicle had been the subject of an earlier carjacking, about a month before the crash. I wanted to know if this could have factored into Diana's death.

I got lucky and found out where the real death car was located and headed to the outskirts of Paris. In receipt of my latest invaluable gem of information and aided by an efficient rail system, I traveled the 10 miles north to 38 Rue du Doctor

Bauer, Saint Ouen, and the dealership that had carried out the mechanical repairs and services on the vehicle. Luckily for me, English is widely spoken even in the outskirts of Paris.

Half an hour after arriving, I was at lunch with the dealership's service manager. With a basic worker's meal ordered and a glass of Beaujolais in hand, he confirmed what I already knew about the Mercedes. It was a standard Class S280 sedan, black in color, with a 2.8-liter, six-cylinder engine. Fitted with seat belts to the front and rear passenger seats, and airbags to the front passenger and driver seats, it was a current model and less than one year old. Selling in France for 347,500 francs ($59,237), it was the least expensive of the range. Then a silence fell. We sipped our wine. Despite the familiarity we had established during our opening repartee regarding the local rugby scene, there was the beginning of a hesitation in his voice. I guessed that he was starting to wonder who I really was. I went on to explain that I had traveled from Australia, not to sensationalize the accident, just to reach a better understanding of the tragedy. And perhaps if I were to find answers, I continued, they may offer some comfort to those, who like me, held the Princess Diana in high esteem. I also explained that my fascination with the Diana case was stirred, mostly because I was on vacation in Paris and had the opportunity to find answers for myself. He started to relax again. I held back the many questions I had hoped to put to him for a moment, opting to finish my meal.

I reopened our dialogue. Was there a lot of street crime in Paris then? And so it went. Pretty soon, his reticence had lifted, he spoke freely of the recent carjacking, adding that not only was the radio and cassette stolen from the center console of the ill-fated Mercedes-Benz, but all the wheels and tires were also missing. This led to that and pretty soon he explained that as a result of the accident at pillar thirteen, the engine had been forced into the vehicle's cabin. He considered the Mercedes must have been traveling at up to 200 kilometers per hour—or 124 mph. And only days earlier the French police had been in touch with him regarding foreign paint found on the front left-hand side of the car. There was a collective opinion that the paint was from a white Fiat Uno sedan. Aha, the second car, I thought. Things were starting to firm up.

Apart from the knowledge of the paint markings, he was unable or perhaps unwilling to offer any further information. I paid the check, and we returned to the dealership. With apologies, he then went back to the paying customers, leaving me with the mechanic who had worked on the vehicle to tidy up any loose ends. Bingo. Just the man I wanted to see.

A strapping fellow with the requisite overalls, he gesticulated his way through a proud declaration that the Mercedes was unreservedly roadworthy after the carjacking repairs had been completed. Recalling clearly the necessary work, he attested that four new wheels and tires were also fitted, and he made the hand motions that left me in no doubt of his sincerity. Then, as a matter of course, he instructed that the car be taken to the police prefecture office where it was checked over and issued a certificate of compliance.

Only then had it been given the okay to be returned to the Ritz-Carlton limousine fleet for guest chauffeur work. Knowing that I was standing within meters of the vehicle, it was a heartfelt disappointment that I was not permitted to inspect the wreckage. Its resting place was an outside car compound, but the police managed the compound, and it was well and truly locked. Putting my personal disappointment to one side, had I been able to view the carnage it wouldn't really have changed anything. At the end of the day, the car was still just a standard S Class Mercedes-Benz. The princess had been traveling in nothing more than a German family sedan. So much for the armored car stories.

By late afternoon, I was back on my train traveling toward Montmartre and my hotel room. I was feeling pretty pleased with myself, having once and for all settled the riddle of the Mercedes-Benz. But I had a twinge of guilt for having to employ some old covert police skills to solicit information from the thoroughly decent Mercedes-Benz people. As the train whizzed me through the subway tunnels, I kept drifting off into the next piece of the jigsaw: the second car. Was there a second vehicle involved? The short answer had to be yes. The glass fragments I had found at the scene confirmed the presence of another vehicle. And the scrapes on the retaining wall above the glass were well out of the trajectory line of the Mercedes.

So where was that car now—and where was its driver? Surely the grief and remorse associated with this accident would be enough to flush out the most hardened of persons? Or was the driver working for someone else—someone or something more sinister?

CHAPTER EIGHT

We know the forces that Diana had angered. We know the specific men she chose to spend her time with, and what the implications were. Now—even though it may be difficult—we must focus on how Diana and Dodi's behavior impacted the night of the crash itself.

By reviewing what is established—and what has not yet been established—we work our way toward staggering new revelations.

If you believe Mohamed Al-Fayed, tears of happiness misted Diana's eyes as she accepted her lover Dodi's marriage proposal over a candlelit dinner—an hour before the accident that brutally claimed their lives.

It's the final heartbreaking tragedy of Diana's life, if Mohamed is to be believed: she found true happiness after years of tumultuous breakups, including her toxic split from Prince Charles that had dragged on for years.

Confirming Diana and Dodi's wedding plans, Hassan Yassin, a Paris-based relative of the former playboy, said at the time, "Dodi told me the night he died that he was going to marry Diana. I felt Dodi had found himself in her—and she in him."

Dodi also confided to his close pal Michael Cole, who worked for his billionaire tycoon father, that he planned to spend the rest of his life with the princess. "I'll never have another girlfriend," he vowed.

But there are serious questions about whether or not the "engagement" was real. Diana, sources have said, tragically knew Dodi was cheating on her with another woman and could only have accepted his proposal, if indeed she did, to avoid upsetting her lover.

Diana died nursing gut-wrenching grief over her discovery Dodi had a secret fiancée she branded "Camilla Mark Two."

For you see, Dodi brazenly spent his nights sleeping with model Kelly Fisher, while seducing Diana during the daylight. Dodi had been seeing Fisher for months before he met Diana. And Fisher, then thirty, was, in those days, wearing a $237,000 diamond-and-sapphire engagement ring Dodi had bought her—promising her, in 1996, that he would marry her in August 1997.

It's always been thought that Diana had no idea Dodi was cheating with a gorgeous Calvin Klein pinup when they started seeing each other, and while the Egyptian heir was smarming his way into the hearts of her two sons.

A source said:

> Diana may have seemed deliriously happy on her final night with Dodi, but it was all just an act. The whole evening was tinged with inner pain and sadness for Diana as she knew Dodi was a liar and a cheat. It brought back so many memories for Diana of Charles's cheating with Camilla she was close to tears a lot of the time with Dodi—frustrated that her hopes he would be "the one" were being shattered.

But another insider, speaking confidentially for this book, added that Diana was determined not to "roll over" and lose Dodi to another woman, as she had done with Charles and Camilla. It was almost like it did not matter to her, at least on the surface.

They said:

> Despite constantly claiming she was "thick as a plank," Diana was actually very smart, especially when it came to matters of self-publicity and emotion. She was determined to hold on to Dodi and not telling him she knew about his affair was one of her tactics. Diana was using her experience of Charles's affair to plot a different set of tactics to win Dodi over for good—and playing dumb and acting overjoyed at everything he did was one of her key moves.

On July 14, Dodi's Harrods tycoon father summoned him from Paris to join him on holiday with Diana in Saint-Tropez on the French Riviera. The Egyptian merchant, who in 1985 had bought the Mecca of London shopping, Harrods, in the hope of storming the British establishment, still dreamed about royal connections.

His pointless dream drove him to tell Dodi that wooing the princess was an urgent imperative. After Mohamed Al-Fayed's directive was issued, a baffled Fisher was kept out of sight.

While Dodi worked on seducing Diana and played with her sons in the sun, the model was holed up on his father's B-list boat, the *Cujo*. She was also on the vessel when Diana and Dodi were first pictured romping aboard the *Jonikal*—feverishly refurbished in time for Diana's visit.

Dodi visited Fisher at night in secret after days spent charming Diana at his billionaire father's thirty-bedroom villa, Castle St. Therese, in July, and then on the *Jonikal* in August.

After learning of Dodi's romance with Diana, Fisher phoned her ex to vent her fury. A twenty-minute recording of the call was played in London in 2007 during the inquest into Diana's death. It captures Fisher screeching:

> You even flew me down to Saint-Tropez to sit on a boat while you seduced Diana all day and f****d me all night.

The model had justification to complain. She had been featured on the front covers of *Elle* and *W* before meeting Dodi in Paris in July 1996. He convinced her to give up her lucrative work and gave her a $2,600-a-day allowance. Dodi also bought her a $6.8 million home in Malibu, where she thought they would live together, and gave her a $237,000 engagement ring in February 1997.

In the call played at Diana's inquest, Dodi insists they had already split by the time he was romancing the princess. Fisher rages that they had still been talking about their wedding.

She is also heard to say, "You told me you didn't even like her. Why do you suddenly like her?"

Dodi responds by dismissing Fisher as "crazy" and "hysterical."

He finally dumped her on August 7, 1997—the day his relationship with Diana hit worldwide headlines. When Fisher realized she was being used, she tried unsuccessfully to sue Dodi for breach of contract over his promise they would marry.

And on August 10, Fisher was sickened when she woke to photos of her love rival romping with Dodi aboard the *Jonikal* in pictures dubbed "The Kiss," first used by the US publication the *Globe*. It would be a photograph that horrified the British establishment.

Our insider revealed the sensational pictures were not as spontaneous as they seemed.

"Diana was extremely savvy when it came to the media," a source said, adding:

> The photographer who captured her and Dodi in passionate embraces said she had spotted him in the distance. She seized the opportunity to play up to the camera—first, to shock the royal family back in Britain and give two fingers to Charles. And, secondly, to kill Dodi and Kelly's love. She had been told by her many moles in the press that Dodi had been spotted sneaking in and out of the boat where Kelly was staying. She then asked her closest confidants to investigate and found out Dodi was engaged to the model. It never came out at the time that Dodi was engaged as Diana did a deal with her moles to give them future stories if they would keep their investigations into Dodi and Kelly's relationship private and between them. She soon got word back that not only was Dodi cheating with Kelly—they were engaged. But once Diana got over her devastation that her latest lover was a cheat, she hatched a plan to put an end to their relationship without ever confronting Dodi. Getting photographed for images she knew would make global headlines with Dodi was a masterstroke by Diana, as it achieved all her aims—shocking Prince Charles and the royals, while leaving Kelly so furious she no longer wanted to marry Dodi.

***

Diana's quiet revenge on Fisher was a product of the way she had dealt with Prince Charles's callous infidelity.

The soft-cheeked English rose was tormented from the beginning of her relationship with Charles by the knowledge he was in love with Parker Bowles—an upper middle-class housewife from Wiltshire far lower on the aristocratic rungs than Diana.

Instead of staying quiet and manipulating Charles into loving her—as she did with Dodi—Diana cried in public and had a series of bitter confrontations with the prince over his cheating.

Less than a week before her wedding to Charles on July 29, 1981, Diana was photographed weeping while watching her fiancé play polo—against a team that included one of her aforementioned and future lovers, James Hewitt.

Her tears came after she discovered Charles and Camilla had been sending each other gifts ahead of her wedding day. She confronted Charles after her public display of devastation, pleading with him to tell her if he loved Parker Bowles.

When Charles refused to give her a direct answer, she started to babble to royal courtiers about her relationship woes, asking them, "Does Charles love me?"

In a ham-fisted attempt to try and resolve the situation, Diana's flunkies arranged for her to have lunch with Parker Bowles—unbelievably, at a London restaurant called "Ménage à Trois."

They felt the name of the restaurant was a clear signal to Diana that Charles intended to keep a mistress for the duration of their marriage—an unwritten tradition within blue bloods that would never sit right with Diana.

When she discovered Charles was wearing a pair of silver cufflinks on their honeymoon given to him by Parker Bowles, Diana said she "cried and cried."

A source told our investigation, "The experience of being so open with Charles about her feelings over his affair with Camilla made her change tack when she found out Dodi was cheating. She decided to launch a quiet war against Kelly—and won. Diana felt her survival depended on winning Dodi for herself."

The main reason Diana felt she needed her relationship with Dodi to work is she saw him as a modern prince with the means to provide the security she needed.

But, on the following pages, many of her closest friends describe their final conversations with Diana and insisting she didn't love Dodi and never intended to marry him, only accepting his gifts out of embarrassment.

Before she got together with Dodi, her humble heart surgeon lover Hasnat Khan had run for the hills—petrified at being drawn into Diana's world of global celebrity. Diana realized she needed a man who could match her wealth and fame and provide her with security at the same time.

Dodi checked off all those boxes.

His father's wealth gave him the resources to keep the world's most famous woman from getting bored while providing her with up to eight security goons on their nights out.

His yacht, his cliffside compound in the South of France, his Ritz hotel in Paris were Diana's new castles. Diana once confided in her friend Rosa Monckton, "He has all the toys."

The sense of security Diana thought Dodi could offer her allowed her to gloss over the truth: he was a tacky Egyptian lounge lizard with the same sense of "style" as Al Pacino's Scarface.

But Diana had reached the point in her life where she finally realized a relationship with someone such as Khan was an impossibility. She could never go from global fame to living an "ordinary" existence, and, eventually, a domesticated existence with a man devoted to being a surgeon would have bored her to death. A man like Khan could also never protect her from the motorbikes of the paparazzi.

***

According to the Fayed camp, Dodi proposed before getting into the car where he would die instantly in the crash that left Diana with catastrophic internal injuries.

It was 11 p.m. when Dodi allegedly asked Diana to be his wife, as they sat under the stars at a secluded garden table at L'Espadon. The spot was one of Paris's most exclusive restaurants and a feature of the five-star Ritz Hotel in the city of love.

Diana and Dodi had just dined on a feast that included scrambled eggs with wild mushrooms and asparagus, sole tempura, baked turbot, fresh white summer truffles, and wild Scottish salmon. Their meal was washed down with a $425 bottle of 1998 Taittinger champagne and mineral water. Red roses and white carnations decorated the table and a harpist strummed songs of love in the background.

Even ultrarich Dodi had trouble picking a ring for the world's most famous woman, who was used to access to the crown jewels of England.

He decided to tell Diana he wanted her to select her engagement ring herself—after he spent hours at the Repossi jewelry store, across the street from the Ritz, where he picked up two rings he'd previously ordered in Monte Carlo.

His father Mohamed Al-Fayed is supposedly now in possession of the ring purchased from Repossi jewelers—a gold band with diamonds forming the shape of star from the firm's range known as "Dis-moi Oui" ("Tell me Yes").

But Dodi also left the Repossi store clutching a brochure—deciding the most romantic thing to do was let Diana pick her own band.

The witness went on:

> When they finally left the restaurant, they were holding hands and looked like they were walking on air.
>
> As Diana said goodbye, she turned to a member of the hotel staff and told him, "Thank you for a wonderful night."
>
> Then she glanced at Dodi and added softly, "I'll never forget it. This was such a beautiful night because of you." Those were her last words before getting into the car that would take her and Dodi on the last ride of their lives.

On the fateful day of their deaths, the lovebirds had arrived in Paris at 4:30 p.m. on Dodi's dad's private jet, after cruising the Mediterranean on the *Jonikal.*

It was the couple's fourth romantic cruise in just seven weeks. In a tragic irony, Diana had originally intended to fly back to Britain immediately after the idyllic week of sailing the Med with Dodi.

But the seemingly besotted princess didn't want to break the magic spell of her happiest vacation ever, and the couple decided to spend one last night in the city of lights before she flew home to Britain to be with her beloved boys.

She planned to spend a week with sons William and Harry before they returned to school for autumn—and was going to tell them of her momentous decision to marry Dodi, said a source.

When Diana and Dodi arrived in Paris they went straight to the $10,000-a-night Imperial Suite set aside for them at the Ritz Hotel.

After their seven-week whirlwind romance, Diana was confident Dodi was going to propose that night because of hints he'd dropped, including during the last telephone call she ever made to excitedly tell a friend how she was looking forward to beginning a bright new chapter in her life.

Diana put in the surprise call from the Ritz to the London home of Richard Kay, a famed royal journalist who had been her confidant throughout the stormiest patches of her life. In a cryptic conversation she told him she had decided to "radically change" her life by completing all her public charity and good-cause obligations by November. Then, she confided, she would completely withdraw from her formerly public life.

Kay disclosed to our investigation that:

> She talked about wanting to come home. She asked me a bit about Dodi and what the media were reporting. My relationship as a journalist (with and to her), it was very much about the media and media coverage.
>
> But she did talk about her plans for the future. She said she was honestly fed up with working as sort of a semidetached member of the royal family, and she was going to give all that up.
>
> She got the idea to launch a chain of worldwide hospices for dying children and Mohamed Al-Fayed, Dodi's father, was going to help finance it. She told me that she was going to do a lot of fund-raising for that. She also said she was going off on another land mines expedition to I think Vietnam.
>
> She said, "It's time to get back, get back to work."
>
> One of the last things she said to me that night was, "Get a good night's sleep and I'll see you tomorrow." [The pair had planned to rendezvous on her return to London.]

He added:

> I think she was looking for something that she couldn't find in Charles. I think once you've been married to the prince of Wales, it's very hard to consider what you might do next and who might fill the void in your life.
>
> What she didn't want, I know, is to be a trophy wife of a rich man. What she wanted was this companionship and friendship, but also love. She told me shortly before she died, the reason she was attracted to Dodi. He understood her world. Dodi had a fairly privileged upbringing and had been in that world of Hollywood glamor over many years. He had also been a rich man's son and had had a lot of privileges and perks growing up. Lots of money and wealth around him, so he understood "society." Diana said to me that helped her realize he was the guy who could take care of her.

Deliriously happy Diana would then, Kay said, be able to live as she'd always wanted to live: not as an icon (she hated to be called one) but as a private person. It was a "dream sequence," Kay said he'd heard that from her before, but this time he knew "she meant it."

> It was complete contrast to her relationship with Hasnat Khan, and the fact that he was another Muslim was obviously very fascinating.
>
> There was Khan. Dedicated. Hospital worker. Doctor. Then there was Dodi Fayed. What was he? He was a rich man's son who put his name to a few films in Hollywood and had never had to scrape a living together. He was entirely different. I could see that she would find him and his world very intoxicating. She was very fond of his father, Mohamed.
>
> She liked that sort of Middle East warmness that families have. She felt very welcome in their embrace. She had—by then—changed a lot from the young woman who married Charles. She found British families chilly and off-putting and cold. Whereas in Fayed (and in the Khan family, too), she found a deep welcome. I think that is what attracted her to him as much as anything.

Just before that call, Diana had phoned another close pal in England and gushed to her, "At last I can see the future clearly. I finally know what I want—and what I want is Dodi. It's all happened so fast, but I've never been surer of anything in my life. He's made me happier than I've ever been before."

Yet even in her happiest moments, there is very powerful evidence to suggest Diana felt an undercurrent of sinister doom. Her day of bliss was a fleeting distraction from it—one hopes—but only a distraction. Diana was a woman marked, and she knew it. She knew it both by the powers of her own observation, and by supernatural powers as well.

Diana's reliance on psychics, spiritualists, "energy healers," and astrologers near the end of her life has been attributed to everything from her desperation for love to her suspected borderline personality disorder. The lonely royal lost herself in a bewildering cocktail of alternative therapists—including astrologers, reflexologists, psychoanalysts, and soothsayers. Diana's psychics say they predicted Diana's violent death, but none of them were able to use their powers to stop it.

Diana's obsession with the spiritual led her to have treatments such as fortnightly colonic irrigation and massage.

One astrologer persuaded Diana to strap fossils to her legs to put her in touch with her ancestors. All they did was leave white scrapes along her calves.

Diana's psychics also sent her into paranoid frenzies by predicting there were plots to kill her in car crashes, while another of her clairvoyants, Simone Simmons, told her she could see a "vast black whirlwind of energy" on the side of Diana's bed where a partner might sleep.

Diana also once sat under a Perspex pyramid with a healer called Madame Vasso, who told her the practice would produce "good energy." Vasso is believed to be one of two psychics (the other is Rita Rogers) referred to by Diana as sister-in-law Sarah Ferguson's "witch-woman."

Vasso later published a kiss-and-tell book on Ferguson in which she dished the dirt on her extramarital affairs, the squalid state of her finances, and her views on her in-laws. The princess's former private secretary Patrick Jephson said that Sarah Ferguson's medium also told Diana that Prince Charles would die in a crash.

Patrick—a former lieutenant commander in the Royal Navy who worked for

Diana from 1990 to 1996—revealed the princess told him in 1990, "Fergie's witch-woman says my husband is going to be killed! She sees mountains and a helicopter!"

He said he tried to treat such predictions as a joke and added, "A little later on, I give my response to the princess as being, 'Yes, ma'am, any tips for the 3:30 at Kempton?'"

But Patrick said psychics had a devastating effect on Diana's mental health, revealing the paranoid princess fell for more and more outlandish claims toward the end of her life.

The identity of the other candidate for Diana's "witch-woman" nickname is Rita Rogers, who met Diana through the duchess and told her the brake cables of her car would be cut.

Patrick said he was worried Diana put so much faith in astrologers and soothsayers because this "fed the paranoia that never lurked far beneath the surface."

Other spirituality skeptics such as Diana's former bodyguard Ken Wharfe put her obsession with them down to her hunt for "solutions and answers" to a mass of problems—including the royal's tormented childhood to divorce and failed relationships.

Others still—including Prince Charles—believe she suffered from a borderline personality disorder that convinced her she could hear voices she thought were coming to her from some form of afterlife. Many believe she was so neurotic that she hated being alone and was on a relentless search for those who would listen to her problems. Others thought she was trying to fill the voids she felt from Charles's cruelty and her early abandonment by her mother, who chose to leave her family for her lover.

But Diana's fixation on the spiritual may also have been connected to her constant fear the royals were plotting to take her out in a violent hit. She may have seen getting in touch with psychics while she was alive as a way of learning how she could stay in touch with the living after she was killed.

Along with the fact that psychics played into Diana's paranoia and gave her people to speak to (for a fee), the royal was probably also fixated on their world, as she had a morbid fascination with death and dissection that bordered on an interest in the occult.

Diana once helped her best friend, Rosa Monckton, bury her stillborn child in the grounds of her Kensington Palace home. Business executive Rosa—now aged sixty-six with two children—and her newspaper editor husband, Dominic Lawson, tragically lost their daughter to stillbirth.

When Diana heard of the heartbreak, she suggested the pair choose the palace grounds as their child's final resting place. But it wasn't only an act of kindness—the ceremony was tinged with touches of the occult. Diana had her two most loyal butlers, Harold Brown and Paul Burrell, secretly dig the child's grave.

She had told security it was a hole for a dead pet.

And, in a misty early morning ceremony in March 1994, Diana, along with Rosa Monckton and Dominic, then editor of *Spectator* magazine, crunched over the gravel drive from Diana's apartment to mourn a child her friends had named Natalia.

In the shadow of Kensington Palace's vast west wall, Rosa read a verse over the dirt grave by Rabindranath Tagore, India's greatest poet and Nobel Prize winner. Afterward, Diana gave Rosa a key to the garden, which she still owns to this day.

Diana's fixation on the afterlife only grew in the three years leading up to her death.

On that fateful Saturday, August 30, 1997, Diana and Dodi flew from Olbia airport in Sardinia to Le Bourget airport on the outskirts of Paris, arriving at about 3:20 p.m. They were not alone.

With them was Diana's holistic healer Myriah Daniels, along with bodyguards Trevor Rees-Jones, Kieran "Kez"' Wingfield, René Delorm (Dodi's butler), and Deborah Gribble (Chief Stewardess on the *Jonikal*).

Masseuse and spiritual healer Myriah had been introduced to Diana while holidaying on the *Jonikal* with Dodi.

"I have a natural gift for being able to fix the human body," she told the inquest into Diana's death. "I do treat the whole person—I am a minister of natural spiritualism."

There were four practitioners of the supernatural who were linked most closely to Diana.

Here, the royal's three most prominent psychics—together with her personal astrologer—reveal what was behind the princess's obsession with the afterlife.

Three of the four have one thing in common—all claim they predicted Diana's death just before her crash—and all admit their spiritual powers were not enough to save her.

***

SIMONE SIMMONS

Simone would speak to the princess for up to ten hours straight on the phone and claims to still hear her voice now—opining, in Diana's afterlife, on her family, Meghan Markle, and global politics.

Like other psychics, she claims to have predicted the Mercedes crash in which Diana died—but got the color of the car wrong, saying it was blue and not black in her vision of her friend's final moments.

The Londoner, fifty-nine, once told a journalist from *The Guardian,* she would "NEVER, EVER" talk about Diana.

Yet one year later she wrote a book about her four-year friendship with the princess, called *Diana: The Secret Years.*

Undeterred, in 2005 she published another book, *Diana: The Final Word* and has become a "rent-a-quote" in Britain every time there is a major royal event—tabloid speak for a source who will spill without pressure.

When Meghan Markle announced that she was pregnant, it did not take psychic abilities to predict Simmons would soon be channeling Diana's spirit so the dead royal could share her opinion on the news with the world.

The resulting conversations from beyond the grave made easy headlines, with Simmons sharing in-depth observations from Diana such as the former princess's joy that Meghan's mum is around to give her security.

In the past year, Simmons has also made news by using her psychic powers to predict Harry and Meghan will be divorced in less than three years.

An alternative healer who claims to have recognized her powers as a child when she used touch to cure a cat of kidney disease, Simmons met Diana in 1992 at the Hale Clinic, an alternative medicine center in Marylebone, London.

She was close to Diana until a year before the royal's death, becoming one of the friends she purged from her friendship circle as she became increasingly isolated and withdrawn, filled with dreams of moving abroad. On her many visits to

Diana at Kensington Palace, she cleared the princess's head—and apartment—of "magnetic imbalances."

Simmons says she recently chatted with Diana's ghost about Brexit, and her former client told that although she thinks Kate Middleton is "perfect," she doesn't believe Meghan is the ideal woman for Harry.

In an exclusive to this book, she sheds light in the passage below on the princess's life based on their intimate chats when the royal was living. (She insists she was never romantically involved with Dodi—despite photographic evidence to the contrary—and says her desire was to settle in the suburbs with her heart surgeon lover Hasnat Khan.)

Here is Simone Simmons speaking of Princess Diana in her own words.

> She saw lots of wacky astrologers.
>
> Some of the things she did were beyond the pale. One time she came in to see me and she had white stripes on her leg. She said she had been to see a healer recommended to her by the duchess of York who had taped fossils to her legs, and she had to walk around with them.
>
> One time she was driving home from seeing me and she said her brakes failed in heavy traffic.
>
> She bumped into the car in front of her and after making sure the driver was okay, she abandoned her car and jumped into a taxi to go home. She was terrified. She said, "They're trying to bump me off."
>
> By they, she said she meant M15 or M16. She didn't have any evidence whatsoever. All she knew is that they saw her as a loose cannon. I told her she should get her brakes checked. I said she should check to see if they had been tampered with.
>
> Diana wrote me a letter that read, "Dear Simone, as you know, the brakes of my car have been tampered with. If something does happen to me, it will be MI5 or MI6 who will have done it."
>
> She wrote that letter sometime before the report came back from the garage. She said she was writing it as a precaution, just in case something happened to her. Until she had that report in her hand, she was terrified. She was looking over her shoulder all the time. She said

she had a funny feeling she was not going to make old bones. She said that repeatedly over four years.

She heard other psychics deliver premonitions that she would marry one of the European princes. She consulted dozens of psychics asking the same question, "Would she and Charles get back together again?" They all said yes, including Rita Rogers.

That was the worst thing. She was totally ripped off for thousands of pounds by people telling her what she wanted to hear. What she was looking for was someone to say, "You will fall in love, you will live happily ever after." She wanted to know if it would happen and more importantly, when. She wanted genuine love more than anything.

Diana once got a threatening phone call telling her to stop her support for anti-land-mine campaigns during which she was told, "Accidents can happen."

She shrugged it off. She had an inkling who it was . . . she recognized the voice as one of Charles's supporters.

I had a vision of an accident with a blue Mercedes with four people in it. I told Diana and Paul Burrell. I didn't know who was in the car—but I did see a blue Mercedes. The saddest time was the state of shock I was in when I heard of her death. For days it was a total surreal experience. For days, it was like everything was going in slow motion around me. I was at home when I heard the news, and I was totally in a state of shock.

Diana was a good psychic—and a sensitive and great healer. She told me of the results of the people she had healed. She was good, very good. There was a lovely picture of her when in Pakistan with her hand over the head of a little boy. That's Diana in healing mode. Diana also kept a copy of the Quran by her bedside.

First, she thought of moving to Australia, then she thought about America, which she was hoping would be a lot less intrusive than the UK. Being the princess of Wales and the mother of the future King of

England, she had her duty to perform by being here. Basically, it's called catch-twenty-two.

I considered Diana to be my best friend. I saw her five times a week. We spent God knows how many hours together on the phone every day. I was Diana's friend, not Paul Burrell's friend. Paul was a member of the household. He and I became friendly—but I would talk to him in Diana's presence because Diana was my friend. I really miss Diana because Diana was a beautiful person with a beautiful soul.

It's very strange how I can still hear her—it's very weird. I hear her voice speaking to me about world events and being desperately in love with her grandchildren.

Diana was just trying to be Dodi's therapist. It wasn't even a fling. She didn't fancy him in the slightest. Why on earth would she have tried to make Hasnat Khan jealous if she really liked Dodi?

From that point of view, she was really naive emotionally. She shouldn't have been with him, but she saw how I was when I was trying to help people with addictions. He was selfish to the core.

She was still in love with Hasnat Khan and she's not that sort of person. Diana had a type. Dodi was certainly no brain surgeon.

She tended to go for more intelligent men, especially as she got older. She was always attracted to men with intelligence who were thoughtful. She didn't especially like men with hairy backs. You know how you talk about these things with your friends. When we started talking, we were both saying, "Eww."

All Diana wanted to do was make the world better. Dodi was, I suppose, a little distraction to that. She was trying to get him healed because he wanted to get married to this woman Kelly Fisher (who Dodi became engaged to before dumping her in favor of Diana). That's why they went out looking at engagement rings.

She tried to tell people there was no relationship and nobody took the blindest bit of notice. She always kept her love affairs secret. Hasnat was secret for two years, except for me and a few others. While she was with the heart surgeon, Diana dreamed of a very different life away from the spotlight. When she was with Hasnat she quite often talked about the semi in suburbia, two up two down.

We had to be realistic. It was nice to dream. Everyone likes to dream when they're happy and in a different world, in a dreamworld, she could do it. But she wouldn't have had a quieter life, she'd always have been doing her humanitarian work.

Her next massive project, and she'd already had meetings with Benazir Bhutto, was to stop child slavery in Pakistan. It was a huge project, really huge. She wanted the government to put the children into education and make doctors, scientists, lawyers to make the country leaders in the field. Can you imagine taking on a project like that?

When Diana was alive, she was the bright, spiritual healing in the world. When she died, that went—and look at the state the world's been in ever since.

You don't see celebrities going out in the middle of nowhere where it's dangerous.

She used to fork out money from her own pocket for charity.

Of course, in addition to her charity work, her main focus in life was her sons William and Harry. Sometimes Harry (he was twelve when Diana died) would skip school so that he could have Diana all to himself, so he didn't have to share her with William. He'd sit on her lap with his head snuggled into her shoulder, sucking his thumb. Even at ten or eleven, he liked to be with her. His mother was his best friend at that time. Harry didn't have any best friends. She was. He was really cute. He wanted me to decide what color his bedroom was going to be.

She always loved Charles, even before she died.

She got angry with him of course, but I don't think there was ever a minute she stopped loving him. Before she died, he kept popping over for cups of tea or to use the toilet. Any excuse. I even said, "Oi, what's going on here?'

After Hasnat had called it off with her, she did wonder if her and Charles could ever get back together but it was no, "Camilla will never let go."

In 1996 she told him to make her an honest woman and he didn't. For Diana it meant a lot even though he was free to do so. It was quite symbolic in many ways. I think it speaks volumes.

He was still in love with Diana. If they would have got married maybe six years later, she would have grown up a bit and they had the same interests, they had so much in common—organic farming, alternative medicine.

They would have made a go of it. I don't believe there would have been any split. She wouldn't have allowed Camilla to come between them. She truly was naive. She didn't know.

Before Diana died, we did have a very long talk, and she said, "What do I tell my boys about love and marriage, because mine didn't work?"

We decided that as far as love goes, the best match would be to be married to their best friend. Someone they can talk to and share everything with, offload on to. Someone they can lean on because of the pressure of their job. Just being princes is really hard work. So, they need someone they can totally depend on.

***

SALLY MORGAN

The sixty-eight-year-old psychic Sally Morgan claimed to have predicted Princess Diana's death in 1997. Specifically, she claimed she'd foreseen a woman being pulled from a car wreck in a tunnel, who she first thought was the queen, but later realized was princess of Wales. But Sally—known as "Psychic Sally" and who self-identifies as "the UK's best-loved psychic"—failed to tell Diana of her premonition.

She also, damningly, failed to foresee her own bankruptcy approaching. And for this reason, some have cast doubt on her Diana claims.

In 2018, Sally Morgan Enterprises went into voluntary liquidation following an £2.9 million accelerated payment notice claim by the taxman. And for the paycheck, on August 16, 2018, Morgan entered the *Celebrity Big Brother* house, a British reality television staple, finishing fifth place.

Yet her bankruptcy came directly as a result of being hit by a string of scandals that called into question her psychic abilities.

In 2011 at a show in Dublin, Sally was troubled by a voice from the other side—the other side of the curtain at the Grand Canal Theatre.

An audience member accused her of being fed every line she spoke from an assistant—something Sally later denied, but which earned her death threats. At a public show in 2012, Morgan gave a reading to two members of the audience, Drew McAdam and his wife Elizabeth. The reading described a man called Toby who had died in an explosion. However, prior to the show, Drew and his wife say they fed Morgan this information by emailing her website and leaving notes in a box provided in the foyer for so-called "love letters."

Two years later, in March 2014, Morgan became embarrassed during a performance after contacting the spirit of a woman who was still alive in the audience.

It's unlikely the controversies would have put Diana off using the medium.

When she first met Sally, Diana gave her an old-fashioned green milk bottle she kept as an ornament at Kensington Palace after the psychic admired it—which Sally still has now at her home in a leafy crescent of Reigate, Surrey in southeast England.

And, poetically, Sally continued to milk their relationship.

In fact, Sally's relationship with Diana led her to fill two-thousand-seat theaters with $40-a-ticket shows before sitting in the foyer afterward signing her DVD, *Psychic Sally On the Road*.

Among her other celebrity clients were Uma Thurman and Diana's friend George Michael.

Here, in her own words, are her claims regarding the princess:

I am quite well-known for having seen the princess of Wales for at least four-and-a-half years. I was her medium and would speak to her almost on a daily basis. I used to see her sister as well, her sister, Sarah McCorquodale. She was the go-between, really, for us. I met the princess of Wales through her dresser, who was called Helena.

I spoke to Diana nearly every day for four years, including on Christmas Day and Boxing Day.

I predicted something the year before and was told by a member of the royal family four days after Diana's funeral that they'd listened to the tape of the reading the year before, and it was basically predicting that.

I did predict the princess of Wales's death. What happened was that she visited me, like she did every week, really. Sometimes three times a week she would come to the house. At this particular time, I said to her, "Oh, I can see the queen, she's going to die." Sarah said, "Oh, what do you mean? How?" I said, "Well, I feel as if she's being pulled out the back of a car by her legs, and her shoulders, and her head is in the stairwell at the back of the car. And I can see a gray pavement, and it's very dark above her." So, I said, "She's definitely in a car, and she's definitely being pulled out onto a pavement, and I can see people trying to give her CPR, or bashing her chest." Then I went, "I think it might be a tunnel. It was dark."

Sarah went, "Okay." She wasn't that shocked.

"Okay." I said, "And about a week later, the Queen Mother will die."

It didn't even dawn on me. Then four days after the funeral of the princess of Wales, I received a phone call one morning, and it was from Sarah and she said, "Oh, hello, Sally." And I was really shocked that she just called me, and because to be very honest, I doubted I'd hear from any of them ever again.

She said, "Oh, I guess a couple of things I wanted to sort of just say to you."

I said, "Yes?"

The first thing she asked me was, did I think it was an accident. Then she said to me, "You do know that you predicted the princess of Wales's death."

I said, "I did not." She said, "Yes, you did, Sally. I have the tape." Because I used to record it when she used to come. I said, "Well, what did I say?" Because I couldn't remember. She said, "Well, you actually said you could see the queen being pulled out the back of a car onto a pavement and being given CPR."

A week later, at the princess of Wales's funeral, was the Queen Mother's funeral, because the royal family and heads of state and people of that ilk, they rehearse their funerals all the time, no matter what age they are.

Because that was the next funeral that had been rehearsed: The Princess of Wales basically had the funeral of the Queen Mother, even though the Queen Mother was still alive. All the pomp and pageantry that went with it. That was rehearsed for the Queen Mother. So, she said to me, "We feel you predicted it." So, I said, "Oh, really? Who's that, then?" And she said, "Well, we've all . . ." She didn't say, she just said, "We've all listened to the tape."

Diana would definitely want the facts to be revealed.

She'd be torn between it all being dragged up again and upsetting her boys. But William and Harry are men now, so they can handle it. I think they want the truth, too. But I think it'll be two hundred years before it comes out. It'll be Prince George's grandchildren who'll allow the truth to be printed.

I was never really able to be friends with Diana, as she was being closely guarded by the royal family. If you ever are involved with the royal family at that level you never ever are friends with them, there will always be a massive lead door between them and you.

They literally live in a *Big Brother* house. From the moment you sign up to be in that family you are in a *Big Brother* house. I think she was looking for someone to tell her everything was going to be okay and that she would find love.

***

RITA ROGERS

Romany psychic and self-declared "priestess," Rita Rogers did little to ameliorate Diana's fears of being killed. Self-styled spiritual adviser Rita, who had regular sessions with the princess, has confessed she warned Diana she had a forewarning that the brakes of her car had been tampered with.

It was far from her last prediction of doom issued to a terrified Diana.

She also made the extraordinary claim at her first meeting with Dodi she had "a feeling of danger" about Diana.

Warming to her story, she claimed she saw a black Mercedes and a tunnel, and "felt a connection with France."

Diana was put on to Rita by none other than the duchess of York, who was said to have turned to the psychic for advice after separating from Prince Andrew.

The duchess was consoled by a prediction she was not destined to remain alone, but that she would marry a US president.

Diana started to use Rita Rogers to try and contact her deceased father to heal her childhood wounds. Three years after their introduction, Diana and Dodi flew to Rita's home on the warm Tuesday evening of August 12, 1997. The couple's cream and green helicopter aroused the suspicion of locals when it hovered over the small Derbyshire village of Lower Pilsey looking for the correct address.

Finally, the helicopter landed in a field, normally a paddock grazed by several horses.

Diana and Dodi had dropped out of the sky to spend 90 minutes in the company of Rita, an unremarkable-looking woman then in her mid-fifties. She was working as a discreet psychic charging $45 a session, whose card read, "Rita Rogers, Medium. Private sittings and phone readings." Diana and Dodi's visit came only nineteen days before the couple died.

Rita was one of the last people to speak to Diana, in a call on Saturday, August 30, 1997.

Here, in her own words, she tells how she warned Diana to come home during their conversation and how she is still puzzled why her psychic powers failed to save the princess's life.

> Diana rang at least once a week to see how I was as well as for readings. She was very fond of Dodi. She rang me at 4 p.m., nine hours before the crash, to tell me she was in Paris and Dodi had gone to get the ring. But I know she was still very fond of Charles.
>
> She was the same age as one of my daughters and I was a bit of a mother figure for her. She used to tell me, "As soon as I hear your voice, Rita, it calms me down."
>
> You couldn't pull the wool over Diana's eyes. She could spot a fraud from twenty paces and would have quickly sussed me if I hadn't been genuine.
>
> I'd told her she would meet a man of foreign descent with the initial D on water—and that the man would be connected with the film industry.
>
> Not long after, she rang me one days and said, "Rita, guess where I am? I'm on a boat with a man I've just met called Dodi Fayed."
>
> Diana had visited several times before on her own, and we spoke regularly as friends. I'd read for her several times, of course, but not on this occasion. She wanted me to meet Dodi, and while I did a private reading for him, she sat in the sunshine on the patio with Mo and waited until we had finished.
>
> As she came in, Diana said, "We've got about an hour, Rita, before the press get here"—she was well aware of the problems with the press, and never wanted to make things difficult for me. That was her way, thinking of others.
>
> Sure enough, the press came.
>
> Diana rang several times, saying how sorry she was for the trouble she'd caused me—although, Lord knows, it was nothing to what she experienced every day—and the next day a motorcycle courier arrived from Kensington Palace with a package for me.

Inside was a gold necklace of interlinked hearts because, as Diana told me, "You have a heart of gold." I was bowled over by it—it was such a lovely gift.

The necklace, from Diana's favorite jewelers, Van Cleef & Arpels, was accompanied by a handwritten note on her personalized Kensington Palace notepaper.

It read, "Dearest Rita, This necklace was made for you and comes with so much love to a very special lady with an extraordinary gift . . . from, Diana xx."

She didn't pay for readings and always sent me pink lilies on her birthday. But this was something really special, because of the thought behind it.

I'd read for Dodi before over the phone, but on this occasion, I read for him in person. He was so interested, because of what Diana had told him about me, and had asked to visit me.

When I read for him that day, I warned him about the accident—specific details of the color of the car, the tunnel, and told him to always use his own driver. Although I had no idea of the timing or the fact that Diana would be with him when it happened. My reading had been for him, and not for her.

Dodi was so in love with Diana, there's no doubt about that. And they were very happy—it warmed your heart to see them together.

Would they have married? I don't know, but I do know that Diana would never have done anything that would have caused a problem for her sons. They were her absolute priority.

But there's also no doubt that they were in love. She was radiant, the happiest I'd ever known her.

She wasn't interested in my work with celebrities but in my work with bereaved parents and parents of missing children. I've sometimes been asked to help with cases like that.

I woke up at 1 a.m. for some reason and saw on the television that Dodi had died in a car crash. I rang her mobile, but only got her voice

> mail. I have helped to save so many lives in the past by giving warnings in time.
>
> I don't understand why I couldn't save her.

***

DEBBIE FRANK

Poring over Diana's astrology chart during their meeting at Kensington Palace on July 30, 1997, Debbie Frank and Diana spotted an eclipse—an occurrence that can lead to a life-changing episode.

Diana interpreted it as something positive happening for her. A month later she was in Paris with Dodi.

Debbie and Diana were first introduced by a mutual friend in 1989 and stayed in regular contact, with Diana using astrology as "therapy."

After their first meeting, Diana called Debbie, who also read for British television presenter Anthea Turner and *Carry On* actress Barbara Windsor, to ask what her chart said about her then-husband Charles's affair with Camilla Parker Bowles.

Diana got so hooked on Debbie's readings she even rang her public hotline if she couldn't get through on the stargazer's private number.

She'd also call every Christmas from Sandringham before her separation from Charles in 1992.

The astrologer, who lives in southwest London, first met William and Harry during one of her visits to Kensington Palace in 1991, and also read their charts for Diana.

Here, she tells of the day of the eclipse reading, Diana's desperate calls for readings, and her pain over never getting the queen's approval.

> Out of the blue I got a call. I was stunned.
>
> She was so candid and open. She said, "Can you talk me through all of the difficulties I've been going through? My husband has gone back to his lady, it's been hell."
>
> We immediately hit it off. She'd call up to three times a day and say, "I'm just checking in," or "I just wanted to hear your voice." She would

even ring my hotlines if she couldn't get in touch with me. She wanted to know if everything was going to turn around in her life.

I remember once, in 1991, she was on a yacht off the coast of Greece having a second honeymoon with Prince Charles.

She was worked up because she'd discovered Camilla's number was the last one dialed from their shared telephone. Diana said, "This marriage is a sham, what's the point, so much for a second honeymoon."

She would say she was having a "grim" time and tell how the royals competed to give the "meanest and stingiest" gifts. She'd sneak upstairs to avoid the rigid family traditions. One year she said Charles bought her some hideous earrings.

Diana always looked glamorous and made-up but she liked to relax. She never cooked for herself, but she'd eat dinner in front of the television watching *Coronation Street* or classic films. Her favorite was *From Here to Eternity.*

Diana lavished her with presents including an enamel Asprey box and a scarlet Celine handbag, as well as flowers, jackets, and scarves.

Diana confided in me about everything.

She was always respectful about the queen but wanted her approval and never got it. She was infuriated that it couldn't work between her and Charles.

After the divorce, which Diana described as a big release, she discussed her new partners. Diana described heart surgeon Hasnat Khan, who she dated for two years, as utterly drop-dead gorgeous.

Initially she said Dodi Fayed was a flash in the pan but later said she had grown really fond of him and his family. We were looking at her chart and I said to Diana, "Oh there's an eclipse." Diana was happy because we decided it was the start of a new life.

Significant things happened to her when there was an eclipse—like the separation announcement from Charles and the birth of William. She seemed calm, happy, and optimistic about the future and told me, "My life is moving in a different way."

> She saw it as a positive. She was really happy with Dodi, was spending more time with the boys and embarking on more work as an ambassador. We thought the alignment could be a positive.
>
> I had taken Camilla's chart too because Diana wanted to read both.
>
> I remember the day vividly. She looked radiant, full of life; she had put on weight from the gaunt person I'd first met.
>
> She was in a pink Versace dress with a tulip neckline, in tribute to her friend, fashion designer Gianni, who had been killed days before. We had an impromptu review of her life.
>
> We then looked at Camilla's chart and I told her that Camilla had a tough time ahead. She said, "That will be because Charles always blows hot and cold."
>
> We had no idea Diana's fate would be linked to that tough time. Then we went through hers. I didn't think for one minute that something so dreadful would occur. I gave her a big hug and she waved me off.
>
> I spoke to her after that meeting, in a final phone call, and she sounded wonderful and told me, "I'm the happiest I've ever been."
>
> I had no idea she would die. I would never have been able to stop it. Let's get one thing clear—astrologers can't predict death.
>
> So, I couldn't tell her not to get into a car, or to stay at home. Some things are tragic fate.

Diana's strong connection to the supernatural and otherworldly could not have done otherwise than to foreshadow her death—a death which would shake the foundations the world's most powerful entities. Some energy from the other side seemed to be reaching through. To guide her? To warn her? It is impossible to know. It is likewise unknowable if Diana could have altered her fate.

Was her doom her destiny?

Yet what remains clear is that the forces reaching out in the aftermath of her accident—from the land of the dead, living, or make-believe—were the most powerful on earth. And they wanted a very precise story told.

***

DETECTIVE'S NOTEBOOK

DATELINE: The next day, investigation week two, September 1997

I woke early the next morning refreshed, and keen to tackle any new angle: the possibility of a second car. I'd need to comb the eyewitness accounts for clues about where to start.

Having purchased my usual range of newspapers during my dawn perambulations, I positioned myself in a cozy arcade coffee shop near my Hôtel Chopin and settled in for a long breakfast. I had maintained a habit of scanning the daily press for anything new, anything on the paparazzi. To date nothing had caught my eye; it was all starting to repeat itself. Being the ninjas of the media, the paparazzi had made their comments in the early days, insofar as they pursued the Mercedes from a distance as it raced from the Pont d l' Concorde and after losing sight of the vehicle, they came upon it in the tunnel after the crash. Had the paparazzi witnessed anything sensational or of evidentiary value I felt sure they would have been clamoring to sell it to the highest bidder. Such is the nature of the beast. No such stories appeared. There was no smoking gun; there were no tales of suspicious characters fleeing the area or odd behavior, just another dead end. I needed a new direction, a way through the forest and into the clearing and I needed it soon.

I folded today's addition to my paper collection under my arm and headed back upstairs to my room. There I began the search in earnest, even scanning some of the older broadsheets I had kept hoping for something, anything. Many of the witness accounts of that night in August were actually recorded by journalists and ended up plastered all over the newspapers and the electronic media. In quite a few ways the journalists were acting as the investigators, albeit without the training to sort the false from the true.

I found an account from a local taxi driver, Malo France, who declared to the world's media that he had found himself in the tunnel seconds after the collision had occurred. Working the night shift, he had been taking a fare to a hotel in the sixteenth arrondissement and had navigated the obvious shortcut, through the tunnel at Pont de l'Alma. As one of the very first at the scene, only moments behind the Mercedes, he claimed to have made the sign of the cross as he stepped toward the mangled mess. Malo recalled "seeing a woman's blonde hair . . . she seemed to have fallen into the front of the car . . . she was crawling back to her rear seat when . . . (he) heard a woman cry." Rescue workers a few minutes later found the princess in the rear of the vehicle on the floor, lodged between her seat and the back of the front seat. The taxi driver insisted that the princess appeared to have been tossed around the cabin. This proved important confirmation of a theory that had been circulating since the tragedy: that Lady Diana Spencer had not been wearing a seat belt at the time of the collision.

Inside Malo's taxi cab were two Americans: Mike, a rock-and-roll promoter and his buddy, Stan, a personal injury lawyer from Ohio. They too were caught up in the melee of mayhem that followed the tragedy. Both recalled the appalling conduct of the paparazzi, taking photographs over and above rendering assistance to the injured and dying. Mike believed that the Mercedes had flipped over. He offered no substantiation for his conviction other than it was an impression he gathered from the ruinous condition of the car (again, an indication of the extraordinary speed at which it was traveling). None of these first three witnesses at the scene offered any information indicating foul play or suspicious activity. As I read, I began to ponder whether any other international visitors may have witnessed the accident. Paris was a huge tourist-based hub; upon reflection, it would have been unlikely not to be the case. As I let this notion take root my attention was captured by one of the more dog-eared publications in my possession.

One of the first witnesses to surface with a story for the newshounds had been a Frenchman by the name of François Levi. On the face of it, Mr. Levi's story suggested damningly that the paparazzi had a great deal to do with the three deaths. On the night of the accident, the former harbor pilot, according to

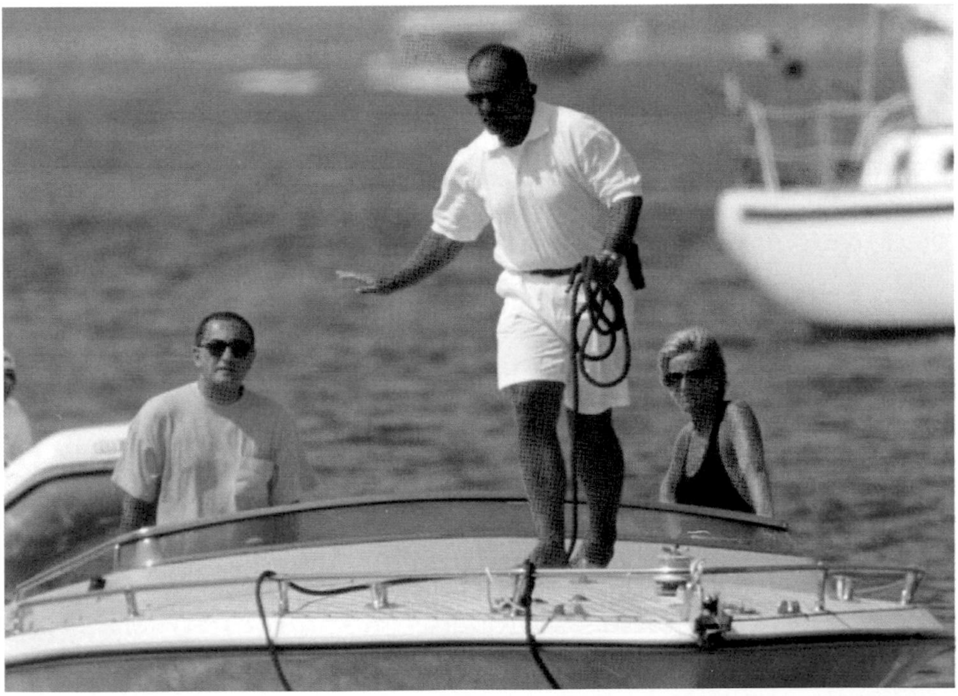

Princess Diana and boyfriend Dodi Fayed vacation in the French Riviera in July 1997, just one month before their horrific death. (Photo credits: Mega Agency)

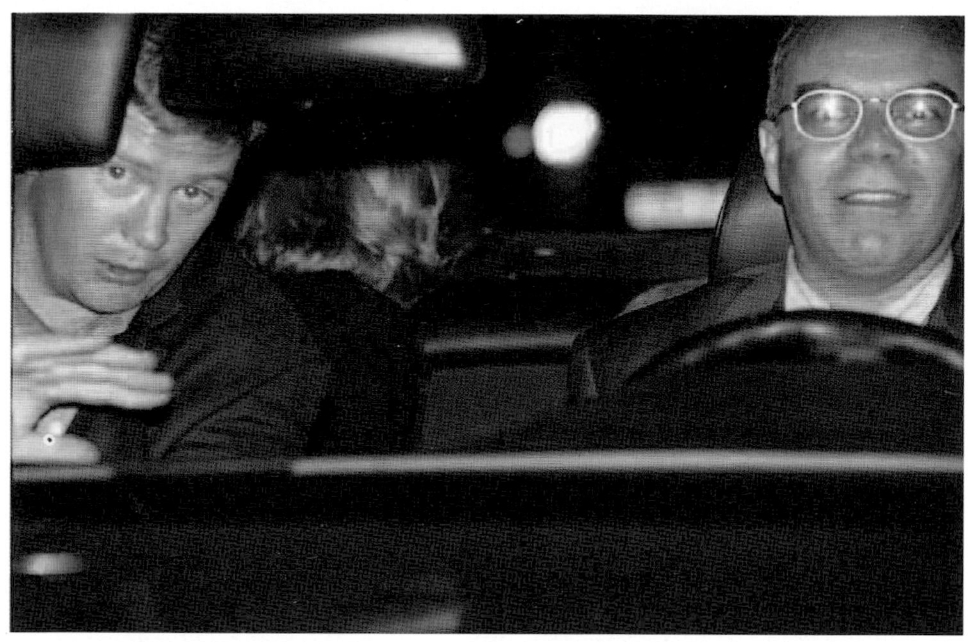

Photo taken minutes before the car accident by following paparazzi. (Shutterstock)

The gruesome images of the wreck that took the lives of Princess Diana, Dodi Fayed, and driver Henri Paul on August 31, 1997. Emergency workers are on the scene tending to the victims trapped in the mangled Mercedes. (Shutterstock)

Side view of the wrecked Mercedes. (Shutterstock)

An overhead shot of the mangled Mercedes being loaded onto a tow truck. (Jerome Delay/AP/Shutterstock)

Close-up image that shows the immense extent of the damage. (Shutterstock)

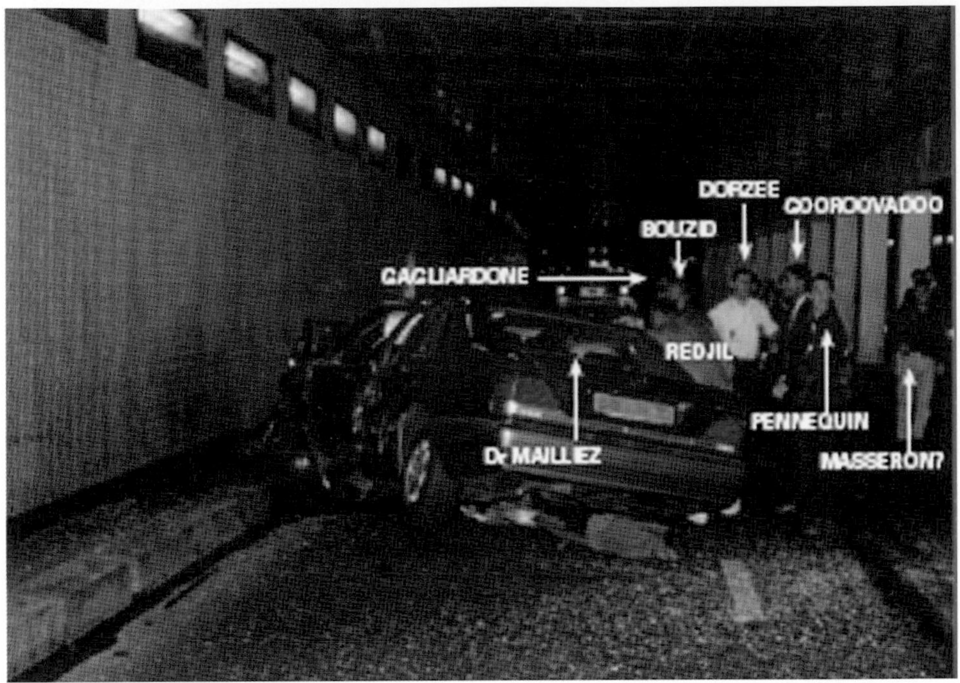

Photographers and emergency workers on the scene of the accident, with their identities noted. (Shutterstock)

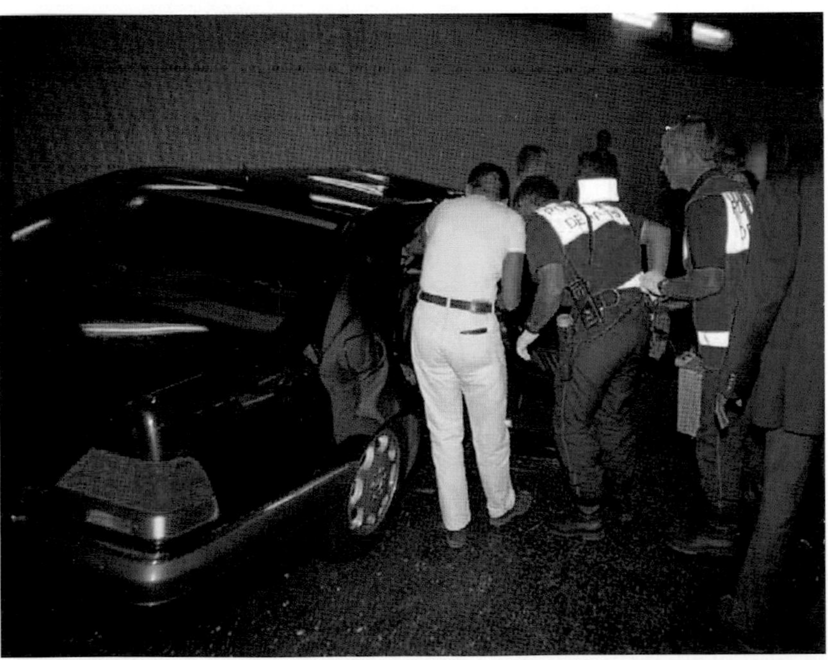

Another view of the accident, with emergency workers tending to the injured passengers. (Shutterstock)

Mohammed Al-Fayed at the funeral of Princess Diana at Westminster Abbey. (Mike Forster/Daily Mail/Shutterstock)

Sir John Stevens, Commissioner of the London Metropolitan Police, who headed the inquiry, Operation Paget, into the death of Princess Diana. (Shutterstock)

Diana's bodyguard and the lone survivor of the wreck, Trevor Rees-Jones, arrives for questioning at Palais de Justice in Paris. (Photo credits: Michel Euler/AP/Shutterstock)

Le Van Thanh, who drove the Fiat Uno that clipped Diana's Mercedes, sits in the vehicle that was painted from white to red the night of the fatal crash. (Paul Cooper/Shutterstock)

The Flame of Liberty (Flamme de la Liberté), which became an unofficial memorial for Princess Diana. (Shutterstock)

newspaper documentation, had enjoyed a Saturday evening out with his wife at the Planet Hollywood nightclub in Paris and was on his way home to Normandy, a region of France three hours to the west of the capitol. I read the story with great interest and began to track Mr. Levi's comments in my notebook, making bullet points, checking for logic and feasibility.

François claimed to have been two cars ahead of a dark Mercedes when, in his rearview mirror, he noticed a motorcycle with two riders dart out in front of the car. His eyes, he reported, were then momentarily dazzled by a brilliant flash of light. He went on to disclose that he heard, but didn't see, the impact as the Mercedes careered into pillar thirteen. I felt my brow furrow as I pondered how Mr. Levi could have known that the Mercedes had hit the pillar when he claimed to have already left the tunnel by then. I reread his statement noting the fact that he clearly indicated that he and his wife, upon hearing the collision, had initially pulled over to the curb outside the tunnel and stopped for a moment. I had walked that exit many times over; the roadway has a sharp ascent making any view to the rear highly improbable. He couldn't have seen the pillar if he were outside the tunnel. My crackpot senses began to tingle.

Mr. Levi continued stating that both he and his wife feared that the accident was a "terrorist attack." A terrorist attack? I had considered the possibility while back in Melbourne but had seen absolutely nothing at the crime scene to give any credence to pursuing this line of inquiry. Still, here was a local Frenchman and his wife offering suspicion of a terrorism link in the deaths of Dodi, Princess Diana, and their driver. The plot was thickening. François didn't attempt to explain how the couple had come to their conjecture; he just stated that this was their firm belief. And his sensational comments had naturally found him on the front page of virtually every newspaper in the world. What was this "witness" up to? Curious to see what else he had to say, I read on.

The Levis, François continued, had then elected to drive on home, all the way to Normandy. This would have had them arrive well after 4 a.m. And it was not until twelve hours after their tunnel experience, "lunchtime Sunday," that he and his wife became aware of the identities of the persons involved in the accident, when they turned on their TV at home. Continuing to bamboozle with his logic, Mr. Levi then boasted of recounting his tale to the Fayed family lawyer that very day. There were now so many questions racing at me. Why would a Normandy man go to Paris for a Saturday night out and then suffer a three-hour drive home, after midnight? Why not stay the night in a hotel? More worrisome, how would a native from Normandy know who the lawyers for the Fayed family were? And how did he manage to make contact with the law firm on a Sunday? Perhaps only minutes after finding out the accident involved Lady Diana. Mr. Levi would surely become more infamous for proving that he could contact a lawyer on the Sabbath than he would be for witnessing the accident that claimed the life of Princess Diana. But the most disturbing segment of his statement for this detective would unquestionably have to be: Why didn't he report his observations to the French cops immediately after he saw the lunchtime news, as would any average citizen? Surely locating a policeman on a Sunday would have been easier than tracking down the Fayed family lawyers?

Reading François's account stirred feelings of suspicion; not for terrorists at the scene, but for meddling from the wings. The Fayeds' lawyer, on the basis of the statement had called for an investigation for manslaughter, quoting chapter and verse from a statement still unseen by the police. François did not enlighten his country's law enforcement officers with his account until later in the following week. The whole matter of this testimonial smacked of skullduggery, causing me to ponder if perhaps all was not what it seemed in downtown Paris. Why was the Fayed family attempting to manage François, and when does a Frenchman use the word "curb," listed in the Oxford dictionary as an English word, to describe the side of the road?

Frustrated, I gathered up a large stack of francs and marched purposefully downstairs offering them up to Charles at the reception desk of my hotel. He had a payphone on the wall at reception. My goal: to telephone Mr. Levi. To talk over his revelation, and most of all to ask him how he came to the conclusion that the accident was a terrorist attack. Did he possess a skill, a sixth sense that no detective worldwide had; one that allowed him to sense terrorists? Despite the efforts of a kindly telephone operator, the emptying of Charles's own pockets and several trips to local stores to replenish my supply of coinage, I was never able to locate him.

Yet, despite being invisible, his sensational story was being used to sully the waters and create a backdrop of terrorism. But why? Who was behind it, who was pressing his buttons? I had my suspicions. The fact that the newspapers reported his statement didn't add any credibility to his story; it merely informed the world that there were stooges out there, willing to place their good names on documents to advance the motives of others who chose to remain veiled, behind the shroud of a lawyer's door or a family's dynasty. I knew enough about reporters to know that they would convey (mostly) whatever came their way; after all, it's not for them to judge. And on the face of it François Levi's account seemed plausible until you analyzed it.

I have long known that witnesses can be a strange lot. Some are full of good faith and assistance; others are notorious for keeping quiet about what they saw or heard, too scared, too indifferent, reluctant to become involved, or fearful of being questioned by investigators. Still others, not realizing the importance of their information, remain silent almost unknowingly. In the case of the Andy Warhol witness, the investigator may well believe that the witness has fabricated their story, but he must prove it incorrect and discredit the witness, otherwise the witness may discredit the investigation. I thought again about Mr. Levi and whether this could have been his motivation. However dubious his account in reality, it remains a fact that mud sticks, and in the mind's eye of future generations there would always remain the possibility of terrorist involvement in this calamity thanks to a man and a wild story.

Of course, it was to be expected that a tragedy such as this would attract its fair share of crackpots as well as conspiracy theories. In only a matter of hours after the collision, the media gossip pot had already begun to bubble and in no time was ripe to overflowing with an endless run of outrageous conspiracy stories fueled by a myriad of sources. All pointed a finger at one or other individual groups deemed desirous of the death of Princess Diana and her companion. From Arab terrorist organizations to Muslim extremists, MI5 and MI6 British Intelligence, and the most absurd of all, that the royal family and Prince Charles himself had orchestrated the tragedy. While these conspiracy theories were never elevated to any status above tabloid nonsense, they troubled the millions of grieving citizens who followed the progress of the case. It is worth noting that despite there being not a smidgeon of evidence to give any of these theories any basis in fact, again, that shadow of doubt remains over the history of the investigation. I feel the need to reiterate here that terrorists, almost without exception, will boast of their involvement (if they have one) in the assassination of a world figure. There were no such attestations from any in the case of the death of Princess Diana.

I put Mr. Levi and terrorism to bed and went back to my research, returning to my tried-and-true practice of methodically reading and rereading. I noted that various newspapers made mention of names, hometowns and country of residence of several international tourists who had been in town late in August. I considered the idea of contacting some of these possible witnesses. It would be a simple matter of asking an international telephone operator to locate and place a call to them. I let the notion roll around my sensibilities a little, conscious of the cost of my last telecommunications endeavor. As I mused, my frustrations intensified and the disdain I felt toward the French law enforcement system grew exponentially. Had they taken control of the situation when the accident first occurred, surely this scenario would have had no opportunity to spin quite so out of control.

Unlike the French police, the River Seine, it seemed, had been doing its job that balmy Saturday night, drawing the general public to its banks for a romantic stroll or cruise. Chris Gallagher was one such reveler, on a cruise that night with friends. Standing on the open deck, he was admiring the view and soaking up memories before he had to head home the following day. As his cruiser motored toward the Alma Bridge, Mr. Gallagher recalled hearing the sound of a massive crash. Looking instinctively at his watch, 12:30 p.m., he recalled that the lights to the Eiffel Tower had just been extinguished. His recollection here was correct; they are turned off at exactly half past twelve. Chris accepted another glass of wine and turned back to his crowd, unknowing of the significance of the noise he had just heard.

Strolling the banks of the river at the same time were lovers Tom and Joanna. Also hearing the sound of a massive crash, they ran to the tunnel, where the Mercedes' horn continued to wail and smoke streamed from its twisted form. They recalled a distraught man walking away and uniformed police arriving, weaving their way between far too many sightseers. The account from Joanna and her man was, in effect, more of the same, more evidence indicating nothing but an accident, followed up by a pack of paparazzi and their 35-millimeter weapons.

Jack and Robin Firestone, a couple from New York City, were vacationing in Paris on the night of the accident. Having enjoyed a long dinner in a classic restaurant, they were in a taxicab, attempting passage through the tunnel only moments after the accident. With their soft bed seeming only minutes away, their cab came to an abrupt halt; the wrecked Mercedes barred their path. As Jack and Robin stepped from their taxi and cautiously approached the fatal scene, they recalled seeing five paparazzi snapping photographs of the mangled car and its occupants. They looked on feeling helpless as a blonde woman, obviously Princess Diana, hung out of the car's window and the paparazzi clicked away frame after frame.

Then there was Mark Solomon, who was in the area and also heard the terrible explosion as the Mercedes careered into the thirteenth pillar. Drawn by the cries for help, he was unaware that it was Princess Diana behind a mask of blood and horror. Mark was particularly disturbed by the lack of effort to save life on the part of the first police to arrive, as was Mr. Culbreath, a British national who stumbled upon the scene. The more I learned, the more aware I became of this as a common complaint by passersby: the slow reaction time of police and their lackadaisical manner, more concerned with crowd control than initial response duty. However, in fairness to the efforts of the emergency workers, at a scene where there are multiple casualties, mere minutes can seem like hours and perceived tardiness may simply be assistance being rendered with utter precision.

CHAPTER NINE

The crash was horrendous, but the response by French police was an abomination.

Shockingly, the wreck that killed Princess Diana and Dodi Fayed wasn't treated as a crime scene by the French authorities, who quickly removed the car and washed down the road ready for rush hour the next morning—and with it, literally all evidence critical to understanding what really happened.

More than this, the accident scene itself was allowed to devolve into a place of chaos.

American-born witness Robin Firestone was in a cab that passed into the Alma tunnel very shortly after the accident. In an exclusive interview, she describes what she saw when her taxi got up to Diana's wreck.

> I noticed these dark formal cars and they weren't moving; they were parked.
>
> I didn't see anybody in them. To my recollection, the windows were dark windows, blacked out windows, so I just thought it was a bizarre sight to see. And I didn't focus on that too much because I really now started to see some action and activity as we made that bend and noticed motorcycles and a lot of photographers at that point.
>
> There were paparazzi—five, six paparazzi from what I recall. One was very specific; I could see it right now in my mind. He was standing in the median next to his, I presumed it was his motorcycle because it was right next to him, and he definitely had a camera on his shoulder. But he had a phone in his hand, and he was talking on the phone.

There were also police already on the scene, which initially led Firestone to believe the matter was being handled. But as her cab continued to creep past the accident site, the level of disorganization became increasingly clear:

> I initially thought, "Wow, the police got here really quickly."
>
> One of them was having an argument; there was like a little push fest—physical pushing back and forth—going on with one of the paparazzi.
>
> It was just absolute chaos. There was no protection of the scene at all. At all. We did not witness ever at any point anybody offering to assist or give help. We did not see anybody aiding or assisting. There was no ambulance there, there was no police tape closing off that entrance to the tunnel.

Looking back now, this seems unthinkable. However, the public seemed willing to accept the immediate version of the events that was released. Instead of wondering about the possibility of a sinister cause of the wreck, everyone's focus was on whether or not Diana's life could be saved.

The first physician who treated Diana from the private medical service SOS Medécins called the Service d'Aide Médicale Urgente switchboard at 12:26 a.m. to order an ambulance. According to French policeman Sebastien Dorzee, who arrived at the scene with a colleague around 12:30 a.m., "Blood was coming out of her mouth and nose. You could see a deep wound to her forehead. At the same time, she was rubbing her stomach. She must have been in pain. She turned her head towards the front of the car, and saw the driver. She became agitated. Then she put her head down again and closed her eyes."

Despite the initial lack of blood on her body, Diana had sustained disastrous head and chest trauma—a hole ripped in her heart by the force of the crash.

The small tear, less than an inch long, to one of four of her pulmonary veins that proved fatal as it stopped blood being pumped to her heart and body.

Emergency surgeons rank damage to the delicate vessels as more serious than almost any other wound.

Dr. Jean-Marc Martino, the emergency specialist who oversaw the princess's treatment shortly after the crash, recalled that after Diana had groaned "My God" when she realized the horror of the crash, she continued to "shout and say things in English which were comprehensible yet incoherent."

Her agitation was so extreme that at 12:45 a.m.—twenty-two minutes after the crash—Dr. Martino injected her veins with midazolam and fentanyl—an opioid analgesic eighty times more potent than morphine—to "calm her down."

Despite the power of the drugs, Diana was so "agitated" she managed to tear the first IV drip out of her arm while still trapped in the vehicle.

She was thrashing around so forcibly that a medical assistant had to hold her down while the drip was reinserted.

After the drugs kicked in and Diana's bruised and sedated body was gently moved out of the Mercedes, she went into cardiac arrest at around 1 a.m.

Martino performed endotracheal intubation—forcing a tube into the princess's windpipe through her mouth—to open her airway, placed her on a respirator to ventilate her lungs with oxygen, and performed external cardiac massage to reestablish her cardiac rhythm.

By the time Diana was gently moved into an ambulance at 1:18 a.m. The so-called "golden hour," within which critically injured patients are most likely to be saved if they have reached the hospital, was almost up. Medics spent about thirty more minutes after Diana's heart attack treating her in the tunnel.

The ambulance didn't depart the scene until 1:41 a.m., and traveled at a snail's pace to the Pitié-Salpêtrière Hospital as the driver did not want to subject the fragile cargo to shocks and bumps that could send her again into cardiac arrest.

Yet Diana's blood pressure plummeted, prompting the ambulance to stop within a few hundred yards of the hospital so it could be treated—leaving Diana within about a thousand feet of surgeons at 2:06 a.m., an exact 103 minutes after her accident.

There were no recorded cases of patients with her same devastating internal injuries arriving at the hospital alive, Diana's inquest was told ten years and three months later.

Her final two hours grew more horrific.

Though she had no serious external injuries, X-rays taken at the hospital indicated internal hemorrhaging that was compressing her right lung and heart.

Ten minutes after her arrival, at 2:16 a.m., Diana suffered her second cardiac arrest, prompting the doctors to inject large doses of epinephrine (adrenaline) directly into the heart.

At around 2:20 a.m. they performed an emergency thoracotomy—opening up her chest cavity to find and suture the wound.

The source of her internal hemorrhaging was a single lesion in her left pulmonary vein at the point of contact with the left atrium.

Diana's bleeding heart was sutured, and the hemorrhaging stopped.

For the next ninety minutes, surgeons conducted internal manual massage of her heart, combined with electroshocks.

It was impossible to reestablish a heartbeat.

The patient was declared dead at 4 a.m. on August 31, 1997.

Dr. Stanley Zydlo, a prominent American emergency physician from Northern Illinois and pioneer in prehospital trauma systems dating to their origin in the late 1960s and early 1970s, said the seventy-minute prehospital delay in Diana's case "certainly took away all of her chances" of survival.

And what came after that?

***

For the purposes of our investigation, we established the following minute-by-minute time line for the aftermath of Diana's horrible "Death Day." It runs like this:

Sunday, August 31, 1997

3:15 a.m. UK time / 4:15 a.m. Paris and Cape Town

> In South Africa, Diana's brother Charles Spencer hears the news his sister is unlikely to survive surgery while on the phone to his sister, Jane. Jane's husband, Sir Robert Fellowes, is the queen's private secretary.
>
> Charles is at the queen's holiday home of Balmoral, Scotland, and

hears Sir Robert on another line in the background suddenly say, "Oh, no."

The prince turns to Stephen Lamport, his private secretary, and mumbles, "They're going to blame me aren't they? The world's going to go completely mad, isn't it?"

Operation Overlord, the official plan to bring back the body of a member of the royal family from abroad, swings into action.

***

4:10 a.m. / 5:10 a.m. (Paris)

On the Scottish island of Seil, Diana's mother, Frances Shand Kydd, has been told her daughter is dead. She has also been told not to tell anyone else until the news has been officially announced.

Distraught at not being able even to call a friend for support, Frances howls at the television news, "Come on! Come on! Tell the world!"

The queen writes a note for the Queen Mother to be given to her when she wakes up, telling her of Diana's death.

In France, one of the country's best facial reconstruction surgeons, Dr. Luc Chikhani, continues to work on repairing Trevor Rees-Jones's smashed face.

He is closing wounds, wiring Rees-Jones's jawbone temporarily back in place, and taking casts of his teeth.

***

4:55 a.m. / 5:55 a.m. (Paris)

Mohamed Al-Fayed is picked up by his bodyguard Kez Wingfield at the Ritz hotel he owns to drive to a helicopter at Le Bourget airport.

Wingfield does something he's never done before. He puts his arm round his boss and says, "I'm sorry for your loss, sir." [Wingfield was approached to speak to us, but declined, saying, "I'm sorry, sir. We're finished with that. Thank you. Sorry about that."]

***

5 a.m. / 6 a.m. (Paris)

An autopsy has been performed on Diana and her body taken to a bed in a first-floor room in Pitié-Salpêtrière, a white cotton sheet pulled up to her neck to cover the thick stitches over her chest cavity cracked open by surgeons during a thoracotomy two hours and forty minutes earlier, so medics could try and massage her heart back to life.

***

5:30 a.m. / 6:30 a.m. (Paris)

Wearing dark glasses, Mohamed Al-Fayed arrives at the Pitié-Salpêtrière Hospital to be told Dodi's body is being taken to a nearby morgue.

At Kensington Palace, a bouquet of lilies wrapped in newspaper has been left at the gates—the first of many thousands.

Inside apartments eight and nine in Kensington Palace, Diana's butler Paul Burrell is collecting items owned by his former employer to take to Paris. He looks at the princess's desk with its fountain pen and bottle of Quink, next to a list of words to improve her vocabulary.

Burrell picks up a set of rosary beads given to the princess by Mother Teresa, draped over a small statue of the Virgin Mary, and puts them in his pocket. He also picks some of Diana's makeup and places it in a leather Gladstone bag with a gold "D" on the side.

Burrell puts her jewelry in the safe and draws all the curtains. Together with Diana's driver Colin Tebbutt, they seal the apartment doors with strong parcel tape to protect everything from being disturbed.

***

6:10 a.m. / 7:10 a.m. (Paris)

Prince Charles is walking alone in the grounds of Balmoral. For the past few hours he's been making calls to his mistress Camilla Parker Bowles and to friends.

Charles knows he must soon break the news of their mother's death to William and Harry.

Inside the morgue in Paris, Mohamed Al-Fayed looks down at the body labeled No. 2146.

He thinks Dodi looks like a little boy again, at peace.

***

6:40 a.m. / 7:40 a.m. (Paris)

The first Princess Diana tribute website appears on the Internet.

***

6:45 a.m. / 7:45 a.m. (Paris)

In Dodi's Paris apartment, Diana's possessions are being collected. Butler René Delorm discovers the Repossi engagement ring made for her by the firm of the same name, silver cufflinks that had belonged to Diana's father, and a silver-framed poem given to Diana by Dodi.

***

6:53 a.m. / 7:53 a.m. (Paris)

The first Princess Diana conspiracy website appears on the Internet.

***

7:15 a.m. / 8:15 a.m. (Paris)

Prince Charles wakes up William and tells him his mother has died. Together they walk to Harry's room.

***

8 a.m. / 9 a.m. (Paris)

Traffic is running through the Alma tunnel once again, less than eight hours after the accident. The only evidence of the crash is a large hole in the thirteenth pillar after French authorities had arranged for the area to be cleaned by road sweepers.

At the Institut médico-légal in Paris, the postmortem on the body of drunk driver Henri Paul begins.

***

9:30 a.m. / 10:30 a.m. (Paris)

At RAF Northolt to the west of London, then fifty-one-year-old Squadron Leader Graham Laurie is told he will be flying Diana's body home in one of the Royal Squadron's BAe 146 jets.

It necessitates a "coffin fit"—the insertion of a modified floor in the rear hold. Fitted with ball bearings, this floor enables the coffin to be maneuvered in and out of the hold more easily.

Laurie, who flew Diana more than three hundred times, tells the ground crew to prepare plane ZE 702.

Prince Harry would often join him on the flight deck, and the princess would chat to the service staff about their families and occasionally play cards with them.

***

10 a.m. / 11 a.m. (Marbella)

Diana's former lover, James Hewitt, wakes with a hangover on holiday with friends at a villa in Marbella.

Hewitt sees his mobile has seven messages and so assumes there's a story about him in the British papers.

Hewitt plays the first message, from a friend.

"Listen, I know where you are, so you may not have heard this. There's very bad news. Diana's dead. She and Dodi were killed in a car crash in Paris during the night."

Groaning, Hewitt replays the message.

***

10:15 a.m. / 11:15 a.m. (Paris)

A scarlet people carrier pulls up outside the small church of St. Mary Magdalene in the mining village of Trimdon, County Durham, and Tony Blair and his family get out.

The prime minister, dressed in black suit and tie, walks up to the microphones. His notes include a phrase his press officer Alastair Campbell told him to stress. It was first used by royal biographer Anthony Holden—"the people's princess."

***

10:55 a.m. / 11:55 a.m. (Paris)

On his way to Aberdeen to take Prince Charles to Paris, Squadron Leader Graham Laurie, at the controls of the BAe 146, lands at RAF Wittering near Peterborough to collect Diana's two sisters, Lady Sarah and Lady Jane.

***

11 a.m. / 12 p.m. (Paris)

Diana's butler Paul Burrell and her driver, Colin Tebbutt, arrive at the room in Pitié-Salpêtrière Hospital where Diana's body lies.

For a moment they think she is alive when a rotating fan blows up strands of her blonde hair.

***

Midday

At Kensington Palace there are now more than a thousand bouquets on the ground and jammed into the railings and gates.

One says, "Rest in peace. Our candle in the wind. Love eternally."

***

1 p.m. / 2 p.m. (Paris)

Reporters have taken over flats across the road from the Pitié-Salpêtrière Hospital, so the medical staff has put sheets over the windows of Diana's room. For confidentiality, the chart by her bed bears the name "Patricia," the saint whose day it is on August 31.

In addition to the red roses that have been sent to the room, there are lilies sent by Prince Charles—his ex-wife's favorite flower.

In Calcutta, frail Mother Teresa sits in a wheelchair for an impromptu press conference.

She reads from a handwritten statement, "Diana was extremely sympathetic to poor people—and very lively, and homely, too. All the sisters and I are praying for her and for all members of her family."

***

5:10 p.m. / 6:10 p.m. (Paris)

Chief nurse Béatrice Humbert leads Prince Charles, Lady Jane, and Lady Sarah into the first-floor room where Diana's body lies.

A picture of her sons that was in her handbag has been placed in her hands, together with the rosary.

Diana is wearing the jewelry recovered from the car—but an earring is missing.

The Prince and Diana's weeping sisters bow their heads and pray by the coffin.

Charles asks to be alone with Diana.

***

5:30 p.m. / 6:30 p.m. (Paris)

Usually composed, Charles is agitated by the missing earring.

"She can't go without her second earring!" he keeps saying.

***

5:35 p.m. / 6:35 p.m. (Paris)

The crowd outside the Pitié-Salpêtrière Hospital watches in silence as an Anglican priest leads out Diana's coffin.

For the journey to England, the coffin has been draped in a Royal Standard, being carried by four pallbearers toward a dark blue hearse. Hundreds of staff and patients, some attached to portable drips, have come outside to watch.

Just before the cortege moves off, a member of the medical team runs forward with a plastic bag and puts it in the trunk of Prince Charles's car. It contains the clothes Diana was wearing when she arrived at the hospital.

***

6 p.m. / 7 p.m. (Paris)

At Villacoublay military airfield, Princess Diana's coffin is placed in the hold of Squadron Leader Graham Laurie's BAe 146. He takes off and heads toward the setting sun before turning north toward England.

As tea is served in the cabin, the passengers can only think of the body of the princess in the hold.

***

6:55 p.m. / 7:55 p.m. (Paris)

Nineteen million people watch on television as the BAe 146 appears out of a cloudy sky above RAF Northolt. Hundreds of people are pressed against the perimeter fence.

Ten-year-old Kirsty Lawley is there with her mother, Tina. Kirsty—who met Diana when she was a patient at London's Great Ormond Street Children's Hospital—insisted they walk from their nearby home across a field to witness the plane arriving.

***

7:05 p.m. / 8:05 p.m. (Paris)

Diana's coffin is removed from the belly of the plane by six RAF pallbearers from the queen's Colour Squadron and carefully lifted onto their shoulders.

They adjust the Royal Standard covering the coffin, then make a slow march to the waiting hearse.

Little Kirsty Lawler hangs to the perimeter fence and sobs.

***

7:12 p.m. / 8:12 p.m. (Paris)

Police outriders from the Special Escort Group lead the hearse onto the A40 into London. Normally, this road is full of traffic but now nothing is moving.

Hundreds of cars have pulled over and their occupants are standing watching the cortege pass by.

As the hearse drives under bridges, people drop flowers onto the road.

***

8 p.m. / 9 p.m. (Paris)

As planned in Operation Overlord, Diana's coffin arrives at Bagleys Lane mortuary in Fulham.

Her body is formally identified by her sisters, and a postmortem examination takes place.

***

9 p.m. / 10 p.m. (Paris)

In New Zealand, eight-year-old Renee Peihopa receives a telegram sent by Princess Diana. Ironically, it is to comfort her over the deaths of her father and sister in a road accident.

***

10:30 p.m. / 11:30 p.m. (Paris)

A short funeral service for Dodi at Regent's Park Mosque is coming to an end. Mohamed Al-Fayed, wearing sunglasses, watches as about fifteen worshippers help carry the coffin to the hearse waiting outside.

A few miles away in Knightsbridge, all eleven thousand light bulbs that decorate his Harrods store have been turned off, and the flags on the store's roof fly at half-mast.

***

11:50 p.m. / 12:50 a.m. (Paris)

Dodi is buried at Brookwood Cemetery near Woking, Surrey, just before midnight, in accordance with Muslim tradition.

***

After all this, the royals exacted one last blow on Diana: dressing her in a morbid funeral dress.

Diana was laid to rest in a long-sleeved black coatdress and a simple rosary given to her by Mother Theresa in her hands that were crossed on her breast.

Even though Diana's final gown was made by one of her favored designers, Catherine Walker, sources say the princess would have hated the idea of being laid in her coffin swathed in black.

One friend of the princess—speaking on condition of anonymity—confided to us:

> If you look at Diana's style, she rarely wore black. She loved pastels and vibrant colors that brought out her fair hair, pale complexion, and blue eyes. She also found the color black terribly depressing and associated it with terrible times, doom and—of course—death. She would have hated the idea if her sons having the final image of her dressed basically as a nun.

One of the major moments Diana stepped out wearing black was in 1994, when she wore her so-called plunging "F**k You Dress" to the Serpentine Gallery summer party. It was the night Prince Charles publicly confessed to his affair with Camilla Parker Bowles [via an interview with Jonathan Dimbleby for a show called *Charles: The Private Man, The Public Role*]. Diana used that gown, with its revealing neckline, to show him what he was missing. But the use of the dress was bittersweet for her, and she later auctioned it off as a show that she was erasing evidence of her old life with Charles. After that she rarely wore black—and the royals knew it. But they still went ahead and laid her to rest in something they knew she would have hated.

"It was their final insult to her," a palace aide told our investigation.

***

As the circumstance of the world's most-watched funeral played out for millions in London and billions around the world, Colin McLaren's investigation led him to Gary Hunter, a London lawyer with connections to Mohamed Al-Fayed and his family.

Immediately, Colin's suspicions were heightened following a meeting with London solicitor Gary Hunter, whose story of car chases, explosions, and supposed terrorists had made him a media star . . . all while the world mourned.

* * *

DETECTIVE'S NOTEBOOK

DATELINE: Investigation week two, September 1997

No sooner had I sat back, confident that I was abreast of all those who could lay claim to having firsthand knowledge of the accident, before an extraordinary new storyteller popped up. Mr. Gary Hunter, a lawyer with a small-time London legal firm, made it to the front page of the majority of my usual array of local and international newspapers with a chronicle of his holiday in Paris on the weekend of August 30 and 31. Gary was to gain the sort of instant notoriety that would be the envy of most public relations experts, and if proven correct, his observations could hold the smoking gun to the death of the queen of hearts and may well alter the entire course of the investigation.

I sat in my usual breakfast nook with Gary's hometown broadsheet, the well-respected *London Times.* According to their commentary, Mr. Hunter had been staying with his wife on the third floor of a hotel building less than a hundred meters from the Alma Tunnel. At 12:25 a.m. on that fateful Sunday morning, Gary had been watching television and heard, "an almighty crash followed by the sound of skidding, then another crash. . . . (He) went to the window and saw people running towards the tunnel. . . . (He) saw a car turning from the area by the tunnel exit and roaring down the Rue Jean Goujon. . . . (He) heard the screeching of tires. . . . (He) saw a small dark car . . . it was racing at 60–70 mph. . . . There were people in a hurry not to be there."

Interestingly, only a few days earlier the French National Police had released the news that they were searching for a second car, a Fiat Uno. And the street Mr. Hunter mentioned, Rue Jean Goujon, I knew very well; I had knocked on every door and spoken to every resident. I only wished the article had been more specific. I wanted to know exactly where Gary had slept that night. The street had several accommodation options: bed-and-breakfasts and hotels. I sensed another round of door knocking in the not-too-distant future and unconsciously glanced out of the café window to see what sort of a day Paris was throwing up at me. All fine, I smiled, sipped my coffee, and picked up the next version of Mr. Hunter's exploits.

The information he came forward with was blunt and straight to the point. There were two other cars involved in the accident and both disappeared immediately afterward, roaring down a street into obscurity. According to Gary, something very suspicious caused the accident, something deliberate and menacingly calculated. His narration claimed categorically that "it was obvious that they were getting away from something and that they were in a hurry. I was confident they were getting off the scene. It looked quite sinister. It could have been a Fiat or a Renault. The car was being shadowed by a second vehicle, a white Mercedes."

Gary went on to say the smaller car was traveling in close conveyance with the white Mercedes:

> They were bumper to bumper. . . . They turned from the area by the tunnel and went roaring down Rue Jean Goujon. . . . They both spun around together and sped off down the street at suicidal pace, more than a hundred miles per hour. . . . (He) thought it was very strange that they were traveling so dangerously close to each other. Their behavior made me wonder exactly what they had been up to in the tunnel when the crash happened.

My detective's radar was starting to twitch again. This was all sounding a little too much like dialogue from an espionage movie. I noticed that the recorded speed of the missing vehicles altered dependent on version perused: from sixty miles an hour to one hundred miles an hour and down a skinny one-way street, going the wrong way!

My first thought was why hadn't Malo France, the Parisian taxi driver, seen the "sinister" actions of the other two cars? After all, according to Gary, they were far from inconspicuous, treating the area like a grand prix circuit. And where were Malo France's passengers' eyes, the two men in the back of his cab who lent a hand? Realistically, could they also have missed the near demolition derby? Then there were Tom and Joanna, the lovers strolling the riverbank; why didn't they observe the spectacle? After all, they were almost on top of the accident scene, in the ideal position. As were the New York diners, on their way home in their taxi. I thought a little more about the topography of the tunnel. At over one hundred meters in length, how could anyone see any vehicle, sinister or not, exiting onto the highway at the far end?

As an officer of the courts of London, Gary Hunter would have to be aware of the correct procedure when making a statement. And once sworn and signed, he would also be aware to whom that statement should be served. In fact, he would have the contact details of both the London Metro police and Scotland Yard at his fingertips. Yet Gary made his evidentiary document three weeks after the event, and to the lawyers acting on behalf of the Fayed family. Here we go again, I thought.

Back up in my hotel room, I located the telephone number for Hepburn Lawyers in London, the workplace of this intriguing witness, and put through a call. My recent experiences had led to an upgrading of my technological equipment; I now possessed a phone card. After only a few short rings a pleasantly efficient voice informed me that Mr. Hunter was unavailable, but could anyone else be of assistance? I was connected to another lawyer, Gary's immediate boss, who greeted me in a lighthearted manner. Feeling confident that Gary's workmates must all be enjoying the usual banter of his newfound celebrity status, I launched in, boots and all, with this jovial fellow.

He listened to my bullet-point version of Gary's story and claimed in return to know nothing of the article. Further, he had heard no talk in the office of Gary's observations, nor was he even aware that Gary had been to Paris that weekend. Then the phone went silent. I imagined him reaching for a tall glass of water. I, in turn, became more fascinated by Mr. Hunter by the minute.

Apparently now recovered, Gary's boss confided that Gary was busy, that I would need to wait but he would attempt to fetch him. Not one for telephone hold music, I zoned out for a few minutes as I mentally processed the news that Mr. Hunter was keeping his media tidbits hush-hush from those closest to home. My musing state was broken by a cheery hello from the other end of the phone line. Initially Gary seemed buoyant. For a moment I thought he believed me to be an Australian journalist. I explained that I was simply an Australian tourist, on holidays in Paris, and that I had read his quotes in the world newspapers. He sounded chuffed, almost pleased. I went on to explain that I'd had a long career in criminal investigation, having worked on many police task forces, and that I would dearly love to catch up with him to discuss his observations. Gary seemed to have trouble clearing his throat.

We suffered an overly long pregnant pause, so I switched tactics, congratulating him on his observations and his honesty in coming forward. He sounded nervous, a little unsure of his himself and his story. I heard a stutter in his voice and a sinking feeling settled in the pit of my stomach, a feeling that detectives dread when questioning a man with a story. I was losing him; he would rather be elsewhere.

I offered to fly to London that very day to meet with him, perhaps we could share a pint and he could fill me in on his remarkable experience? Gary was not so enthusiastic. This was hardly necessary, he offered. I countered, casually letting slip that I was traveling to London anyway to visit relatives, so catching up was easy really, my shout for a beer. Reluctantly Gary acquiesced and we locked in a time, agreeing to meet at his office the following day before lunch. He rang off, no doubt to take a few deep breaths before suffering a myriad of questions from his superior. I admit to a few deep breaths myself. But I wasn't ducking questions; I was scrawling them in my notebook, the ideas popping into my head faster than I could get them down on paper. Mr. Hunter would have a whole lot more answers to come up with tomorrow.

I threw a few essentials into my shoulder bag, added the Gary Hunter press cuttings, and sprinted downstairs to reception, where I begged a favor from Charles, who was on the desk. Could I rebook my room for the next week and, more importantly, could it be left as it was, strewn with papers, sketches, and newspapers? By now Charles had a good sniff of what I was up to and gave me the nod. He would keep the cleaners at bay until my return. So, with a surge of adrenaline, I headed for the airport. I had one decent-sized fish on my line, and he wasn't getting away.

Arriving in London late that night, via Heathrow, I found a hotel close to the center of town, close to Gary Hunter's law firm, and took a room. Up early, I spent little time over my stodgy English breakfast and arrived outside Gary's London law firm well before lunchtime. Nestled among an eclectic mix of studios and small businesses, I took in the charm of the quaint low-rise office and then stepped inside. I asked the receptionist if I could see Gary, explaining that I had an appointment. She seemed to tune into my Australian accent and hesitated. She looked around at nothing in particular and I sensed an oddness. It was then that I was served an English ace. The receptionist explained, "Mr. Hunter is unavailable." And I was livid.

I gave the woman my name and repeated that I had an appointment. My protests fell on deaf ears; Gary wasn't keeping my appointment. No longer in the mood to gloat of his narrative, he had become celebrity shy overnight. The receptionist looked embarrassed as she handed me a plain white envelope containing a type written note: a briefly worded apology from Gary. It read, "Sorry to inconvenience you, Colin, but I cannot speak of this matter with you, nor can we meet. I hope you understand." I stood alone in the foyer; my shoulder bag slumped to the floor. I was gutted.

Shuffling over to the plush two-seater guests' lounge, I dropped my weary body and reread the note over and over. My dismay turned to annoyance, and I demanded to speak to the senior partner. My request was denied. There would be no one available to see me, that day or any other day. The receptionist started to get herself busy. The room fell silent, and I left the building feeling totally duped.

I found a nook nearby that allowed for a few hours of surveillance and sat observing the handful of people who came and went. It was only a small firm of lawyers, but none of those who wandered in or out had the appearance of a forty-one-year-old male lawyer. I fully intended to approach anyone that looked like he could have been Mr. Hunter and force my meeting. Before long I gave my knuckles a run, knocking on a few of the neighboring offices using the wrong address routine, asking if anyone knew Gary Hunter, a lawyer. I was hoping for a better description, so I never missed him, should he leave in a crowd. No one in the neighboring businesses knew him and I was starting to become a pest. I had Gary's number in my back pocket so I found the nearest pay phone and with the ruse of a new client recommended to Mr. Hunter, I rang his office. Feigning a dodgy English accent, I got past the snooty receptionist and was placed on hold. Gary answered. His game was up. I explained who I was, and let him have half an ear full, stating that I wanted a word, a chance to go over his story. Initially he stayed silent. Then he made the simple, nervous comment, "Please Colin, I can't talk to you, I am under instructions. . . . I must ring off." There was a pregnant sense that Gary was about to hang up. I needed to get him to talk, to open up, but I felt he was shutting me out. With nothing to lose, I went for broke, I told him that I would be waiting out the front of his office all day and night to see him. He did not reply. I believed I had a mere few seconds remaining before he did ring off. I added that I considered his evidence of seeing cars fleeing the tunnel as unlikely. My livid state returned as Gary's silence hung. It was then that I knew Gary Hunter was never going to voluntarily meet me. I offered my suspicion outright and said, "I have been told your law firm does occasional work for the group of companies owned by the Fayed family, is that correct?" It was only my belief, but Gary didn't know that. He remained silent. "If I'm wrong, say so." More silence, which acted as confirmation.

I went on to tell him that I considered his statement to be a fraud and that I intended to prove it. Gary's reaction was predictable: he slammed down the phone.

Deciding that he had to come out sometime, I paced on a street that I was sure now had eyes. But by the close of business mine were the only ones left, staring at locked doors, including the one at the rear. The London lawyer who claimed to have seen so much had evaded me. With a little less pride than I'd had the day before, I set my direction finder to the London underground, destination Heathrow, and decided to go back to Paris.

As I waited in line at the train ticket office, the revelations of the past few days circled my brain: a second car, questionable statements from witnesses tied to the Fayeds. The thought of losing stirred me to back away from the ticket seller and think it through. I had to make use of my time in London, despite the setback. There was one other major player in this game that I couldn't afford to leave on the bench. Electing to stay one more night in London, I had it in mind to knock on the door of Harrods the following morning. It was time to meet up with the inner sanctum: the Al-Fayed group, which, it was beginning to appear, was never too far away from any new exposé concerning the accident on August 31. First it was François Levi, and now the scarlet pimpernel, Gary Hunter.

I couldn't put aside a nagging suspicion that the Al-Fayed camp was aware of my independent investigation and I considered that the camp was also aware that I had spent my whole day standing out the front of a nervous, small-time London lawyers' office looking like a banished colonial. I needed to go shopping at Harrods!

At 10 a.m. the following morning, I climbed the stairs to the administration section of one of the world's great department stores and entered a very stylish outer office. Behind an equally impressive reception counter sat a young woman who welcomed me with her classically upper-class English dialect. I asked if I could speak to Mr. Mohamed Al-Fayed. She neither confirmed nor denied his presence in the building; instead, she posed a number of polite questions as to my reasons to see him. I replied with my standard answer. Visiting detective—Australian—undertaking an independent study—the tragic deaths in Paris. She smiled, again noncommittal, and showed me to a seat, handing me the top few of a mess of glossy magazines. Opposite, a wall clock ticked loudly for half an hour. Then the man himself appeared.

Mohamed Al-Fayed was probably better dressed than any man I have ever seen of his age. We shook hands, exchanged plastic smiles and introductions. He seemed to accept my qualification as a detective as he glanced me up and down; I was dressed more for golf than a high-level business meeting. His eyes then locked onto my shoulder bag. I took the opportunity to pull out a number of my dog-eared notebooks to indicate my bona fides. I flicked through my most complete book, highlighting maps, sketches, and measurements, explaining that I'd just come from Paris after much research at the accident scene. I looked up to gauge Mr. Al-Fayed's reaction and was distracted by the presence of a dour-faced man standing directly behind him. He was edging his way into our conversation, like a man who needed to hear. I soon learned that he was one of Mohamed's security executives, although he didn't appear to have his boss's tailor. An ex-cop himself, he still favored the powder blue shirt with poorly matched tie. Mr. Al-Fayed suggested that I sit with the cheerless fellow and discuss my findings. I didn't want that and moved in closer to the main man, as if to confide a notation, or measurement from my book. And with that the Egyptian-born billionaire was gone, disappearing behind the interior design.

Both old brigade law enforcement officers, we started with a little awkward small talk, chewing the fat, searching for a war story in an attempt to break down the barriers. It wasn't working. Chatting resulted in a one-sided, five-minute interrogation, enough time for the security executive to ascertain my career qualifications and to pose one question, twice, "Have you got any evidence of Muslim involvement?" I answered in the negative. He crossed and uncrossed his legs and followed up by suggesting that my final report into the Paris tragedy would be interesting if it included some suggestion of Muslim terrorist participation. The starkness of the comment hung thickly in the air. He stared at me, as if waiting for me to nod, to talk or to do . . . anything. My eyes then followed the pattern in his tie. He then stood, adjusted the crease in his trousers, as was probably an employment requirement, and commenced to move away.

Baffled by his lack of professional interest in my findings, I also stood and attempted to redirect the conversation to the facts as I had documented them. He smiled dismissively, handed me his business card and suggested that should I find "any material of interest" perhaps he would accept a copy of my report. Then he too disappeared. I looked at another English receptionist, but this one was an expert at looking busy. I shook my head, stuffed my books in my bag, like a failed door-to-door salesman, and descended the grand stairway, then turned out of the side street entry and caught that overdue train for Heathrow.

Back in Paris later that night, Charles, my hotel receptionist, unlike Gary Hunter, was true to his word. My cozy little hotel room was a sight for sore eyes after enduring a long wait for what proved to be a bumpy flight back to Paris. Gary had proven himself far from a man of honor, failing to show his face for our meeting, but he had succeeded in wedging himself a spot way deep up in the back regions of my nostrils. So, although bleary eyed, I awoke the next morning determined to sift through his "evidence" and either prove or disprove his story once and for all. I may not have him, but I still had the newspapers with his chapter, verse, and quotes of his story. I got to work and bullet pointed every word of his verbatim yarn. My first box to check off: find the hotel room from where Gary Hunter claimed to have made his spectacular observations.

There were several hotel buildings tucked away in the backstreets, but none with a view of the tunnel or the Place de l'Alma. That was my most worrisome problem. Added to this there were no hotel buildings of any kind on the Place de l'Alma itself. Gary mentioned that the street below was Rue Jean Goujon and of his being less than a hundred meters from the Alma Tunnel, but this did not gel with local geography. For his observations to have been "100 meters" from the tunnel, he would have to have been staying at "apartment building one" on Cours Albert. I knew that to be incorrect.

I recalled my visits to the apartments along the way and the fully mature leafy elm trees that dominated the area, obscuring any views. I oriented myself to the tunnel exit where Gary claimed to have seen the two "sinister cars." Four hundred meters farther west, it was impossible to see from Cours Albert or Rue Jean Goujon. I spent the better part of the day treading the pavements, up and down the maze of one-way streets, dead ends, and narrow laneways, knocking on doors and reacquainting myself with French smiles.

Having endured repeated small talk on my trusty subject, French and Australian rugby, by late afternoon I was rewarded. At the sixth accommodation facility I had visited, after the sixth guest register I had checked page by page, I found one "G. Hunter" listed toward the back of that belonging to the Royal Alma Hotel. A smallish establishment, it was situated around the corner from Place d l'Alma, 300 yards farther up the one-way street of Rue Jean Goujon. The receptionist was kind enough to confirm Mr. Hunter's attendance for the weekend of August 30 and 31, and offered to show me the room he occupied—room 304 on the third level. Gary's room faced the street and overlooked a tall and impressive post–art deco apartment block immediately across the road. A quick tour of the interior indicated that none of the hotel rooms offered any views, in any direction.

However, to give Gary the benefit of the doubt, had he leaned himself precariously out of his tiny window and looked sharply down the street he might have been able to catch just a glimpse, in the midnight darkness, of a clump of elm trees that surrounded a small public garden. Beyond that, if the trees were cut down, and massive spotlights lit up the distance, there might have been a slim chance of seeing a fraction of the roadway that travels past the Place de l'Alma and over the River Seine. Certainly there was no possibility of seeing anything to do with the tunnel or immediate surrounds. As for seeing people running, in any direction, to or from the tunnel, that too was a complete impossibility. As for having any view of either end of the tunnel or for seeing two cars roaring out of the tunnel exit, the story was a complete fabrication. It would be highly unlikely with the distance involved, for Gary to have even heard the accident from his room. His statement just didn't stack up.

Again I asked myself why. Why did someone invent such a story? Why did this London lawyer construct a vivid set of observations and hand his statement to the Al-Fayed family lawyers? And, more importantly, who was really behind it, trying to sully the water and trying to promote terrorism as the motive behind the death of Princess Diana?

CHAPTER TEN

Even though Colin had systematically debunked Garry Hunter's story, a campaign of misinformation—or, dare we suggest, fake news—was being spread into the landscape that surrounded the death of Princess Diana. Someone who wanted to create a smoke screen, away from the simple question of how the world's most prominent woman could be killed in a car accident with a driver traveling at breakneck speed and riddled with drugs and alcohol? And, more troubling, the question yelled out to be answered: Who employed the driver and came up with this deeply flawed plan?

There is no doubt that Princess Diana was being spied upon by both British and American agents at the time of her death. Her increasingly controversial public profile, and her relationship with Dodi, meant that she was being tailed by both CIA and MI6 officers—up to and including at the moment her tragic life ended.

"The British government and the royal family were worried about Dodi," one former intelligence agent who spoke under conditions of strictest confidentiality confirmed. "They had painted a sinister picture of Dodi as being a drug user, a serial philanderer, and a highly unreliable figure. There had been talk in those final weeks that Diana was thinking of getting married to Dodi. That set alarm bells ringing at Buckingham Palace. It was unthinkable that such an inappropriate figure should become stepfather to the future king, Prince William. Plus, he was a Muslim. If Diana had children by him, they would have to be raised in that faith, which could cause huge embarrassment to the British royals."

Dodi's reputation took a hammering when it was revealed he had been thrown off the set of the film *Chariots Of Fire*, on which he had a nominal role as an executive producer—thanks to his billionaire father—after it was discovered he had been handing out cocaine to the cast and crew on set.

"Dodi had other things on his mind than developing a film career for himself, of which girls and drugs rated pretty highly—and not necessarily in that order," producer David Puttnam has observed.

If Dodi's inappropriateness as a mate for the princess of Wales was of concern to the British, it was Diana's outspoken attacks on the arms industry that worried the Americans, and brought her under observation by the CIA and others.

"She had already successfully rallied public opinion against the use of antipersonnel land mines—to the extent she persuaded British Prime Minister Tony Blair they should be banned," an intelligence source mused. "Now she was pushing for President Clinton to follow suit. The American arms industry was becoming hugely concerned about the way she was swinging public opinion, and wanted to know what her next moves were going to be. If Clinton agreed, then what next? This is an all-powerful, multibillion-dollar industry yet, weirdly, it saw as its chief enemy that pretty blonde princess."

So, two countries were focusing their spying efforts on the princess and her playboy. The two intelligence agencies, CIA and MI6, were probably pooling their information. Colluding against her. And Diana knew she was being listened to—constantly ordering sweeps of her private quarters in the years before her death.

She also harbored suspicions she might die as a result of a car accident and had revealed these suspicions in a letter—as we have established—to her butler, Paul Burrell, as well as to her solicitor, Lord Victor Mishcon.

For example, in a letter written ten months before the accident in the tunnel—and divulged years later by former butler Burrell—the princess wrote that "this particular phase of my life is the most dangerous."

As Burrell himself tells us:

> She was often careful about her car. She said to me, "Get underneath and see if you can see anything. Is there a pipe cut where the brake fluid goes in?" I said, "Your Royal Highness, I'm not an engineer. I don't know these things."

> "Well, have a look. Is there anything unusual underneath the car?" So, I'd scramble underneath the car in my uniform, or my suit, and try and find something which looked out of place.
>
> Of course, I never did, but she was convinced that the system was out to get her. She wrote me a letter one night. She sat at her desk often late at night and wrote me notes. This letter goes on for ten pages, and part of it reads, "This is the most difficult part of my life. I fear that Charles is going to organize an accident in my car. I am going to die of head injuries, and be killed in order that he can marry Camilla."

In the same note, she painted Charles as a murderous fiend who not only wanted her, but also his own mistress—Camilla Parker Bowles—out of the way so he could marry another woman: nanny to princes William and Harry, Tiggy Legge-Bourke.

Meanwhile, the royals circulated stories that Diana was delusional and had developed a mental illness.

"Charles, Philip, and senior bureaucrats spread stories that she was crazy," one palace aide told our investigation, speaking on the condition of anonymity. "They were always pushing the line that Diana had a screw loose and no one should listen to her."

It should be observed that this would also suit the interests of the nations and arms dealers who felt threatened by Diana's crusading.

Investigator Noel Botham, author of the book *The Murder Of Princess Diana*, claims another reason Diana was marked for assassination was that she had an affair with a relative of Prince Charles in 1991, which was documented in a series of passionate love letters.

It's said the fling lasted six months and began on a skiing vacation in Austria. Some thirteen letters total between the two were discovered, Botham said, at least one of which begins, "My darling Diana."

These sort of pressures—from within and without, from royals and from governments—found their culmination in Diana's so-called accident. It is easy for contemporary readers to wonder how the suspicious death of a woman so obviously embroiled in romance and political intrigue was taken at face value back in 1997. Yet it is also easy, in hindsight, to forget how gradually these truths came to light.

As each year since Diana's death has passed, more information has been leaked to the public and to journalists. At first, many of these tawdry truths seemed simply no more than that: isolated incidents of indiscretion. Yet as the magnitude of the web has been revealed, the sinister interrelations between the revealed secrets have become bracingly clear.

Investigative journalist and former BBC royal correspondent Michael D. Cole—in an exclusive interview for this investigation—shares that he also believes there were sinister forces behind Diana's death, and that the princess herself had some inkling of what was coming. . . and thought that Prince Charles would be involved.

> I personally think that there is much more to be found out about this. It was not an accident. It was a profound tragedy. It lives with me every day. It is my fondest hope, before I die, that the full truth of this will come out, because I don't believe it has yet.
>
> Princess Diana herself believed strongly that she was going to be murdered, and she predicted how she would be murdered. She said that she would be murdered in a car crash, orchestrated to look like an accident, and she very firmly blamed her husband for being behind that plot.

Perhaps, no single person has done more to bring the truth out into the open than Dodi's father, Mohamed Al-Fayed, who has poured an estimated $14 million into investigating 175 separate conspiracy theories surrounding Diana and his son's death.

He has no doubt that the royal family were one of the parties involved in plotting the deaths to prevent Diana from marrying a Muslim. More specifically, he blames Prince Philip and Prince Charles. He is desperate to prove what he thinks is the truth before Philip dies.

Mohamed Al-Fayed isn't the only one to smell a rat.

Conspiracy theories about the crash have grown in credibility and urgency in the years since the crash.

One place where many investigators start is the timing. Incredibly, it took a staggering total of 101 minutes to get Diana to the hospital after the initial emergency call. Mohamed Al-Fayed believes British secret service agents had infiltrated the paramedic crew and purposefully delayed the ambulance to slash her chances of survival.

President Ronald Reagan suffered the same pulmonary tear as Diana in the assassination attempt against him in 1981—yet he was saved and lived until age 93.

Suspicion surrounds the accident itself and also the vehicles involved in it. That's vehicles, plural. For example, the mysterious white Fiat Uno that numerous witnesses say sped into the tunnel after the dark blue Mercedes and bumped it from behind, causing the fatal wreck. Investigators found paint and plastic in the wreckage that matched an Uno owned by Jean-Pierre Andanson, a French photojournalist supposedly chasing the princess. After police bizarrely ruled the Uno out of playing any part in the crash, the story took another unexplained twist when Andanson's burned remains were found in his locked BMW in the South of France three years later. There was a rumor that Andanson had boasted of working for both British and French intelligence services, using photography as his cover.

In *Princess Diana: The Evidence*, authors Jon King and John Beveridge assert that when Andanson's corpse was found, his head was detached from his body and he had a hole in his temple—wounds almost impossible to be caused in a suicide. A month later, armed men stole laptops and cameras from the French photo agency that represented Andanson, but detectives still ruled the death a suicide and denied any link to the break-in. Rumors persisted that Andanson was a shady operative in the murky world of espionage. At the very least, we know that he was someone whom powerful forces wanted destroyed.

"Many people think he was a liability who had to be taken out," one source close to the investigation revealed.

There are also lingering conspiratorial questions about the condition of the driver Henri Paul, and if the blood samples taken from him were tampered with. Some experts claim the samples contained such high levels of carbon monoxide that Paul wouldn't have been able to walk, let alone drive a car.

Diana and Dodi were forced to abandon their usual chauffeur and travel in a replacement vehicle driven by Paul that night, ostensibly for security reasons. But experts suggest that the limo was deliberately sabotaged, and the replacement vehicle was rigged for the fatal crash.

And a further complication—how did Paul come to have nearly $340,000 in his bank accounts despite being on a $30,000-a-year salary?

Some of his old friends claim he was a clandestine operative for the Direction de la Surveillance du Territoire, France's equivalent of MI5, paid to snoop on famous guests at the Ritz hotel.

A British probe led by former Scotland Yard Police Commissioner Lord Stevens dismissed these conspiracy theories, pinning the blame firmly—and solely—on the boozed-up chauffeur. At the belated 2007 inquest, a jury ruled the cause of Diana's death to be the grossly negligent driving of Henri Paul and the following paparazzi.

The 832-page document published after the Metropolitan Police investigated scores of conspiracy theories surrounding Diana's death discounted all of them. Still, there remains a strong suspicion that Diana was a victim of a meticulously planned murder.

The British documentary, *Diana: Story of a Princess*, screened after the princess's death, underlined just how hated she was by shadowy senior advisers to the royal family known as "the gray suits."

The monarchy has an ancient bloody history of beheadings, incarcerations, and a litany of cruel and ruthless punishments meted out to anyone posing the slightest threat to the crown. Diana, with her beauty, her effervescent personality, and her enormous public popularity, was perhaps more a threat to the old order at Buckingham Palace than any other figure in modern times. For that reason alone, the crash at the Pont de l'Alma tunnel is suspicious.

And just look at the way the royal family treated her. They cast her aside after her divorce to Charles, and, as her former royal protection officer Ken Wharfe put it, the queen "signed Diana's death warrant" by failing to persuade her to keep on her Scotland Yard bodyguards instead of relying on Dodi's calamitous security detail.

There's no denying that the royals snared naive seventeen-year-old Diana Frances Spencer to be Prince Charles's virgin bride and bear his children. But when she turned out to be a rebel strong enough to stand up to them, there is strong evidence to suggest she became a sacrificial lamb, finally meeting her death accordingly in a Paris tunnel.

"Princess Diana was the victim of an arranged marriage," says Harold Brooks-Baker, one of the world's leading authorities on royalty and publisher of the famed aristocrats' bible, *Burke's Peerage*. "She was a seventeen-year-old child pushed into the arms of Prince Charles. What starry-eyed girl would refuse a marriage proposal from a dashing prince? But the shadowy powers behind the throne failed to manipulate their beautiful palace puppet and eventually drove her to her death. They have blood on their hands. Charles should not become king. He should hand the throne over to his eldest son, Prince William."

Clearly, these royals were not a group to tolerate transgressions. They expected obedience, and they expected Diana to bear the children of Prince Charles. So, what, then, of the ultimate disobedience? What of Mohamed Al-Fayed's claim that Diana was pregnant with her Muslim lover Dodi's baby when she died?

It's an explosive idea. Yet, explosive or not, there is copious evidence to suggest it is true.

Consider firstly the images of the two published earlier that year. Her head resting lightly on his bronzed shoulder—Diana's supple, tanned body relaxed in his tender embrace; the pictures of two lovers resting on the deck of a luxury yacht after an afternoon frolic in the warm waters of the Mediterranean shocked the world.

Diana's face is etched with a deep, satisfied glow, basking contentedly in the arms of new love Dodi. Free of her royal shackles, the playful princess hugged her lover after unleashing a wave of passion for her Egyptian playboy.

"I am yours forever—you have changed my life," lipreaders confirm that Diana whispered to Dodi as one of the snaps was taken of their lips parting after a long, passionate kiss.

Dodi is seen in these images hugging the beautiful royal, locking his sun-kissed arms around her waist and striking her shapely bottom.

"I can't believe this is happening to us," sources say he said when the images were captured. "You are the woman I always dreamed would be mine someday."

They embraced on the deck of the yacht *Jonikal* moored off the island of Sardinia—oblivious to the watching world around them.

The lovers held hands and let the shimmering warmth of the Mediterranean enfold them as Italian photographer Mario Brenna captured the magical sense of romance that had the whole world talking in 1997—when the snaps were released. Insiders said at the time the perfectly captured Diana deliriously in love.

Veteran royal-watcher and editor of *Majesty Magazine* Ingrid Seward explains why Diana was so comfortable with Dodi:

> I think he was just someone that Diana could really enjoy herself with. The whole affair with Hasnat Khan was conducted in the utmost secrecy, but Dodi was glamorous and fun, and I think she was enjoying herself. I think it was as simple as that. It was in the open, and I think she was literally enjoying herself.

Diana was a woman caught up in a whirlwind of passion as she and Dodi slid into blue waters for a swim, and she wrapped her long, slender legs around her sweetheart beneath the lapping waves. Surrounded by holidaymakers, who didn't recognize the couple, they were free to frolic like lovestruck teens.

Mario said of the images, "They show a princess truly in love. I'm sure they knew I was taking photos, but they didn't care. They were so in love they wanted the world to know."

On the deck of the *Jonikal*, the couple were seen slowly massaging each other with sun lotion. At one point, Dodi eased down the straps of Diana's swimsuit so he could rub cream into her shoulders.

The pair smooched, kissed, embraced—and in one tender moment, Dodi lovingly slipped a bracelet over Diana's wrist as she chatted on her mobile phone. His excitement with his new love even boiled over into unbridled passion as he followed her on the yacht—with his arousal showing through his shorts. At the time, media outlets were forced to censor those shots.

A royal source said at the time of the snaps taken in August 1997, "That cruise sealed their love. The photos show Diana is free from her emotional prison. She's boasting a new, unfettered sexuality. You can see the gleam in her eyes. And her figure has taken on a rounder, more voluptuous shape."

The magical six-day trip started on July 27 on the luxury love boat from Nice, France, to the crystal-clear waters surrounding the fabled islands of Corsica and Sardinia. The *Jonikal* was manned by a staff of sixteen, sailed by Bonifacio, Corsica, and anchored off the wealthy resort town of Porto Cervi, off Sardinia's Emerald Coast. The lovers stayed onboard all the next day. They ordered a pasta dinner from Pedrinelli's restaurant, delivered by boat.

The *Jonikal* then headed to Cavallo, where Princess Caroline of Monaco had vacationed the week before. In Dodi, Diana had finally found the man who unleashed her pent-up sexual frustration after her tortured years with Prince Charles.

Dr. Lois Mueller, the renowned clinical psychologist from Tampa, Florida, who studied the couple's body language when the images were printed, declared that in her professional estimation:

> Dodi is the ideal lover for Princess Diana. She fell in love with the power and passion of a Middle Eastern man."
>
> Just like her lover before Dodi—Pakistani heart doctor Hasnat Khan—Diana found her new Egyptian lover captivating. Middle Eastern men are known for their sexual prowess and energy. Dodi has that exotic passion and love of women that comes from his culture.

And after Diana's painful, sexless marriage to cold Charles, the rebounding royal doubtless delighted in the attention and appreciation of Dodi.

"Dodi is also younger and better looking than Charles," added the shrink, speaking more informally and abruptly.

Dodi also loved Diana's plumper body as she packed on fifteen pounds after her breakup with Hasnat, and increased her curves—leading Dr. Mueller to further comment, "Middle Eastern men love their women well rounded."

Whether the double meaning is intended there, is, truly, anybody's guess.

Despite Diana and Dodi being so obviously in love, there may have been a motivation for allowing the photos to be taken above and beyond wanting a public celebration of their feelings for one another. Insiders have claimed she purposefully posed for the photos to infuriate Charles.

"Dodi set out to woo a woman who was trying to get over a lost love—and he succeeded," a source revealed at the time. The pair moved in similar circles and had seen each other at polo events and film premieres in London's West End. However, it wasn't until July 1997 that Diana and Dodi started a relationship during their luxury summer break in the south of France. Diana was still reeling from her split from the surgeon Hasnat when she accepted Mohamed Al-Fayed's invitation to stay at his palatial villa in Saint-Tropez with William, fifteen, and Harry, twelve. It was there Diana started to see a different side to Dodi and realized he had the makings of a dream stepfather for William and Harry.

"Dodi was a real charmer, and William and Harry took to him at once," an insider noted in a well-documented 1997 tell-all. "He went swimming with them, played games with them, and laughed at their jokes and pranks. Diana saw another side to the smooth playboy, and they started talking intimately for hours, going dancing, and then became inseparable."

Dodi's dad had been a friend of Diana's father, the late Earl Spencer. Diana's stepmother, Raine, the Countess of Chambrun, sat on the Harrods International Board. Throughout the summer of 1997, a carefree Diana loved being showered with gifts and affection by Dodi. And once the pictures started to spread around the world, Diana was, according to friends, relaxed about the publicity over her new relationship.

A source quoted at the time revealed, "Diana told friends: 'It's the best sex I've ever had.'"

They added about her plan to use the photographs as a parting shot to Charles:

> This was Diana's revenge. This was the woman who might have been queen of England revealing a new love from a foreign family with huge wealth and none of the royals' restrictions.
>
> The royals thought they had gotten rid of her. But she came back on top and was threatening to start her own kind of royal dynasty with the tremendous wealth and power of the Fayeds behind her.

Every publication in the world wanted to print these sizzling snaps of Diana and millionaire boyfriend Dodi passionately playing in the Med. But the *Globe* scooped them, forking out a reputed $210,000. It was a huge payday for photographer Mario Brenna, who was said to have made up to $3 million worldwide with the pictures.

He usually did fashion shoots, but when he spotted Dodi's yacht sailing between the islands of Sardinia and Corsica, curiosity made him take a second look.

"I'd seen the yacht in my home base of Monaco just two weeks earlier," he said. "Diana was on board then with the Al-Fayed family so I thought, 'Maybe she's back.' Sure enough she was—alone with Dodi. I couldn't believe my eyes. They were all over each other. They kissed for 10 seconds and after that her head went back. It was almost like she was putting on a show for the camera. I don't know if she saw me, but I made no attempt to hide. She looked so happy."

In addition to their celebrated nautical romp, there is also evidence of their strong affections—and the royals' disapproval of it—that comes from a very different source. Namely, a dog breeder.

Dodi was planning to give Diana a schnauzer pup named Juliet—believed to have been a gift to celebrate the conception of his child with the royal. Dog breeder Marlene McNeill, who supplied the touching gift, said, "He wanted the new puppy to grow into a living, growing symbol of his love for Diana. It was a wonderful, romantic gesture for the princess. It's utterly tragic that she never got to receive the little puppy that was being bred for her as a gift of love."

Marlene was fifty-four when Dodi ordered the dog for $950 from her Tassajara kennels near Portland, Oregon—and swore her to secrecy about the gift.

"He wanted it to be a big surprise," said Marlene.

Dodi chose the dog as Diana loved his giant schnauzer Romeo, also sold to the playboy by Marlene in 1991.

She said he wanted Diana to name the dog Juliet so their dogs could be just like the lovers in Shakespeare's play.

But we see the dog was not only a romantic gift.

A source close to Mohamed Al-Fayed said, "It was thought the gift was going to be handed to Diana as her pregnancy developed. Al-Fayed was convinced Diana was pregnant, and the dog was going to be like 'training' for her ahead of the new arrival—something to cuddle that would then be replaced by her and Dodi's baby."

Dog breeders are one thing, but what about someone with a medical degree?

Dr. Richard Shepherd—who reexamined Diana's body for the official inquiry into her death—has also raised questions about whether she was pregnant.

He left the issue hanging when he admitted Diana could just have become aware she had conceived shortly before her death.

At the time, Dr. Shepherd said, "Pathologically there was no evidence that Princess Diana was pregnant, but some women say they know they're pregnant from the moment of conception. Was she one of those?"

Others believe Diana's pregnancy was far more advanced when she died—with the child being the reason she was assassinated.

For example, in *The Princess Diana Conspiracy*, author Alan Power said that Diana was between six and ten weeks pregnant, and the fetus was "clearly visible" by staff at the Pitié-Salpêtrière Hospital, where Diana was taken after the crash.

What's more, both radiologist Dr. Elizabeth Dion and nurse Jocelyn Magellan claimed they saw a fetus in Diana's womb. There is some controversy surrounding the question of whether or not a fetus can be accurately identified by the naked eye at such an early stage. However, Dion and Magellan were both experienced medical professionals. Furthermore, it's true that a fetus of six to ten weeks would be very small, but it would not be impossible to identify—especially if you were a healthcare practitioners who knew what you were looking for.

Dr. Dion told friends that her evidence was "incontrovertible"—or undeniable—but she was never called to testify about it in court, according to author Power.

"It was most definitely Dodi's child and this was most definitely one of the motives for murder," wrote Power.

He added that the pregnancy also "explained Diana's illegal and speedy embalming" after the crash so tests to confirm a pregnancy could not be performed.

Meanwhile, the French police officer, who did not want to be named, said the authorities conspired to cover up the fact that the princess was expecting Dodi's child in order to spare embarrassment to her family.

The fact Diana's shattered body was embalmed just hours after her tragic death is thought to be the most striking piece of evidence to prove that she was pregnant. That question remains unanswered to this day.

Jean Monceau, who did this embalming, says it was performed to prevent the body from deteriorating so it would be "presentable" to Prince Charles and other family members who were on their way to Paris.

But countless crime experts, investigators, family, friends, and hospital personnel where Diana died believe dark forces within the palace wanted embalming to cover up the fact of her pregnancy at all costs.

Alarmingly, other witnesses at Pitié-Salpêtrière Hospital say the princess was pregnant but miscarried the baby as she lay clinging to life during her final moments on Earth.

"I was told that Diana was *enceinte* ('pregnant' in French) but had lost the baby," confirmed one nurse at the hospital. "That was even before the news circulated that Diana had not made it. People who heard of her death were weeping, not only over losing such a beautiful person, but because it happened when she was pregnant."

As if protesting suspiciously too much, within hours of her death, hospital authorities began taking unprecedented measures to squelch word that Diana was with child.

It is said that senior hospital bureaucrat and high official from the French ministry of health quickly called together the doctors and nurses who'd attended to the dying princess and told them that to protect her privacy, her pregnancy was not to be mentioned to anyone.

"A phony story was then circulated that there had been no miscarriage—that it had all been a mistake due to confusion surrounding her blood loss," reveals a hospital source.

The cover-up is said to have been orchestrated by a top government diplomat, under direct orders from senior palace officials.

"It's believed that during this process, all remaining indications of the pregnancy were removed," said one well-placed investigator. "It's likely that the strong chemicals used in the embalming process disguised the bodily changes that would have shown a pregnancy."

It wasn't until after Diana's body was flown to back to London that an autopsy was finally performed by royal coroner Dr. John Burton. He claims there was no sign of a pregnancy, but that was no surprise to medical experts who insist that the miscarriage and embalming would have removed all evidence. But the cover-up couldn't silence friends of Diana, who were in on the joyous news that she was indeed expecting a child—and had suspected it was a baby girl.

"It's almost beyond belief that her life was snuffed out so brutally at the moment of her greatest happiness," says a family friend. "She longed for a baby girl. It was a profound wish she kept deep in her heart. She felt something within that was different from her previous pregnancies, and when a psychic friend of hers told her she was pregnant with a girl, she was sure."

Diana had just spent six idyllic days cruising around the Mediterranean with Dodi, and a telltale photo taken during this last vacation clearly shows the slender princess sporting a baby bump while walking along a beach in a bathing suit.

"She was blissfully happy," recalls the family source. "Her little bump was showing, and she was so proud. She'd even told reporters that she had some happy news to report."

Pregnancy claims were also brought up during the 2007 inquest into Diana's death.

Pitié-Salpêtrière Hospital anesthesiology professor Bruno Riou and cardiac surgery professor Alain Pavie were both asked about speculation that hospital staff claimed they saw signs of a pregnancy during an ultrasound scan of Diana's abdomen. If true, it would support contentions made by Mohamed Al-Fayed that his son—and the beloved princess—were murdered to cover up their impending child.

Royalists, including friends of Prince Charles, have strenuously refuted claims that Diana was pregnant at the time of her death.

But a palace insider claimed the princess's condition was hushed up at the request of senior royals—just as other conspiratorial signs that would claim she was murdered were also hidden from the world.

***

DETECTIVE'S NOTEBOOK

DATELINE: Week three of my investigation, September 1997

The last thing I felt like doing was making more inquiries around the Place de l'Alma. I was certain that during the last two weeks virtually every immediate resident had heard my pro forma introduction and my half a dozen standard questions. There was simply nothing more there to glean. I was up for a stroll along the Seine and a good read of anything but the newspapers on the death of Princess Diana. I grabbed the only novel I had taken with me in my travel kit, a book I had thus far ignored, and went in search of breakfast.

Despite my good intentions, I found myself unconsciously pacing upstream alongside Paris's great waterway and by lunchtime I was almost adjacent to the tunnel entrance. Out of habit I resumed my favorite position on the capping beside the roses and turned to page one of my reading material. John Grisham's *The Runaway Jury* was not a runaway success with my mood. I tossed it aside and refocused on the three words that were dominating the airwaves and were now circling endlessly in my brain, "the second car." Where was it? But more importantly, where was its driver? I was fascinated that in a month since the accident the driver had neither been located nor come forward. In an attempt to understand a serious incident such as the crashing of the Mercedes-Benz a detective will often sit alone at the crime scene with a head full of facts and a hungry mind, looking for answers. It works. Somehow it gets you closer to the unraveling than sitting on a swivel-less swivel chair at an overladen desk in a tired squad room.

So as I adopted this approach, staring almost absentmindedly in front of me, my eyes cast downward to the road surface. I noticed that the tire markings were fading quickly and again felt thankful that I had taken my notations when I did, as it would be fraught with danger to attempt any measurements at this point. I looked over at the merge lane and imagined the little Fiat Uno slowly motoring along the service way behind the close-knit avenue of trees that obscured the view of the main highway. My head flicked to the right and I pictured the Mercedes-Benz hurtling toward the tunnel at that exact same millisecond. The Fiat's brush with the juggernaut was unavoidable; the driver could not have taken any preventative action as the Mercedes was simply traveling too fast. Similarly, Princess Diana's chauffeur would not have expected the little Fiat to dawdle out onto the highway in front of him, hence the skid marks from Henri Paul's desperate attempt to avoid their imminent collision. I was under no doubts that the presence on the carriageway of the second car had played a part in the chain of events that led up to the tragic accident. However, I had come to the realization that the driver of the Fiat Uno, whoever it may be, was not at fault. But then why was he missing? What was his mind-set?

The shock that an innocent party would experience, having been involved in what may have appeared to them to be a minor collision, only to hear in subsequent hours of the resultant deaths of three people, would normally have them seeking counselling, wanting to talk with someone—and soon. To suspect that they may have had a hand in the death of the princess of Wales would add to their burden exponentially. They would be reminded of such sadness and horror every minute of the day through the saturation of the world's media, workplace chatter, and neighborly gossip. The whole world was on to it; it was too much for any one person to handle. Grief would be followed by depression, whether it was accidental death or otherwise. For those reasons I found it even harder to accept that there might have been passengers in the Fiat Uno. I concluded that I was looking for a lone driver. But our driver was going against the archetype of those involved in a fatal accident. He or she had gone to ground. I asked myself why would a citizen unquestionably innocent of any wrongdoing disappear like this, and more importantly, how would they? And where was their car? Paris was not a city of garages; almost all vehicles were parked on the street. A Fiat was a common sight; any number could sit out the front of someone's house or apartment block and be completely inconspicuous, except this vehicle was now seriously dented from its collision with the Mercedes and its impact with the retaining wall. It could no longer park unnoticed; it could no longer be an anonymous common car. So where was the nearly ruined white Fiat when millions of eyes were looking for it, talking about it? This puzzling issue was working its way through me as the traffic buzzed by. Occasionally a mourner would amble from the overpass to sit beside me on the retaining wall. After a few moments of mutual silence I would repeatedly face the ridiculously obvious query, "Did you like Princess Diana?"

Frustrated that my two most troubling questions remained unanswered, I wandered off despondently. As I strolled toward the eastern gate of the Brazilian embassy, I was halted by the sound of the massive security doors swinging open. The engine of a little transporter had just come to life and I watched as it slowly exited the embassy grounds. On the back of its tray was a small container, no larger than a sofa, just the sort of thing an ambassadorial office would use to ship home documents or old furnishings or any other unwanted rubbish. Diplomatic immunity guaranteed unhampered transportation of literally anything. My heart raced with a new possibility. I imagined a bigger container, one that would fit a small motorcar. Nothing too difficult there; containers come in all shapes and sizes up to forty feet long. How easy to be free of any involvement in the death of the princess of Wales, however innocent. Just secrete the Fiat Uno in a diplomatic shipping container and toss it out with the rubbish. I stared at the rear of the transporter as it rumbled toward the merge lane, its brake lights flashing momentarily before it nudged forward, found a gap in the traffic, and disappeared onto the main carriageway on its way to the tunnel.

One missing car, one missing driver, three dead, and a mangled Mercedes.

It was then that I knew it was time to go home. As I walked briskly back to my hotel, I had a sense that the car would never be found, nor the driver. And the farther I walked, the more sure I was that he or she was long gone. I felt a lot like a man who has just placed the last piece of a gigantic jigsaw puzzle. But it didn't fit properly. My diplomatic hunch didn't feel right.

***

Within forty-eight hours I had packed up my room, said goodbye to Charles, and eaten my last meal at my regular dining table. It was time to leave behind a rose garden, tire residue, a tunnel entrance, and a fractured thirteenth pillar. I felt a sense of relief that my work in France was complete; there was no need to stay any longer. Soon I was seated on an Air France jet with my head in a familiar waft of Gauloises cigarettes, my bout of Sherlock Holmes escapism over. I was heading back to the office; as my detective self used to say, once upon a time, "time to go home." And besides, I was starting to get very tired of the same clothes I had suffered for the past three weeks.

As I pressed the recliner button on my economy class seat, lowered the air-conditioning control, and snapped the top off my first airline gin and tonic, I recalled my initial impression of the now infamous French tunnel. Like many of the crime scenes I had visited, there was nothing remarkable to lure the curious to the location, nothing to tell of a tragedy of insurmountable proportions. There was just a mess of civil engineering, asphalt, and concrete capping in an otherwise non-descript roadway in the middle of a very big city where people came and went in too much of a hurry.

With my head and mood now in the clouds and onto my second gin, my mind drifted to an equally infamous location and another tragedy that had stopped the world in its tracks. Back several decades and across a continent to Elm Grove below the Texas Book Depository and the 1963 assassination of John F. Kennedy. I reasoned that history's pages may also group these accident scenes, crime scenes, call them what you will. The thirty-fifth US president's last moments—like Princess Diana's—were as a passenger in a chauffeured vehicle. Another tunnel, another overpass, another inconsequential stretch of motorway . . . it's funny how a handsome president and a beautiful princess had found equality in death.

However, the Holy Grail of investigative enigmas, for all the similarities, was managed very differently by its local police. The Texans swarmed over the area like an army of excitable uniforms and overwhelmed suits, bumbling their way to the facts. In France they played with a different deck of cards. None of the gendarmes appeared to give a damn, the investigative magistrates were missing, and in my three weeks at Claude's rose garden not once did I see a uniform, a suit, or a forensic outfit. I was glad to be done and dusted.

CHAPTER ELEVEN

Sex was central to Diana's death—and not only her own sex life.

Put bluntly, some sources have wildly claimed there was evidence that Diana could have been killed to cover up the seedy sex secrets of the royals—including the truth of Prince Charles's sexuality and a shocking gay rape involving the royal.

For this is the shocking belief of informants who say Diana quietly made a record of her knowledge of scandals that could finish Britain's monarchy on ten never-before-seen videocassette tapes and a series of audiocassettes, and stashed them in a box called the "Crown Jewels," under lock and key in her Kensington Palace apartment. (A signet ring belonging to Diana's lover James Hewitt was also reputedly in the box.) She is also believed to have stashed photographs that show Prince Charles romping naked with a male lover.

As far-fetched as it sounds, the claims were central to the 2008 inquest into her death when her sister, Lady Sarah McCorquodale, strenuously denied she destroyed the box of secrets. Instead, Lady Sarah insisted she gave them to Paul Burrell for safekeeping, adding pointedly, "I trusted him, then."

The princess's former butler maintains, however, that the papers were taken to the Spencer family seat at Althorp, where they are hidden.

Richard Keen QC, counsel for the family of driver Henri Paul, asked Lady Sarah at the inquest, "You opened Pandora's box. Once Pandora's box was opened, all the evils of the world came out and you claim that you gave them to the butler; is that right?

"Are you seriously saying that you took all of these sensitive materials with their obvious capacity to embarrass and cause distress . . . and handed them over to the butler?"

The answer was a terse, "Yes."

Lady Sarah, who was an executor of Diana's estate, confirmed that in March 1998—six months after her sister died in the Paris crash—she and Burrell found the key to the mahogany box hidden inside the cover of a tennis racket. They sat down together to go through it. Its contents were "highly sensitive," she said, and, as she was traveling home to Lincolnshire by train, she gave them to Burrell for "safekeeping."

She said she subsequently asked Burrell "two or three times" for the return of the papers but was given various excuses, including that they were stored in packing cases at his Cheshire residence.

"I asked Paul Burrell to take it home, the evening we opened the box, for safekeeping and he did and that's the last I ever saw of it despite asking him to give it back to me on several occasions," she told the inquest.

Were these recordings compiled intentionally, perhaps as a defense against reprisals the royal family might have been tempted to take based on Diana's other misbehavior? Or did they fall into her hands unexpectedly? Did Charles leave them where Diana could find them, as part of some personal indiscretion?

However they may have come to her, the recordings and images that would potentially shatter the Windsors were squirreled away by Diana in a spot in Kensington Palace known only to Burrell.

Diana's videos had been recorded by her voice coach Peter Settelen.

Only six of the videos were used in the famous bombshell Channel 4 documentary, but the remaining ten have never been seen. Diana also recorded her most intimate secrets on twelve C90 cassette tapes, we can also reveal for this book.

When Burrell collected hundreds of Diana's possessions in the wake of her death, the secret stash of recordings and photographs were among the 342 items he took to the attic of his home near Runcorn near Cheshire, northwest England.

That is what police were looking for when they hammered on his door at 6:50 a.m. on January 18, 2001. They were also the reason Paul Burrell's trial for allegedly stealing the items from Diana never went ahead. As everyone knows, the queen herself stepped in at the eleventh hour to state she had suddenly recalled giving Burrell permission to take keepsakes from Diana's apartment—something

Burrell had claimed all along. It was only an intervention of this magnitude that could stop the world hearing the butler reveal exactly was among the items he had lifted.

Afterward, Burrell was summoned for a three-hour meeting with the queen, during which she chillingly told him "dark forces" were at work and that his life may be in danger from knowing too much about the royal family. Charles—panicked a supposed bisexual affair would emerge—also battled behind the scenes to have the trial stopped and Burrell silenced.

The man who will be the next King of England is rumored to have kept a string of boys on the side during his marriages to both Diana and his second wife Camilla.

In 2003, the future king was embroiled in another well-documented gay scandal when his former manservant George Smith claimed he was raped by a member of Charles's staff, Michael Fawcett. Smith—who worked for Charles for eleven years, until 1997—also said Fawcett was in a homosexual relationship with the prince. He also claimed that one morning while delivering breakfast in bed to Charles, he had walked in on the pair having sex in the prince's bedroom. Charles was forced to issue a statement on the rape story. It did not name Smith as the man behind the story, but said the accuser had suffered from post-traumatic stress disorder and alcoholism after service in the Falklands War. The smear-filled statement said, "He has, in the past, made other unrelated allegations, which the police have fully investigated and found to be unsubstantiated."

Nevertheless, the British tabloids shrieked "SEX, SECRETS, BETRAYAL and SHAME." *The Mail* on Sunday splashed on its front page with the ghastly headline "I WAS RAPED BY CHARLES' SERVANT."

This scandal would never have emerged if Diana had not sat at the end of Smith's bed after he was hospitalized following the alleged rape—and recorded his damning attack on Charles, along with other secrets about her husband.

Diana took her recorder to Smith's bedside in 1990 after Charles told his wife the allegations were "downstairs gossip"—before the footman was given $48,000 as a payoff before he left royal service.

Being an old soldier and loyal to the crown, Smith kept quiet about the incident—even when the trauma forced him to enter a psychiatric rehab center and contributed to the breakup of his marriage. It was while he was in the Priory Clinic that Diana perched on the end of his bed, supposedly to listen to his problems. Yet her real motivation was to capture Charles's most shameful secrets on the whirring tape recorder in her handbag.

Understanding that knowledge was power, the princess—paranoid even in 1990 about her safety—kept the tape with her other eleven cassettes containing royal secrets, locked away. Also among her treasure trove were vicious letters sent to her from her father-in-law, Prince Philip, which have also never been seen. It was her stash of secrets that drove the queen and Philip to stop the Burrell trial. The royal family was said to be "petrified" Burrell would reveal the allegations squirreled away on tape recordings.

But their conspiracy did not stop there—insiders believe Diana may have been killed to cover up the secrets they never thought would emerge.

One aide, who believes Diana was offed (and only spoke on condition of anonymity for fear of recriminations) said, "There's one reason Diana was killed—she knew too much. The royals knew she had been collecting information on them for years, and wanted her out of the way. They just couldn't have their trail of affairs and seedy secrets coming out in the open. She was bumped off, and they thought that was the risk removed. What they never betted on was that she had taped their most intimate secrets—and had photographic evidence Charles was gay. They were stunned when it emerged they were being kept in Paul Burrell's attic, and did everything they could to stop the contents being made public at court."

After Diana's death, Lady Sarah was asked by the coroner's inquest to search the Spencer family's home for a variety of sensitive documents and materials that could have included these tapes. The inquest jury had heard claims that Philip had ordered the killing of Diana, and these claims could not be dismissed outright. However, neither could they be given credence without proof. The tapes and other sensitive materials were never found. Lady Sarah and a police officer who had previously investigated Paul Burrell gave conflicting accounts of what had happened to the secret items. Both Lady Sarah and the police officer were in agreement that the missing items might be inside a wooden box that Diana often kept in her sitting room.

Yet Lady Sarah claimed that the box had been taken into Burrell's possession—for at least some period of time—following Diana's death. Lady Sarah said that she had looked in the box but found it did not contain any of the sought-after letters or recordings. She believed that this was because they had already been taken by Burrell.

At the same time, the police officer claimed that Lady Sarah had previously claimed that the material had been in the box, but that a search of Burrell's home revealed they were not there.

Again, Lady Sarah has denied that she destroyed these materials herself.

At the time Diana made her "rape tape," her marriage to the heir was already in its death throes, with Diana repeatedly telling friends she suspected he may have only married her in 1981 to cover up his homosexuality.

But she also suspected Charles was bisexual, as he also had a disgraceful track record for bedding friends' wives.

Camilla was wed to his friend Brigadier Andrew Parker Bowles, who turned a blind eye to their twenty-two-year affair before they divorced in 1995. The prince of Wales also bedded very-married Lady Kanga Tryon—and cheekily agreed to be godfather to one of her husband's children.

A source for this book said, "There may be hundreds of theories about why Diana could have been killed, but knowing too much is the real reason."

This idea that Diana "knew too much" emerges as a theme in any study of the princess's death. It also begins to suggest the ways in which the "dark forces" that sought to end her once and for all may have found ways to collude.

It is now believed the twelve tapes in question have been destroyed. How and by whom is not precisely known.

* * *

Biographer Tom Bower—who has published a book on Mohamed Al-Fayed and Prince Charles titled *Rebel Prince*—spoke to many involved in the Burrell theft case.

Bower's research reveals just how the royals stopped the court hearing that may have brought down a monarchy.

This time line, constructed from Bower's work, is instructive in understanding the devastating power with which the crown can punch when it so chooses:

January 18, 2001. The doorbell rang at 6:50 in the morning.

Paul Burrell, who was asleep, was awakened by his wife.

Standing at the door was Detective Chief Inspector Maxine de Brunner and three other police officers.

"Do you have any items from Kensington Palace in this house?" Princess Diana's former butler was asked.

"No," he initially lied.

He was told he was being placed under arrest, and then the predawn raid on his home near Runcorn in Cheshire began in earnest.

What the detectives found next was far beyond their expectations.

The rooms were filled with paintings, drawings, china, and photographs that clearly belonged to Diana (who'd died three and a half years before) and her children William and Harry.

"Oh my God," de Brunner is said to have exclaimed.

In Burrell's study, she'd just spotted an expensive inlaid mahogany desk inscribed "Her Royal Highness."

"How did you get all this?" she asked the butler.

"The princess gave it to me," he said, collapsing into a chair and beginning to weep.

As the search continued, the police discovered two thousand negatives.

A cursory look revealed Charles in the bath with his children, and many others showing the young princes naked.

Other finds included thirty signed photographs of Diana, many empty silver frames, a box containing the princess's daily personal notes to William at school, and another box of Diana's more intimate letters to William.

As Burrell's sobs intensified, an officer shouted from the attic, "It's full of boxes, wall to wall!"

The boxes were wrenched open: inside were bags, blouses, dresses, nightgowns, underwear, shoes, jumpers, suits, and hats that had belonged to Diana, including a blue-ribboned hat she'd worn during her visit with Prince Charles to South Korea in 1992.

Her perfume, de Brunner noticed, lingered on the fabric.

Late that afternoon, officers filled a truck sent from London with two thousand items that de Brunner judged had been illegally removed.

The princess, she believed, would never have given away such personal material, and certainly not in such quantities.

Nevertheless, a large number of Diana's possessions remained in the house.

But without orders from Scotland Yard to either seize everything that had belonged to the family or to seal the house as a crime scene, there was no more to be done.

"I want white lilies on my coffin," wailed Burrell as he was escorted to the waiting police car.

There can be few people unaware of the subsequent 2002 trial of Paul Burrell, but it appears that a great deal went on behind the scenes that was never revealed to the public.

News of his former employee's arrest reached Charles about a week after the police raid.

Unaware of the scale of the alleged theft, but knowing that low-paid staff occasionally pilfered small items, he told his assistant private secretary Mark Bolland that Burrell probably did steal some things "because they all do."

Within hours, however, Charles had become more alarmed. After all, police probes into murky palace habits could produce unexpected difficulties.

Charles's senior private secretary, Stephen Lamport, looking beaten and downhearted, confessed to a colleague, "We've got a terrible problem with this man Burrell . . . the prince of Wales is distraught. The prince will say he gave the things to the butler and that Burrell's actions were all right."

Lamport's confidant was unimpressed. Even Charles had to allow justice to take its course, came the reply.

Indeed, the investigation was now well under way.

During his second police interview, Burrell was asked, "Did you tell anyone that you had the property?"

"No," he admitted, still insisting that the items—including all Diana's school reports—were gifts.

Burrell's solicitor Andrew Shaw, for his part, appeared to think the case would never come to trial.

"You're making a terrible mistake," he told Maxine de Brunner. "They won't let Burrell's secrets be splashed in the public domain. They'll never let this come to trial."

In light of what happened subsequently, his comments were not quite as far-fetched as they first seemed to many who heard them.

***

April 3, 2001

Along with a crown prosecution lawyer, Maxine de Brunner arrived at St. James's Palace for a meeting. There was no alternative but to prosecute, they told the royal family's senior officials.

Also present was Charles's divorce lawyer, Fiona Shackleton.

Shackleton revealed that Paul Burrell had sent the prince a handwritten letter in which he offered to return some of the items, provided Charles agreed not to support any prosecution.

The CPS lawyer explained that the case could be closed only if Prince William and Diana's sister Lady Sarah McCorquodale, who together inherited Diana's property, signed statements to drop their complaints.

Shackleton's view was that Charles could not be party to undermining the legal system.

Agreeing to accept the return of some property in exchange for dropping the investigation, she said, would make it look as if Buckingham Palace were participating in a cover-up.

"It needs to be all or nothing," she said.

Sir Robin Janvrin, the queen's private secretary, agreed to tell the monarch what had been discussed, and almost certainly did so.

This, of course, would have been the ideal moment for the queen to recall that she'd allowed the butler to take some of Diana's possessions for safekeeping. But apparently, she didn't say a word.

As for Charles, he was upset when his own private secretary told him the police intended to prosecute.

He could already see the writing on the wall. For who knew what Burrell might say in the witness box? In effect, he was a time bomb, having witnessed the prince's secret meetings and phone calls with Camilla while he was married, and Diana's many rendezvous with her boyfriends.

He told his spin doctor Mark Bolland to try to navigate a way out of a prosecution.

***

May 2

The case against Burrell strengthened.

The police had had time to watch six videos found in Burrell's home, featuring Diana talking about the most intimate details of her relationship with the royal family, her sex life with Charles, and her affair with police protection officer Barry Mannakee. The tapes had been recorded by Peter Settelen, the princess's voice coach, who, soon after her death, had asked her private secretary for the return of not six but sixteen tapes.

Yet he was told, "I am advised by Mr. Burrell that he has been unable to trace them."

What had happened, the police wondered, to the missing ten tapes? (Material from Settelen's six recovered tapes was, again, used in a Channel 4 documentary in 2017.)

And there was another tape that worried Charles. . .

Kept in a box of Diana's and now, he believed, in Burrell's possession, it described the alleged rape of one member of his staff by another of his staff.

* * *

July 19

Burrell's lawyers now issued a warning to Shackleton.

If Burrell were prosecuted, they said, he would have to describe from the witness box not only details of Diana's sex life, he might also read out quotes from letters in which Prince Philip had allegedly threatened her.

Burrell's lawyers later explained that this was not a threat—the defense was seeking only to protect the royal family.

At this point, the CPS and the police asked for a "victims' consultation meeting" in order to obtain the direct approval of Princes Charles and William to prosecute Burrell.

In anticipation of a police visit to Highgrove, Charles appealed to Bolland, reportedly saying, "Mark, this is crazy. You must do something."

The prince was now apparently keen to do anything to avert a trial, especially with William a potential witness.

Burrell simply knew too much. Would he, for instance, dare to describe Diana's reported use of cocaine to the court? The best way to avoid a prosecution, Bolland agreed, was for Burrell to return all the property he'd taken.

***

July 24

A top-secret meeting was now arranged between Bolland and Burrell. Over coffee, the butler said, "I'm sorry."

He wanted to let Charles know that he'd return all the property, but insisted on telling him so in person.

Throughout the twenty-five-minute meeting, the spin doctor reported that he had been appalled by Burrell's "creepy manner." The royals' staff, he thought, were "a slimy, weird group with odd relationships."

Later, he reported back to Charles that the butler wanted "a big hug and an offer of a job at Balmoral. He doesn't want to be cast out."

The prince repeated the words thoughtfully, "He doesn't want to be cast out."

A truth occurred to Bolland then about the royals. Something that revealed just what was at stake, and hinted at what might be happening behind the scenes.

"No one cares whether Burrell is guilty or not."

***

August 3

The police were expected at Highgrove in the afternoon.

What they didn't know, Bolland hoped, was that secret arrangements had been made for Prince Charles to meet Burrell a few hours later.

But before the police arrived, the spin doctor became suspicious that the plan had been leaked to the police, probably by one of Charles's own protection officers.

The meeting with Burrell must be canceled, he advised. Charles agreed.

Next, the prince discussed the approach he planned to take with the police.

He intended to ask, "Does this really matter? Yes, some items may have been pilfered, but just how serious is it? Not very."

In the moment, however, Charles didn't get around to saying any of this. Instead, he was palpably shocked when the police told him two thousand items had been seized at Burrell's home.

It was the first time he'd heard the actual number.

"He's taken the lot!" Charles exclaimed.

After listening to more evidence against the butler, the prince was asked if he supported a prosecution.

"We've got no alternative," he sighed. Before leaving, the police asked Charles not to have any contact with Burrell.

The prince was now in a fix, to say the least. Officially, he had to support the CPS's charge that Burrell had stolen the items. But, privately, he still wanted the prosecution halted.

Another big sticking point was that Diana's sister and coexecutor, Lady Sarah McCorquodale, was adamant that the butler should be brought to trial.

Meanwhile, the police confronted Bolland to ask if he'd talked to Burrell. Yes, replied the spin doctor.

This admission confirmed police suspicions.

***

August 18

Now, in an attempt to avert prosecution, Burrell's lawyer handed the police a thirty-nine-page statement signed by his client.

Among other things, it described the butler's close relationship with Diana—how he would smuggle her boyfriends into Kensington Palace, cancel public engagements so she could be with her lovers, and provide meals for the princess and her man of the moment.

In addition, Burrell hinted that he'd tell what he knew about Diana's nocturnal visits around Paddington, where she tried to persuade prostitutes to give up their trade by plying them with gifts.

Even the police could see that if Burrell gave detailed testimony about Diana's sex life in court, the monarchy would be seriously harmed.

Still, there was nothing in the butler's statement that undermined the charge of theft. So Burrell was once again interviewed.

This time, he claimed that the items found in his house should be seen either as gifts, taken by mistake, or handed over to him to be destroyed. He didn't offer to return anything.

At 2:40 p.m., Burrell was charged with theft.

A month later, Burrell's lawyer wrote to Charles, asking for an audience so he could explain "the extreme delicacy of the situation" if his client had to testify. This was, obviously, pregnant with meaning.

Charles, who'd taken legal advice, did not reply.

The lawyer then sent further warnings about Burrell's intention to speak about events of "extreme delicacy" and "matters of a very private nature."

Again Charles did not reply. This provoked Burrell's lawyer to threaten to summon the prince as a witness.

The nuclear option had been placed on the table.

***

February 13, 2002

Yet another statement from Burrell was delivered to the police—this time about a meeting with the queen.

They'd talked for three hours, he'd said, sitting on her sofa together shortly after Princess Diana's death.

The queen had told him, he said, that his relationship with Diana was unprecedented.

She had spoken about how much she herself had tried to help the princess, and also warned him to be careful—so many people were against Princess Diana, and he had—seemingly—sided with her.

However, the CPS lawyers decided that since Burrell's statement made no mention of Diana's property, it was irrelevant to the case. (Whether the statements were relevant to Diana's ultimate fate, and the plots against her, is, of course, another matter entirely.)

***

August 27

Burrell's lawyer again approached the police, insisting that a message be passed on to Charles.

His client, he said, was offering to return all the royal items in his possession if the prosecution was dropped.

The message was never delivered but, somehow, the prince nonetheless became aware of the butler's offer—and hoped it would stop the trial going ahead.

Legally, however, that was impossible: the CPS now had sole responsibility for the prosecution. Nevertheless, Charles ordered his new private secretary, Sir Michael Peat, to express his concern about continuing with the prosecution if it was a lost cause.

***

October 14

Paul Burrell, then aged forty-four, stood in the dock of Court One at the Old Bailey, and was officially accused of stealing 310 items from Diana's private chambers, together worth $5.9 million.

Other items taken from his house were not listed because they allegedly belonged to either Charles or William, and neither wished to appear in court as witnesses.

The day's proceedings made blazing headlines in all the media, raising increasing concern at St. James's Palace.

***

October 28

Just after 8:30 that Monday morning, eleven days into the trial, Crown Prosecutor William Boyce was reading his papers in a small room adjacent to the court when he was unexpectedly joined by Commander Yates.

"I've just had a conversation with Michael Peat," said Yates, then repeated the private secretary's exact words: "Her Majesty has had a recollection."

Rarely has a six-word sentence meant so very much to a man's fate, or to a royal family.

On the previous Friday, Peat explained, the queen had recalled a meeting five years earlier, soon after Diana's death.

Burrell had come to the palace to tell her about preserving some of the princess's papers.

"The queen agreed that he should care for them," said Peat.

Boyce visibly paled. Taking off his wig, he seemed to shrink.

Only by questioning the queen in court could Burrell's version of the conversation be rebutted, and that was constitutionally impossible.

No reigning monarch could appear in "Her Majesty's court."

"That's the end of the trial," was Boyce's view. Later in the day, Peat told CPS lawyers more about the queen's recollection.

On the previous Friday, she, Charles, and Philip had driven together to St. Paul's for a memorial service for the victims of the Bali bombing.

Driving past the Old Bailey, she asked why a crowd was standing outside. Charles answered that Paul Burrell was on trial. The queen was apparently unaware that he was being prosecuted.

Then she mentioned that, some years before, Burrell had sought an audience with her to explain that he was caring for some of Diana's papers, and she'd agreed that he should do so.

To some in the prosecution and to police at the Old Bailey, the circumstances of the recollection described by Peat lacked credibility.

But "an act of genius," was the judgment of one Whitehall observer who said, "Only a golden bullet could have stopped the trial."

***

November 1

Crown Prosecutor Boyce announced in the courtroom that the trial was over. Charles and Peat breathed sighs of relief.

The danger to them—for the moment, at least—had passed.

What did the royal family fear? What was so harrowing that they were willing to call off the trial? What would have been revealed in open court? Any lawyer can tell you that trials do not always unfold as you expect them to. Anything can happen.

Some chose to believe that, quite simply, the idea of the queen herself being called to testify—and to be challenged openly by a lawyer—was too much for hang-wringing royals to bear. Others believe the queen might have been forced to lie in court. Or—most terrifying of all to those involved in the plot against Diana—that the queen might have grown a conscience in the dock, and chosen to speak the truth about what actually happened and which forces were truly at play in matters regarding the life and death of her former daughter-in-law.

With hungry journalists sniffing around each and every corner, it did not make sense to risk even giving them the slightest scent.

At the time, most qualified observers believed that her sudden recollection stemmed from Burrell's ability to confirm that Charles was not entirely heterosexual. Keeping this kind of information quiet was not without precedent.

Charles's beloved great-uncle Lord Louis Mountbatten was bisexual and famously rumored to have had an affair with Edward VIII when he accompanied the young prince of Wales on his empire tours.

Charles clearly modeled after him. Charles thought of Mountbatten as his grandfather and wept at his funeral after the lord was killed by the IRA.

Another "close friend" of Mountbatten's was an Irish student whom he met at Cambridge, Peter Murphy, who became his close and constant companion until the end of his life.

Lord Louis, who would go on to become governor of India, married Edwina, a fabulously wealthy socialite, who was to have a torrid affair with Panditji Nehru, Prime Minister of India.

Before his marriage to Marina of Greece, the duke of Kent is supposed to have enjoyed the company of thin blond men. He was once even arrested for engaging in homosexual activity but released when his identity was confirmed.

The papers may not have reported on his indiscretions, but all of high society knew about them. To this day his papers are sealed at Windsor Castle, and no researchers are allowed to look at them.

Yet in the weeks and months that followed the trial's abrupt end, journalists involved began to dig a bit deeper. Was there something more than the concealment of bisexuality at play? It felt as though the trail's handling confirmed that the royals were certainly hiding something . . . but what? The possibilities seemed endless.

However, the inability of anyone to ever recover the "Crown Jewels" suggests the pursuit might all have been a red herring—as it is now believed everything hoarded by Diana has been destroyed after the items taken by Burrell from Diana's apartment were seized in their 2001 dawn raid on his home.

A trunk of royal secrets Diana had entrusted to Dodi's dad is also said to have vanished in the chaotic period following her death—and is now suspected by many experts to have been taken by British operatives.

The tycoon's suspicions Diana and his son were killed to prevent the royal family from being "polluted" by his Muslim family further forced British police to investigate 175 conspiracy theories into her death. And his campaign to prove Diana's crash was no accident was driven largely by a hoard of secrets she handed him before her death; they were locked in a box with her initials on the lid that she said contained the reasons she would be assassinated.

Mohamed Al-Fayed has insisted Britain's MI6 spy agency was behind the crash, after which he went to retrieve the box—but he found it was empty.

Private investigators believe British government agents beat him to it and destroyed the contents. Mohamed Al-Fayed now insists Philip and the royals couldn't bear the prospect of Diana marrying a Muslim and having his baby, once ranting to US shock jock Howard Stern, "Do you think this bloody racist family would have allowed that to happen?"

He also told the 2008 inquest into Diana's death, "I will not rest until I die—even if I lose everything to find the truth. Diana suffered for twenty years from this Dracula family."

He also insists Diana was pregnant with Dodi's child and said the couple was preparing to announce their shock engagement the day after they died in Paris.

There is corroboration that files and dossiers related to Diana and the circumstances of her death have—without out a doubt—been destroyed . . . but perhaps not in the way you might first expect.

For example, Diana's personal psychic confirmed that she torched a thick dossier on land mines given to her by the royal—as she feared it would lead to her being killed.

Simone Simmons, the psychic recruited by Diana to give her "energy healing," also revealed the duke of Edinburgh wrote "cruel and disparaging" letters to Princess Diana—that she hinted at having seen firsthand—which have also since mysteriously vanished.

Simone said Diana had given her a copy of a dossier about the land mine industry she had compiled during her campaign against the weapons. The psychic said she had hidden this under her mattress, along with other documents from the princess.

Simone added that the land mine dossier was several inches thick but that she had burnt it after Diana's death because she was afraid of what might happen to her.

She said, "I believed that if they could bump Diana off, then they could bump anyone off—and I value my life."

CHAPTER TWELVE

In the aftermath of Diana's death, agents were everywhere. The royal family colluded with a merciless mob of British spies to collect photographs of Diana's nightmare death scene—as they feared the images contained evidence of their plot to assassinate the tragic mum-of-two. It was a cover-up worth millions.

The agents—handpicked for their ruthlessness—unleashed a campaign of intimidation in the days and years following Diana's death to gather the pictures from some of the world's leading paparazzi.

Now, for the first time through this investigation, *Diana: Case Closed* can reveal evidence of the sinister plot to hide any proof of the royal family's involvement in Diana's death.

We can confirm from multiple sources that veteran photographers in the Paris tunnel where Diana and Dodi crashed at speeds upward of 121 mph were bullied, bribed, and blackmailed into handing over negatives of the images they took to document the horrific crash.

These are the chilling conclusions of two of the world's longest-standing press photographers—who spent years snapping Diana and have finally spoken out about the diabolical plot to murder the princess on the twenty-first anniversary of her death.

They fear the photos were snatched because they contain the faces of Diana's assassins and the agents behind the mysterious beam of white light said to have been flashed into the face of Diana's driver to make him crash.

We here reveal interviews with two of the world's most famous paparazzi photographers that reveal their terrifying belief photos collected of Diana and her death scene were stolen in the wake of the 1997 tragedy—by agents who targeted one of them with bugging equipment, phone threats, and a suspected bomb plot.

In an exclusive interview, one source—who spoke strictly on condition of anonymity for fear of repercussions from British secret services—said:

> The biggest single indication there was a conspiracy to kill Diana is that the images taken the night she died have never come out. That's because spies acting on orders from the royal family either stole the photographs, or used bully-boy tactics to intimidated the snappers who took them into handing over their pictures. I know paparazzi in the tunnel the night Diana died who were paid visits by secret service agents and told to hand over their photos of Diana in the tunnel or face the "gravest consequences" for themselves and their families. Some of them were shown dossiers on their private lives containing personal secrets to force them into handing over their images. Others who had cleaner private lives were threatened with violence and financial ruin if they didn't hand over their pictures. They wanted the images so there would be no photographic evidence of their assassination of Diana and the assassins who were loitering in that tunnel in the aftermath of the crash on the night.

The source added they estimated the royal family and spies spent $10 million to obtain death site photos from paps.

It's thought that a total of twelve paparazzi were in the tunnel where Diana crashed.

Seven of the photographers—Romuald Rat, Serge Arnal, Jacques Langevin, Nikola Arsov, Laslo Veres, Christian Martinez, and Stephane Darmon—were hauled into custody after the crash killed Diana, before being cleared of manslaughter charges in a French court.

The source said:

> This was a classic intelligence community tactic—haul people in under the guise of investigating their movements so they can then bully them into doing what they wanted. The move also started a hate campaign against paparazzi—all to distract from the role spies had in

> assassinating Diana. Paparazzi photographers were to Diana's death what Lee Harvey Oswald was to JFK's shooting—scapegoats for a conspiracy brewed in the corridors of power.

Pictures taken at the time of Diana's crash are thought to contain evidence of a blinding flash of light being beamed at Diana's driver Henri Paul, forcing him to crash.

The source added the violent lengths to which the agents were prepared to go to obtain photographs taken at the scene of Diana's crash is demonstrated by what he and many others are convinced was the murder of one of the world's most profitable paparazzi.

The source also claims the death of Andanson was "100 percent assassinated."

James was a pap some believed to have been recruited by ruthless agents and forced to become part of Diana's assassination team. Though it was a story that Colin had found initially fantastic, the source told us something we didn't know: there were also two bullet holes in Andanson's head when they found him burned. He'd apparently also bragged of secretly taking "explosive" photos of the scene, and even bragged of driving the second vehicle, if you believe the rumors. And for reasons unexplained to this day, Andanson was boarding a plane bound for Corsica less than six hours after the crash. With this new information, it was something we, as an investigative team, would need to focus on, and we did.

In the weeks leading up to James's death, he had a series of meetings with famed French crime author Frédéric Dard to discuss the book that would "blow the lid off a conspiracy" to kill the princess.

In yet another twist, Frédéric also died in 2000, a few weeks after James's apparent "suicide."

Because the critically acclaimed author—beloved in France for writing more than three hundred crime novels—was killed by a heart attack aged seventy-eight, and only a handful of confidants knew of his meeting with James, Frédéric's death was not immediately linked to the web of Diana conspiracy theories.

We can also reveal today how an additional paparazzo believe he was targeted by spies in the wake of Diana's crash.

Darryn Lyons, age fifty-two, dubbed "Mr. Paparazzi" while running

London-based agency Big Pictures during the 1990s, is convinced Diana was assassinated.

He was one of the first people to be sent photographs of Diana's death scene on August 31, 1997—and his offices were then almost immediately targeted in what he believes was a burglary, in an attempt by the secret services to obtain the snaps.

Days later, according to Darryn, he came to his office to find it in darkness, with the cause of the power loss never identified.

His Big Pictures agency was also hit with telephone death threats, and Darryn then heard a ticking noise at the premises he reported as a bomb—before becoming convinced the agency's phones were bugged after hearing "clicking noises on the line."

On September 2, 1997, Darryn handed over copies of the Diana death pictures he had been sent to a police constable from Islington Police Station.

He has since said he feels "lucky not to have been killed in all the cloak and dagger stuff" in the wake of Diana's death.

Interviewed for this book, here is Darryn's full account of the shady circumstances surrounding the incidents:

> Darryn also offers his own bewildered take on the conspiracy behind the killing, based on his firsthand access to the scene, telling us, "The rumors are it was the white Fiat. But it's too many things I don't understand. The whole accident has never been explained to us [photographers] either. No one really, really knows."

> On the night in question, I spoke to Piers Morgan, who was editor, I think, at the *Daily Mirror* at the time. I know Phil Hall was editor of the *News of the World*, and he was talking directly to Rupert Murdoch at the time. I had the world exclusive at my feet.
>
> Not even the editors at the time believed what was going on, and they were making checks anywhere, and nothing was coming through the wire services. These photos were literally minutes after the accident. They were extraordinary and very graphic.
>
> Our information was that Diana was certainly unconscious, and that it looked as if she may have broken an arm or something to that effect.

There's no way we knew the seriousness of it at the time. But we did know that Dodi was in terrible trouble.

I was in communication with the editor of the *News of the World* at the time. Naturally, on such a big story like this, money was being talked about for the exclusive right to publish the pictures.

Because people were still not believing that this had actually happened. It unfolded, very quickly. I spoke to Piers Morgan, and we had a very in-depth conversation. He was an incredible voice of reason for me about the situation.

When we found out that Diana had passed away, those pictures had to be taken off the market. I was inundated—naturally—with calls from around the world about the pictures. But I had made the decision these were pictures that the world should not be seeing.

You wouldn't have said from the photos that I saw coming into our office in London that the princess of Wales was going to pass away. She looked like an angel, serene, with a smile on her face and only a small cut on her forehead. (The photograph has never been published.)

On the second night after Diana's death, things started to get very, very strange. We had worked pretty solidly for forty-eight to seventy-two hours, not only fielding calls about the photos, but from media outlets seeking interviews, and we were trying to get a handle on the fallout of what was going on. You've got to remember, we had seven to ten days of incredible pictures of the princess of Wales. There was tremendous interest in Big Pictures at the time.

I decided—for a bit of a relief as much as a thank-you—to take the staff out to acknowledge their incredible efforts. We went to an establishment just down the road; no more than three hundred or four hundred meters to a courier house.

We weren't there that long. When we went back to the office, I remember unlocking the door and the alarm wasn't set, which was the number one sign that something unusual had happened, because I know we had done it on the way out.

Everything was on, except for the lights were completely out in our building. You'd normally have a grid go down, you wouldn't have a whole property go down, in terms of power.

It was just very eerie—and very strange. I walked through the door with a couple of staff members behind me, and all of a sudden, I hear, it was like a "tick, tick, tick, tick, tick."

Then, I saw with my own eyes a shadowy character. It was like a silhouette of someone. I heard movement, and then I heard this "tick, tick, tick, tick, tick" sound again, and I just screamed, "Get out."

I thought to myself, "Is there a bomb in here?"

As time went on, we could hear other voices on the telephone lines. We could hear tapping on the phones. We were definitely being listened to.

There's no question in my mind that we were under extreme surveillance. I also totally understand that we would've been. But certainly, going back to that night, I had an immense amount of fear. I dialed the emergency services because it was just all very strange.

I've never seen so many police arrive in my life. It was a huge amount of law enforcement, who blocked off the road. The full monty had arrived.

They went in and checked the building out and declared everything was okay. The lights, I'm pretty sure, were still down, but no one could explain to me why that was the case.

We all gave detailed descriptions of what we saw, what we thought, and what we felt.

While we gave answers to questions, we never got answers to our questions.

No question the highest level of security forces would've been extraordinarily active for the hours after Diana's passing, and for many, many, many, many weeks and months after.

> As for our involvement, I do think there was an intelligence operation underway in an attempt to get what we had and download it. Whether that was successful or not, I do not know. I assume yes.

> We began to receive death threats at our office. Every day, nonstop. My management team had to endure horrendous threats, on a minute-by-minute basis.
>
> There's no question that not only myself, but also members of my staff did fear for their safety and lives. Why? What could have happened? Who was behind it? Perhaps we will never know.
>
> I have no idea if Diana's death was a result of a conspiracy. I'm merely saying that there were so many unexplainable issues on why things happened, particularly surrounding the night it happened.
>
> Even though we've had inquiry after inquiry, I still think there's someone that was involved in the accident.
>
> So, am I satisfied that that was just a simple car accident? No, I don't think I am.

Another veteran pap who suspected his home was burgled by spies the night Diana crashed was Frenchman Lionel Cherruault.

He had spent years amassing a collection of images of Diana, and in a book titled *Death Of A Princess* by Thomas Sancton and Scott MacLeod, Lionel is quoted saying a police officer visited his house after the investigation into the robbery—to warn him it was not an ordinary crime.

The book said:

> Next day, a police detective appeared at the apartment. "I must tell you something," he said clutching a sheaf of papers in his hand. "I've just read this report. I have to confirm that you were not burgled."
>
> "You mean they were gray men?" said Cherruault, using a euphemism for intelligence agents.
>
> "Call them what you like," replied the detective. "You were not burgled."

And this conspiracy goes all the way up to the queen.

Her notoriously stiff upper lip finally quivered days after Diana's death as she stood in Buckingham Palace and confessed, "There are powers at work in this country about which we have no knowledge."

Queen Elizabeth's stunning admission was made to Diana's butler Paul Burrell during a conversation about Diana's personal files, tape recordings, and possessions he had lifted from her Kensington Palace apartment just after her death was announced.

As revealed earlier, they are the files and recordings that could have cost Diana her life.

Burrell interpreted the queen's statement as a warning to him in his astonishing three-hour meeting with the monarch that his close friendship with Diana could put his life in danger.

He said, "I told Her Majesty I intended to protect the princess's world and keep safe her secrets. The queen responded by nodding her approval and smiling. There were many she could have been referring to. But she was clearly warning me to be vigilant. She had made clear she was deadly serious, and added, 'Be careful, Paul, no one has been as close to a member of my family as you have.'"

The aide added about the queen's warning, "I think it was a general 'Be careful warning' over many issues. This was unprecedented times and as the queen said to me, no one has been as close to a member of my family and this has never happened before. The queen is a good, kind, devout lady and she looks after members of her staff who look after her on a daily basis. As I had done to her, she extended me the kindness of looking after me."

We can reveal Burrell's interpretation of the warning is believed to be far from the truth.

A source close to the investigation into Diana's death—whose identity must be shielded due to their fear of repercussions, even twenty-one years after the tragedy—said:

> What the queen was really telling Paul was that he should never, ever reveal what was on the recordings he took from Diana's apartments—or he would be next in the firing line.

What she was actually trying to tell him was that Diana had been murdered, and she knew it. The queen would have thought her warning was as unsubtle as she could make it, as veteran royals like her act like high-ranking members of the mob. They never say anything that can incriminate them and speak in an aristocratic code that was obviously way above Paul's plebian head. Even when the queen was clearly giving him a stern warning, he filters it through his ego and believes she is speaking to him as an equal, and not like a subject who could be easily crushed.

The royal family is not called "the firm" for nothing. It's a family in the same way the Mafia is a family.

CHAPTER THIRTEEN

They were everywhere.

From scorned ex-lovers to angered international arms dealers, Diana had an enemies list like few have ever seen—a list much longer than Colin and I, as investigators, put together. Between her own countless premonitions of death to the outright threats against her, it is a wonder she lived so long. Nations, international conglomerates, and the British royal family all stood to benefit from her shutting up and going away forever—and such a thing can be accomplished a number of ways. Yet foremost among them, and certainly foremost in effectiveness, would be snuffing out Diana's life entirely.

Diana was a threat to the establishment for a host of reasons. For the royals, it was a reputation cost. Diana threatened to cheapen the monarchy; to blur the line between acceptable and unacceptable behavior for a member of the family. And most unnerving of all, she threatened to dispel the magic that made outsiders feel as though the royals were exceptional and special. If that were to occur, many in the public might start asking questions about why the royals are followed, tolerated, and subsidized in the first place. Everything the family had built could all come crashing down.

And the powerful international entities Diana threatened saw her as a risk to their very chummy way of doing business. To their racket. Land mines alone were probably enough to get Diana on their watch list.

Consider the following: In Country A (as in the United States), there is a large military defense contractor that makes land mines. In every election cycle, lobbyists in the employ of this defense contractor make heavy campaign donations to politicians who support foreign aid to war-torn Country B. Once elected, these politicians green-light several billions of dollars in aid from Country A to Country B. But there is a tacit understanding. Country B knows that it must use the preponderance of the funds received to arm itself against future oppression. . . by purchasing arms from the defense contractor in Country A. It is a racket in which everybody wins.

The defense contractor turns a few million in lobbying funds into a few billion in land mine sales. The politicians get their election coffers filled and stay in power. And the war-torn country gets a whole bunch of money for arms (with a bit left over to grease the political wheels on their end, too).

It was a nice, "legal" scheme for making money and solidifying power . . . and one idealistic royal threatened to send it all crashing to the ground.

Again, the wonder is not that Diana was killed—and she *was* killed—but that her life was not taken sooner.

One imagines that initially, the players involved must have looked to one another. Can't the royal family handle it? Can't the British government make her shut up and stop speaking out like this?

But they could not, and they did not.

Diana persisted.

But she wasn't killed as a result of an orchestrated execution.

It was an all-too-familiar road accident.

Here is how.

* * *

Our new research has shown that the paparazzi were not to blame in Diana's death, and that it was instead a case of someone being in the wrong place at the wrong time.

Painstaking decades of work, in-person interviews with witnesses and those involved, as well as multiple visits to the crime scene have brought forth revelations that French and/or British police either did not see, or were not in a position, politically, to acknowledge.

We have found that on the night of her death, the $123,000 Mercedes that carried Diana and others was capable of easily out-accelerating every single vehicle that the members of the paparazzi were driving. In short, there was no neck-and-neck chase, as such a thing was an impossibility. The mass of photographers could not have kept up with her car. Period.

Yet as her car neared the tunnel on that fateful night, there were numerous witnesses—many, only auditory—who heard a loud screeching of tires. This could only have been the Mercedes braking suddenly. Why? Had driver Henri Paul simply failed to notice the tunnel that was right in front of him? Even in a somewhat intoxicated state, this seems unlikely.

But something made him brake.

Other witnesses claim to have seen a flash in the tunnel—or in the moments before the car entered the tunnel—just before Diana's death. It would seem easy—perhaps *too* easy—to conclude that this flash was from a photographer's camera. But when we stop and think, we have to ask how this could possibly be. Diana's Mercedes was too fast. The paparazzi could not catch up with it. They arrived after the fact, of course, to take photos of the death car. But none were present when the vehicle literally met its doom.

We can now, in this book, reveal that additional research into the circumstances of Diana's death brought forth two new witnesses—George and Sabine Dauzonne—who were present at the accident and confirmed details to Colin of a particular scenario that has long been floated but never proven . . . until now.

While the motorcycle make and models driven by the photographers were not able to keep up with Diana's car that night, two other vehicles were. These vehicles were in close proximity to Diana's car as it approached the tunnel. The vehicles were a motorcycle and a white Fiat Uno that had joined the road late in the game.

The motorcyclist remains a mystery, but the Dauzonnes got a clear look at the driver of the Uno, as Colin discovered.

In the aftermath of the accident, a fragment of plastic was found by French police. It came from a Fiat Uno. In addition, Diana's Mercedes was found to have a smear of white paint upon it. This paint was analyzed, and found to be paint that was only used by one manufacturer: Fiat. An exhaustive database search of over 112,00 Fiats never found the elusive car. Despite calls to the public, no person ever came forward as the driver.

In the days after Diana's death, during the inquest into what precisely had happened, no less an authority than Sir Richard Dearlove, former head of MI6, poured fuel on the fire that the "flash of light tunnel murder" scenario was not only an established assassination format, but one that the British government itself had considered using in the past.

Specifically, Dearlove outlined a scenario that the British government had contemplated deploying in the early 1990s to assassinate a senior Balkan politician by forcing a crash. When the politician's car passed into a tunnel, a blinding flash device would have been deployed, bright enough to blind and disorient the driver. (In a world in which the CIA has openly confirmed possessing "heart attack guns" for decades, it requires no leap of faith to trust that a blinding device such as this existed in 1997.) The flash would be mistaken by any bystanders as a photograph, but the effects would be deadly. The driver of the car would lose control of the vehicle and crash into the tunnel in such a way that the death of the target would be essentially assured.

A year after Dearlove's testimony, Richard Tomlinson, a former British spy, also publicly confirmed and corroborated Dearlove's account.

What seems possible is that the mysterious lone motorcyclist deployed this blinding device while Diana's car was in the tunnel. In her memoir *Spies, Lies and Whistleblowers*, former MI5 agent Annie Machon confirms her belief that this is precisely what happened.

What was the Fiat Uno's role? Did it somehow assist in the deployment of the device? Did the driver steer his car in such a way so to help the motorcyclist in deploying it? Or was he or she merely an Oswald-like patsy? Was the car only there to soak up blame and attention in the aftermath, to distract investigators from the real clues? Or was it, as we believe, a simple and routine car accident.

We would know the answers to many of these queries if we had, for example, footage of the accident.

There were two CCTV cameras in the Pont de l'Alma underpass, but neither recorded footage of the fatal collision. They were either malfunctioning on the night in question, or not positioned to shoot the correct part of the tunnel. This too unbelievable to be dismissed as a coincidence.

Indeed, a French judicial inquiry into the crash was told that neither camera was working on the night in question. Both, unbelievably, were broken. However, one motorist who came forward to the press shared that he received a speeding ticket after being caught on a tunnel camera just fifteen minutes prior to the accident.

But a lack of cameras was not enough. The flash-attack itself was not enough.

The conspirators had to do more.

French security services who were part of the cover-up leaked information to the press that Henri Paul was a drunk, and was three-and-a-half times over the legal limit on the night of the crash. They also switched his blood sample at the lab, replacing his with that of an alcoholic. This was all but proved when Paul's physician confirmed which medications Paul was taking, and that those drugs did not show up in his system.

If you believe some armchair detectives, however, Henri Paul was sober as a judge when he was attacked and disoriented with a top-secret government light device that likely rendered him more severely disoriented than any amount of drinks could do.

It all comes back to Diana's own words in the death note:

> This particular phase in my life is the most dangerous. My husband is planning "an accident" in my car, brake failure and serious head injury in order to make the path clear for him to marry.

In October 1995, the princess told Lord Mishcon, her solicitor, that "reliable sources" had informed her of the prince's plans "that she and Camilla would be put aside." We find this document today in the National Archive in London.

If the disbelievers are to be believed, Diana was murdered, and she was murdered by forces with leading-edge spy technology, and with the power to create international complicity between governments and government agencies. She was just that dangerous, and just that powerful. Because of her behavior, she had to be stopped. This story could have ended no other way.

Yet our story continues, with a unique and unprecedented encounter with one of the chief players. And what it reveals shines an entirely new light on what happened.

Armed with this information, we knew what we had to do.

***

DETECTIVE'S NOTEBOOK

DATELINE: October 1997, five weeks after Diana's death

It was now just over a month since the horrid accident had changed the lives of so many and caused the biggest outpouring of grief that the modern UK has ever known. The instant I opened the door to my warehouse back in Melbourne I turfed the dog-eared newspaper clippings I had carried for three weeks to one side, scattering them across the floor, to come to rest with the waiting cans of paint. I looked at the cans of paint and looked away, too occupied by my crime-scene analysis from Paris to think of renovations.

My first task, I thought, once I had sidestepped my building needs, would be to seek out an independent expert opinion.

I needed to know who drove that second car!

I also needed an automotive engineer to tabulate and interpret the last journey of the Mercedes-Benz, so I got on with my search for such an individual. Melbourne has a robust automotive industry; back in 1997, there were five major car manufacturers as well as many engineers in allied fields such as motorcycle manufacturers, truck and farming equipment, and the aircraft industries. All excelled in their fields and supplied either components or finished products to the Australian market, as well as being exported around the globe. I burrowed down and, like most detectives, I hit the phones and rang a string of contacts.

I soon discovered an engineer that was a cut above almost all others. Vincent Messina fitted the bill. At that time, he had twenty-five years' experience under his grease-stained belt. With an honors degree in engineering computing and design, he was the proprietor of DAPS Australia Pty. Ltd, a business focused on the creation of specialized vehicle testing systems used by automotive manufacturers worldwide—specifically to analyze speed, inertia, and braking. I knew full well that the answers in the Mercedes lay in understanding the inertia of the car. And the answer to the second car would follow.

Vincent had cut his teeth on the vast production lines of the Ford automotive company, managing crews of as many as a hundred mechanics, body fitters, and engineers. His skill took him to the United States, where he managed a workshop for Ford Atlanta, in charge of hundreds of highly skilled men and women, building today's cars to last well into the future. Vincent would ultimately leave the mainstream automotive industry to create his own high-end equipment, under his own badge: DAPS Australia, the first company in the world to come up with complex computer analysis equipment to enable engineers to read speed, in various forums. To simplify matters, Vincent's technology could dynamically understand the exact speed a car was doing, at any given moment of its journey, by reading the ABS braking system. By 1997, virtually all motorcars were fitted with ABS brakes. Certainly, Mercedes-Benz prided themselves in having the best system available, that of Bosch, from Germany. Further, should Vincent and his team of clever engineers be supplied with evidence of previous speed undertaken by a vehicle, such as video footage or even skid marks, then his analysis equipment could provide, within a high level of certainty, the speed of the vehicle.

A further and somewhat unique feature of my chosen expert's career was his twenty-year involvement in motor racing, holding various national titles for super-bike racing and sidecar sprints. He was not only an automotive expert, but also a practitioner of speed. Highly esteemed in both the worlds of motor sports and engineering, Vincent also built racing machines from scratch and delighted in seeing them win national titles. In time this talented man would go on to build a 417-horsepower motorcycle, which he called the Aurora Hellfire V8, simply the fastest production motorcycle the world has ever seen, a true work of metallic art. Its top speed is north of 340 kph (210 mph). Vincent would prove to be just the man for my task. Constantly on the move, traveling the world, installing his equipment and teaching engineers how to operate his complex gadgetry, and developing his super bike, Vincent was going to be a hard man to pin down.

In the case of the Mercedes-Benz 280 in which Princess Diana was a passenger, I was in possession of what I believed may be two parallel skid marks that belonged to the same Mercedes. My many photographs showed the skid marks in various dimensions; side on, bird's-eye view, and in relation to the road surface and its changing conditions as the road surface entered the tunnel.

A duplicate set of images lay in a folder awaiting Vincent's return to the southern hemisphere; as luck would have it, this coincided with the last foolscap sheet of my notes being added to his waiting pile. I gathered my images together and booked an appointment with the skeptical secretary to meet Vincent.

At the meeting and after what must have seemed like a lecture on the subject, (I went for more than two hours!) he graciously received my notes, sketches, detailed measurements, and photographs. One set of images appeared to worry him, those showing the tire residue on the side of the capping. I presented him with a small specimen canister containing the rubber residue that I had collected from that capping, back in Paris, within minutes of first observing the said rubber residue. I told Vincent how I lightly brushed the palm of my hand across the minute bristles of rubber and how they fell away to the road surface—an indication of fresh the rubber was, as surely had it rained at the time the rubber adhered to the capping (or in the few days since my arrival in Paris) and the force of the raindrops would have removed the bristles.

Vincent opened the tiny canister and tipped the bristles onto his palm and, after rolling the fibers between his fingers, Vincent stated that not only was it unequivocally car tire residue, but that it appeared free from contamination, not weathered. His only comment on the photographs showing the parallel skid marks was at how rich, dark, the rubber appeared, indicating that the skid marks were probably reasonable fresh. He felt my thirty or forty photographs showed the skid marks clearly and that after analysis the wheelbase should be readily identifiable. From there, we would be able to work out the make and type of vehicle that left behind its two telling rubber marks.

Vincent familiarized himself with the photographic depiction of the scene at the Place de l'Alma. My images clearly showed the many scars, fresh scratches and gouges on the vertical surface of the retaining wall that is both left and right of the roadway before it becomes a tunnel. We both agreed that these scars clearly indicated a car out of control. Indeed, we agreed there had to have been two cars to make these harsh markings as, on one occasion, in one position, the scarring marks were opposite each other. No one car could create that sequence of scarring.

Of course, I had always believed there were two cars involved. One feature of the roadway yelled and screamed at me that two cars had to have been involved: the merge lane and its relationship with the two long skid marks. The closeness of these two features smacked of an unknown car trying to enter the fast-moving roadway, which caused the Mercedes-Benz driver to brake sharply, hence the skids.

It was then that Vincent queried a telltale set of markings in the skids. To explain better, skid marks usually show a set of parallel rubber marks, each running in a neat straight line (the tread of the tire). In the two skid marks that I photographed, there was the presence of wavers or fluctuations in the tire residue of the skid marks. The straight rubber line had an interruption to its neat line. This interruption was obvious to the trained eye, to Vincent's eye. As some of my images were taken up close, the wavers or fluctuations were clearly visible, showing the composition of the said fluctuations. At one part of the tire tread they represented a "bubble" shape in the tread, where there should have been a straight line. This fascinated Vincent and a smile graced his face. He offered nothing more. And with that, Vincent gathered up my materials and left, heading off to his factory of sophisticated computers. I went back to my boring renovations.

He hadn't been gone more than an hour or two when a breaking news story that the broadcaster promised was of global proportions interrupted my afternoon's work. The news reader on my small portable television announced that a team of investigative journalists were alleging that Princess Diana and Dodi were "murdered in an SAS-style bomb attack." Certainly, I had seen no evidence whatsoever of any explosion: no soot, scarring, or blackening in the tunnel, on the pillars, walls, or roof of the tunnel in the many days I had spent there just after the accident. Now, I had another twist in the saga that claimed Princess Diana's life. Journalists—not police—alleging it was all part of a bombing attack.

The announcer went on with his tale and all its fascination. The story was bolstered by claims that an explosives expert from Spain believed a pursuing car triggered a deadly device. Apparently, the expert was able to state that another unknown car was tailing the Mercedes-Benz, only meters behind when it had entered the tunnel, and that a remote-control device had been used to detonate the bomb. I stood shaking my head. *How could he look into the past?* I couldn't help thinking of the crazy Hollywood-style story that the London solicitor Gary Hunter once told the world media, and me. A story that ended up being a load of rubbish.

What the bombing story failed to say was that no residue of an explosion was found in the tunnel and the Mercedes, apart from hitting the pillar, showed no evidence of being fragmented. Nor did any of the approaching paparazzi or locals at the scene allude to seeing an explosion. In forensic terms an explosion is an easy thing to detect. Despite the sensational story, the drama of explosives and a so-called expert with explosives, no further "facts," were ever put forward by any worthwhile authority. As the newspapers say, the story came and went after a day. But it was a good story, for five minutes. And I got back to my renovations, eagerly awaiting contact from my own expert, one the wasn't sensational, nor keen to get himself on the television sets in millions of homes.

As I waited, I would read the daily newspapers about many other similar and sensational claims of skullduggery or terrorists surrounding the death of the dethroned princess. It seemed that everyone was trying to attach a bizarre theory into the death of three people in a tunnel in the city of love. Without exception, each story was factually wrong. I felt that I had a very sound understanding of what had occurred as the Mercedes raced toward the tunnel—probably more than any other person on the planet. Certainly more than the French cops.

Now, for all the notes that I had taken, all the measurements I had accumulated, I needed something solid to turn my investigative theory into crime-scene fact. I needed forensics. I needed an engineer to tell me a story that matched my investigative facts.

During my waiting hiatus, a real game changer came into play: the French police finally announced that there may have been a second vehicle involved in the crash, as there was a foreign paint sample lifted from the front right wing of the Mercedes-Benz, yet to be analyzed. The police were feeding the chooks, as detectives say, throwing the media a juicy story to keep them in line. And juicy it was. It would prove my theory was correct. All of sudden, there seemed to be a chase on, between myself and the French cops to unravel what really happened on the night of August 31, 1997. So far, I reckoned I was a few weeks ahead.

A couple of weeks later, out of the blue, Vincent called, proffering a second meeting. He was the type to say little to nothing on the phone, so I sucked in some Melbourne spring air and headed outside. We met at a cozy café not far from my warehouse and sat for most of the afternoon. Several espressos later I had the gist of his report of more than a dozen pages and sketches. His comments were extensive and, obviously, full of engineer jargon. His serious face told me two things: that he was a man of real skill, and that he had given the task his best. My translation of his debriefing went as follows:

> The tread pattern of the skid marks, which were clearing visible in my photographs, were unable to be matched identically to the tire tread used by the Mercedes-Benz motorcar company when manufacturing the 280 SL model.
>
> With the age of the vehicle and the fact that it had had many repairs, services, and been subject to a carjacking, Vincent was unable to say whether the tread related to the exact tires that were initially fitted at the factory when the vehicle first rolled off the production line.

However, he *was* able to say the tread was consistent with tires used by the manufacturing company and listed in the Mercedes-Benz 280SL handbook. Furthermore, Vincent studied the width of the tires, identifiable from three measurements along the 22-foot skid marks. He found they were 200 mm, and stated that the tread alignment was consistent with the wheelbase of the model 280 SL.

To assist his calculations, he was guided by the manufacturer's handbook, which showed the wheelbase center line to be 1,579 mm, a distance taken from the centerline of the rear wheels. He then took the distance I gained, between the inside of the skid marks (1380 mm) and added the width of a factory-fitted tire (200 mm) to come up with a measurement one millimeter less than what it should have been. He seemed happy to allow the one-millimeter difference for fading or my measuring tape skills. I was thrilled at the result of his first analysis. I knew then that the two skid marks I had photographed had come from a Mercedes-Benz 280 sedan. The question could now be asked, with a fairly high level of certainty, as to how many other Mercedes-Benz 280 sedans could have skidded at that exact same location, leaving behind the same two long—in parallel—skid marks? Obviously, the answer was zero; such a coincidence—I confidently suggest—was unfathomable.

As a detective, I knew at that first set of answers from Vincent that I was on the right track to solving this case.

To determine the speed at which the Mercedes was traveling as it hurtled toward the tunnel entrance, Vincent used the overall length of the skid marks to first calculate the speed of the vehicle prior to applying the brakes. He noted that the Mercedes-Benz S280 sedan was fitted with a standard Bosch antilock braking system (ABS). The ABS is designed for high-speed detection of wheel lock. The system is a microprocessor-controlled device that utilizes speed sensors on each wheel that monitor the wheels rotation motion. Once the speed difference threshold is exceeded for a wheel, the detected wheel(s) braking hydraulic circuit is temporarily relieved, and the brake force is momentarily released. And so the process is repeated as the speed varies. The Bosch ABS system can electronically pulse at twelve to eighteen cycles per minute as it reads and reacts to the speed of the vehicle. In real terms, the hydraulic circuit would take around 100 to 300 milliseconds to physically release the line pressure on a locked wheel, dependent on the condition of the road surface: wet or dry, gravel or asphalt. My inquiries confirmed the road surface was dry, and being that it is a good asphalt surface, then the 150 milliseconds was the most reliable time unit that Vincent used in his later calculations, allowing for the slight grading of the roadway and the possibility of late-night dew on the surface. The scene had two matching 22-foot-long skid marks that Vincent believed were the front two wheels of the Mercedes. Using the above-mentioned times against the 23-foot-long skid marks, the engineer was able to estimate the speed at which it was traveling prior to applying the brakes and when the brakes were released, coincidently, at the same point where the road surface commenced to fall away.

He was able to assess that the Mercedes traveled an average speed across the skid marks of at least 168 kph (104 mph), before the ABS unit was disengaged. With media reports suggesting the Mercedes-Benz was traveling at a speed of up to 190 kph (118 mph) prior to the accident (prior to the skid), Vincent was able to state that this estimate was highly likely. He also noted that while it was impossible to precisely say what the speed was, the evidence of the 22-foot-long skid marks made the 190 kph (118 mph) theory credible.

Vincent also believed that with the Mercedes-Benz traveling at 168 kph (104 mph) as it left the skid mark where the road surface started to fall away, a catastrophic ending was almost inevitable. With such acceleration, combined with the fall in the road surface, the car would have firstly become airborne. Based on the data he studied of the road length, fall, and surrounding conditions, the Mercedes would have become airborne for a distance of 28 meters (90 feet). This revelation was consistent with the tire rubber residue found on the capping wall, which (coincidentally) was a similar distance away.

Vincent added that both the impact points and the skid marks confirmed the presence of a second vehicle at the accident scene. He explained that the presence of wavers or fluctuations in the tire residue of the skid marks gave clear evidence that at some point while the Mercedes was braking its inertia was interrupted, causing the fluctuations. The engineer also stated that unless the Mercedes were somehow able to bounce from retaining wall to dividing wall and back again, a distance of over 26 meters (20 feet), it would have been impossible for it to be the only vehicle involved in the accident. The marking and scarring of the retaining walls and the obvious fluctuations in the skid marks therefore confirmed that a second car was involved.

The expert expanded, stating that the Mercedes was lightly clipped by another car that had entered the roadway from the merge lane. He noted that there were no signs of the other car skidding at that point, indicating that the second car was traveling slowly. The "glance" from the second car would have turned or deflected the vehicle into the dividing wall on the left of the roadway, leaving the way clear for the straight-ahead path of the speeding and now out-of-control Mercedes, which catapulted farther toward the capping. Due to the vast differentiation in speed of the two vehicles, the second car would probably have limped along the left-hand side of the roadway and would likely have witnessed the subsequent impact of the princess's Mercedes as it careered into the retaining wall and its resulting carom into the thirteenth pillar within the tunnel.

In conclusion, Vincent noted that the airborne Mercedes and its occupants were unlucky not to have cleared the retaining wall. Had the driver been traveling a mere 10 mph faster, the car would have gained the additional few centimeters in height necessary to clear the capping and run up the adjacent flower bed and grassy ascent. Vincent had little doubt, had this occurred, that the occupants of the Mercedes would have survived.

What follows is Vincent's qualified account of the likely last 3.2 seconds of the princess's journey in the rear seat of the Mercedes.

> Immediately prior to the driver applying the brakes, the Mercedes would have been traveling at a speed of arguably 190 kph, rapidly approaching a left-hand curve with a noticeable descent over a short distance. A proposition that would be of real concern to a professional speed-racing driver, let alone a chauffeur in a drunken state.
>
> At the end of the skid marks as the road fell away the vehicle would have become airborne. The princess would have lurched forward; her unrestrained body would have hit the front passenger seat with a force of up to eight times her body weight. At that point, she would have been a human projectile without any way of stopping her propulsion. Her movement would not have altered until the Mercedes came crashing to the road surface about a second later. At that point she would have been forced forward, slammed past the harnessed front seat passenger, and finished up in the front section of the car over the console area. In another second the Mercedes crashed into pillar thirteen.
>
> At that point the princess would have been flung to the dashboard and possibly the windscreen. On each occasion that the princess was thrown forward the force of her propelled body weight, and that of her unrestrained companion, Dodi Fayed, would serve to crush the manufactured strength of the front driver and passenger seats, causing damage to the mountings.
>
> In effect, Princess Diana was flung about the cabin of the Mercedes-Benz like dice shaken in a cup. While all the occupants may have survived the initial traumas, the force with which the Mercedes hit pillar

> thirteen would not have been survivable for anyone not wearing a properly fitted seat belt.

In sum, Diana didn't have to die. It would be expected that the princess would have received serious cranial, shoulder, and chest injuries. Had she been wearing a seat belt, she would in all likelihood have survived. Further substantiation of the engineer's theory can be found in the knowledge that the only survivor, Trevor Rees-Jones, had been wearing his seat belt at the time of the crash.

Curiously, he had only fastened the harness just prior to the accident occurring. There has been much speculation as to how this is known. The simple answer is that a police speed camera took one photograph of the vehicle as it careered toward its tragic end, and the belted figure of Rees-Jones was clearly depicted.

Here was the most important witness in the entire saga, the only survivor, the man who could answer all the questions. Why were they traveling so fast? What was the demeanor of Dodi and the princess as they entered the Cours Albert? What were they fleeing, and why? But arguably the most important question he could answer was, as the individual in charge of the princess's security—why did he allow an "inebriated" driver to charge of the transport of his own charge? A world waited for the answers that would never come.

Following five weeks of intensive care treatment, it was announced that Rees-Jones had suffered amnesia and would possibly never recall his experience of the world's most infamous accident. Whatever contributing factors he was aware of or involved in appeared to be forever locked in the darkest reaches of his mind. And for Vincent's skills in analyzing speed and braking systems, he too was unable to offer any further explanation for the accident. He simply bade me farewell and headed for the airport. He was off to install his specialist equipment in a Korean car manufacturing plant and I was left holding the sum total of an independent investigation into the death of Princess Diana, Queen of Hearts.

***

By October 1998 and with Vincent's appraisal as evidence, I'd almost finished writing my report on the investigation. Before putting my real report on the crash to bed, I faxed the Harrods executive with the dour face a sample ten pages of my report. It was what I said I would do when I met him the year earlier. In sending the sampler I made it clear that there was no smoking gun, by way of any Muslim terrorist involvement uncovered in my investigation. Not surprising, the London camp sought no further contact with me. It seemed that since Lady Diana's death some folk only wanted to recall a version of the fine Lady that suited them. It was just like Repossi Jewelers in the piazza opposite the Ritz Hotel, whom I visited a week or so after I arrived in Paris to speak about a rumor that they supplied an engagement ring to Dodi, for Diana. Their answer was a firm no, there was no ring. Now, all this time later, history seemed to have changed: Repossi was claiming to all that they were the preferred jeweler to Dodi and Diana, and an engagement ring was ordered. And it was even engraved! I started to see how legend was entering the story of the death of a princess. Even Harrods had created a statue at their front door, in honor of the loving engaged couple. It appeared legend was becoming a focus instead of truth.

As I pondered this sad shift of reality, I had to come to terms with a fact that my report into the death of Lady Diana and her companions would not fit into legend or required reading, but find a home in the bottom drawer of my writing desk. Still, despite this lesson of how history gets written, the circumstances surrounding the case would continue to niggle at me like an errant eyelash.

Two years later, a flurry of reports began to bounce around the media airwaves centering on the suspicious death of a leading French photographer, Jean-Paul "James" Andanson. The fifty-four-year-old paparazzi stalwart had been known to hound Princess Diana, selling his proofs of her to tabloids worldwide. A man at the top of his game, he was considered financially secure. Now it was his image that had made it to the front pages of the grubby press. I pricked up my ears.

On face value, the circumstances of the death appeared simple. A body was discovered in Andanson's car in rural France. Ruled suicide by petrol incineration, the remains were so badly charred that it took a month before DNA could absolutely confirm his identity. Andanson had left behind a distraught family and a shocked collection of work colleagues. Undeniably it was a tragic end to any life, but there was no evidence of a link to the August 31, 1997, accident at the Place de l'Alma.

But no, one man's wretched death was to become a theorist's lifeblood. Andanson was to be the latest name dragged into the sullied waters, his title changed from photographer to suspect, for Jean-Paul had once owned a white Fiat Uno automobile.

British news copy splashed scoops citing paint samples identical to those found on the crashed Mercedes and claimed that, finally, here was the elusive second car. Mr. Andanson's widow, they purported, loosely supported the theory that her husband was involved. Every detail of his movements in August of 1997 was scrutinized, his life was picked over, and his extended family was interviewed, even chased. With clever wording, journalists speculated that Andanson, "for reasons that he never revealed," fled for Corsica on the day of the accident. Some theorists had even stated that the body of Jean-Paul had a bullet wound to his head. The Al-Fayed camp hollered "murder" and demanded further investigations. Rumors began to circulate insinuating that Andanson had associations with secret agents from British and French Intelligence. It wasn't long before the world media jumped on the bandwagon once again, claiming the deaths of Dodi and Diana as criminal. I shook my head in amazement whispering, "Here we go again."

The more I read, the more the tale began to resemble an Ian Fleming novel, with mentions of the CIA, government cover-ups, and even a midnight break-in at a media office. Only a week after Andanson's death was announced, tabloids alluded to "three masked men armed with handguns" who allegedly broke into a newspaper office in Paris. Shooting a security guard in the foot, the bandits then dismantled all the security cameras before stealing laptops and computers. Even the circumstances of a mere office break-in had been exaggerated to fit a theory that CIA agents had staged an elaborate armed robbery to make away with revealing facts.

Pushing the papers aside, I leant back in my easy chair and pondered the nonsense that I was reading. Was this mere fancy, or was there really something here that I had missed?

Unsettled, I delved deeper. Police reports into the suicide showed a thorough investigation revealing that the deceased did own a white Fiat, but instead concluded that it was totally un-roadworthy at the time of the accident, up on blocks in a garage. The evidence for this finding was conclusive. Further, Andanson himself was at home with his family on the night of the crash and had departed early the next morning to catch a prearranged business flight to Corsica—so much for the reports that his own wife had him as a suspect and that his leaving France was in any way suspicious. As for the many hobby detectives stating that the paint from Andanson's Fiat categorically matched that deposited on the Mercedes, they were right. But what they neglected to mention was that the "Bianco 210" paint sprayed on the photographer's car was the same "Bianco 210" paint used by the Fiat factory for tens of thousands of their cars over a two-year period. Fiat was the best-selling small car in Europe, and its most popular color was white.

I was relieved to read the final police reports stating that the suicide of Andanson was genuine and due to the breakdown of marital relations. There was no bullet hole, there was no murder, nor was there any justification for dragging another name into the uncertainty surrounding the death of Princess Diana. Another chapter closed in the growing tome of conspiracy theories. None of these theories were helped by the annoyance that the French cops never bothered to answer them, squash them, or firm them up.

Years on, a coroner's inquest was held in London into the death of Princess Diana and her companions. Not only would an official cause of death be delivered, but by wrestling it away from the French authorities the forum would allow a more probative approach, and hopefully deliver some answers. And perhaps even silence the stooges once and for all.

Much was made at the commencement of the inquest of the need to hear evidence from Le Van Thanh. A man of Vietnamese ancestry, the thirty-two-year-old, a father of two, was a security guard at the time and believed to be the owner of a white Fiat Uno—one of the 4,600 then registered in Paris. And yes, running to rule, the public relations department of the Al-Fayed camp was again stirring the pot, happy to step forward with insinuations that Mr. Thanh had an involvement in the tragedy on the August 31, 1997.

Tabloid media devoured the story. For weeks, dingy bars were abuzz with claims that only hours after the accident Le Van Thanh's Fiat had been sprayed red to mask damage caused by its impact with Diana's Mercedes. Soon what had been nothing more than scuttlebutt began to gain credibility as a series of articles in a more prominent London newspaper, the *Times*, appeared. Quoting Mr. Thanh's father, a journalist reported that the elder Thanh believed that his son had been involved in the accident but had panicked and attempted to cover up by giving his vehicle a new coat of paint. The result of the allegations against Mr. Le Van Thanh and his vehicle set in motion a media and paparazzi chase almost unequaled in Paris since 1997; the man was hounded day and night. Theorists speculated that the paint from Thanh's car would match that found on the Mercedes, but once again the allegations omitted the universal "Bianco 210" information. Oddly, young Mr. Thanh stood his ground and refused to comment. French detectives subjected him to an arrest and escorted him in and out of police headquarters, where his alibi was scrutinized in a six-hour interview.

While it seems impossible to believe Van Thanh's presence was a coincidence, it is possible, in theory, to believe that Van Thanh was a stooge or a dupe. That is to say, that he did not know who he was working for or with. That he did not know who was being targeted that night in a tunnel in Paris. That he was as shocked as the rest of us to learn what the outcome of his action had been.

The coroner's inquest heard from an investigating detective that a journalist had posed as a police officer and had offered Mr. Thanh, Sr. money for his comment. And while Le Van Thanh's car certainly seemed to have been hastily resprayed, it had been done so by Mr. Thanh's brother, a panel beater, and over a series of days after the accident. This in itself was odd; the timing of the urgent respray was in sync with the timing of the accident involved in the death of Lady Diana.

Le Van Thanh claimed, however, that as per his time clock documentation and fellow worker attestations, he had been working night shift at a Renault storage compound at the time of the accident. But he stated that he was unable to recall the name of his coworker. Indeed, he failed to recall much of the that night—a night that his father recalled very well, whereby his son came home with an urgent need to respray his car from white to "beacon" red.

On April 8th, 2008, the English coroner found that the cause of the accident had related to the speed and manner of the driver of the Mercedes, as well as the speed and manner of the pursuing paparazzi vehicles. I myself had formed that same opinion while at Paris in September 1997, and later, at the end of my independent report. The only question that remains unanswered back in 2008 was simple: "Where is the elusive Fiat Uno and where is its driver?" And to a lesser extent: "What will be the next conspiracy theory put forward by the Al-Fayed camp?"

Later, in 2015 and again in 2019, I would have the good luck to meet Le Van Thanh and speak to him, at his home on the outskirts of Paris. It was those two conversations and a face-to-face interview with the witness that identified Le Van Thanh (also in 2015) that would solidify my opinion as to who was the driver of the Fiat Uno that fateful night and how the accident actually happened.

CHAPTER FOURTEEN

Finding the Fiat Uno was clearly the number one priority for any serious investigation into Diana's death. Initially, as has been explained, the search identified photographer Andanson as the driver.

But in November 1997, French authorities located another man who, as we know, had painted his car red hours after the crash: a French Vietnamese national, Le Van Thanh, who claimed he was working security at the time of the crash. But then he was quickly ruled out, despite Colin finding him to be of more interest.

So why would he respray his car? Could he be the key to cracking the case? And why did the French police ignore this vital information? These questions were never answered at the time, but our investigation would eventually circle back.

***

DETECTIVE'S NOTEBOOK

DATELINE: 2015 and onward

Later, in 2015, and again in 2019, I would revisit the death of Princess Diana and pull out my files. Like most unsolved cases or cold cases, this one was like a thistle up my ass; I couldn't get it out of my mind, couldn't let go of it. I had to know the involvement—if any—of Le Van Thanh and why the French authorities chose to shut down their investigation after seizing his Fiat Uno. And why had the English investigation never compelled Le Van Thanh to give evidence at their independent inquiry? Or, better still, hold a special sitting day in Paris, to accommodate Le Van Thanh?

As it turned out, I would have the good luck to meet Le Van Thanh and speak to him at his home on the outskirts of Paris. Twice. No other person has ever been able to get a word out of Le Van Thanh. Since August 1997, he has chosen to doggedly ignore all attempts to speak about that summer night. It was my two conversations with this most elusive person of interest that would ultimately satisfy my twenty-two-year search for the truth. Along with an extraordinary face-to-face, three-hour interview with a female witness that was in the tunnel that night, both would solidify my opinion as to who really was the driver of the Fiat Uno that fateful evening and how the accident really happened.

In any major crime or horrific tragedy—such as the death of Princess Diana—police will, invariably, receive hundreds of calls from the public. Of course, what they are really hoping for is just one call from someone connected to the incident. Public assistance is often the key to solving a crime. The Paris cops were flooded with calls from well-intended witnesses or passersby. I became privy to some of the more important callers, however I never heard about a lady that rang police shortly after Diana was pronounced dead. In fact, no one knew of her until many years later.

Sabine Dauzonne and her husband were dining in Paris that night, on the Left Bank, at their favorite restaurant. It was just after midnight and they both commenced their short journey home, driving their Rolls-Royce motorcar. They crossed over the Seine river at the exact spot where the accident happened and entered a merge lane that fed traffic onto the Cours Albert, the fast-moving roadway that the Mercedes raced along before entering the tunnel. (This merge lane is not the one the Fiat Uno used to enter the Cours Albert. It's actually the merge lane at the exit end of the tunnel.)

As the Rolls-Royce cleared the merge lane, it attempted to take a position on the roadway. It was then that it became stuck behind a small motorcar, a white Fiat Uno. In effect, it was traveling so slowly it was blocking the bigger car's path. There were no other cars on the roadway. The Fiat had come out of the tunnel, just feet behind, and as the Rolls-Royce fell in behind it, Sabine took a good look at the slow-moving vehicle. She noticed the last two digits of the registration plate as "92." This, she knew to be a Parisian registered car, as number ninety-two denotes one of the arrondissements of Paris. Her husband George had trouble trying to pass the Fiat as it was zigzagging around. Sabine and George got a good look at the driver. They later reported this extraordinary observation to police, but they were ignored. Days went by and Sabine contacted police again, to no avail. No one seemed interested in flushing out better and further particulars on this mystery driver and the elusive Fiat Uno. No one except me. Yet, I would discover that Le Van Thanh was arrested, in November 1997, after his Fiat Uno was one of the thousands of white Fiats inspected. The trouble was the Fiat Le Van Thanh drove to the police station was now red in color. The cops underwent a formal interview with the boyish security guard, then raided his home. The raid yielded very little, except a massive Doberman type black and tan watchdog wearing a muzzle. Le Van Thanh would walk home from his police interview as his car went off to the Forensic laboratory for analysis and no one heard anymore. Le Van Thanh and his now red car, resprayed hours after the death of Lady Diana, had become an elephant in the room, and stay that way.

For that first interview, I was back in Paris in 2015 and involved in pulling together a documentary into the death of Princess Diana for an American television network. During my research I came across the snippet of information from Sabine and George and almost fell off my chair. You might guess correctly that I instantly set up a meeting with Sabine, and she obliged, still a little perplexed that no French police had bothered to interview after eighteen years. I met her in her beautiful apartment building and found her to be an extremely articulate woman, highly intelligent and with a very clear memory of the night of August 31, 1997.

In the world of the detective you meet with many witnesses. A great many are very diligent people who have a story to tell. Others are a tad reticent, and you have to hold their hand as the story falls from their lips. And there are a few that I call nuisances, that just want to be part of the mystery. It's a lucky dip, really, when you knock on the door of any potential witness as to whether you will waste an hour of your life or discover gold. Sabine was gold. The perfect witness that had a more in-depth story inside her. A story supported by her husband George. Yet, the French cops missed it all.

I would spend more than three hours sitting with Sabine and filming her recollections of that night. In short, she recalled, after entering the Cours Albert roadway, she and her husband were very careful not to collide with the erratic

Fiat, as it seemed to slowly stagger onward. In an attempt to pass the Fiat, they went to the driver's side and eventually moved alongside the car. It was then that they noticed there were dents and scrapes on the car and scrapes along the entire left side, the driver's side, from the taillight to the front of the driver's door.

Sabine was able to study the driver, as she initially thought he might be drunk. She observed a young man, who spent a lot of his time looking back into the tunnel. He seemed preoccupied with looking backwards, instead of driving forward. Sabine described his behavior as "agitated." She also described the driver to be a small man with short dark hair and a tanned face. Then she mentioned a dog. A very big dog, black and tan in color, a Doberman type, seated on the back seat and looking at her. The dog was wearing a muzzle on its face. Bingo!

Sabine and her husband continued to watch the Fiat for a few more seconds until they needed to increase their speed up to 60 mph. They then drove off, with the image of the driver and Fiat and dog etched into their memory.

I then asked her to look at various photographs, and it was without hesitation the she pointed out the image of Le Van Thanh as the man in the driver's seat.

The picture of Le Van Thanh I showed her was one taken back in 1998, with Le Van seated at his now red-colored Fiat. The image is unusual insofar as Le Van does not have distinctively Asian facial features. He could look Central American, Asian, or an ethnicity that is difficult to determine, at night, in a car, looking around "agitated." He could look French.

Interestingly, Sabine offered no ethnicity in her description, just a young man, tanned skin, and short black hair, which form the facial features of Le Van.

In short, the evidence of Sabine and her husband is remarkable—remarkable in the fact that the French cops chose to ignore it. I would also discover that the English cops—during their investigation some years earlier—also heard sworn testimony from both Sabine and George stating that Le Van Thanh was the man in the Fiat Uno car. Yet, the police, from that point forward, seemed to have ignored the couple as well. I also found out the English cops never got the comments from Sabine as I did, never put the hours into the witnesses. And just as odd, the English investigation chose to keep the name of Le Van Thanh from their final report There is no mention of him, except, bizarrely to say, "the other Fiat Uno owned by a French citizen living in Paris." What's with the subterfuge?

To be absolutely certain about matters, I asked Sabine to dictate a sketch of the Fiat Uno car and where the dog was seated and where the scratches and dents were located. She did so without hesitation. It goes without saying that there are many salient points in Sabine's observation., points that raise questions for Le Van Thanh and also the cops.

Just to name a few of many:

1. The positive identity by two articulate people that the driver was Le Van Thanh.
2. The dog and muzzle descriptions match the police raid and dog of Le Van Thanh.
3. The damage to the Fiat, on the same side as what would be expected after hitting the Mercedes-Benz at the merge lane.
4. The "agitation" by the driver, leaving the tunnel, driving erratically.
5. The exact time of night as the accident involving the Mercedes.

Add to this the signed statement by Le Van Thanh that he replaced two rubber bumpers from his Fiat, at the time he resprayed his car from white to red. (I observed rubber residue on the dividing wall leading to the tunnel, at the merge lane.) So what was going on in the minds of the police, who chose to ignore such a vital witness and her equally vital husband? And, more worrying, what happened to the search for the truth, into how Princess Diana really died? And the causation? And a greater understanding of the accident, as well as the transparency associated with letting a waiting public know what really occurred on the streets of Paris on August 31, 1997?

I now had a blunt realization that the French and English investigators either didn't want the facts to come out, or, due to incompetence, failed to pursue the groundbreaking facts from Sabine and George—facts that would deliver the answers needed to better comprehend this shocking tragedy. This made me remember all the years that I was a task force detective, solving multiple murders and running a team of detectives. I would labor my point, with the investigators, to take time with witnesses and develop a rapport. Get them on the right side, relax them and, ultimately, you would be rewarded. Rush a witness and you'll get limited results.

Reading the pages of the English investigation I discovered that the investigation team became concerned as to why the French police seized Le Van Thanh's Fiat and analyzed it, then eliminated him from further inquiry. I too am concerned! It appears the English contracted a group of global forensic experts who reviewed the process of the French police. They came up with a startling conclusion that upon review, the French analysis of "the Fiat Uno paint, and the damage to the tail light area was NOT conclusive to eliminate the Fiat." Therefore, all of a sudden, we have a forensic scandal on our hands. (You will note they only mention taillight area, not the side of the Fiat, as per Sabine observations of scrapes and dents along the driver's side. More on that later.)

So, based on the forensic reviewers' comments, why was Le Van Thanh eliminated? This damming independent forensic comment came at a similar time to the English coroner's determination that Princess Diana died from "an unlawful killing." The coroner went on to level blame at the driver of the Mercedes, Henri Paul and also the cars following the Mercedes. Surely, in the absence of any sound explanation from the driver of the Fiat Uno, that would include this driver as well . . . whoever that may be.

It was Sabine's evidence that made me push to see, to meet, to force a conversation with Le Van Thanh. Now, eighteen years later, I knew I would have a battle on my hands, to first locate him and then talk to him. It was then that I took the advice of a number of people in Paris, and sought help from the older brigade of the paparazzi. The old boys, the guys that were chasing Diana around, back in the days and months before her death. I would fast learn that the paparazzi of the eighties and nineties period were an enigmatic bunch of photographers. Highly talented, among the best press shutterbugs in the world, most were now my age or older and a good many had made fortunes in the heady days of celebrity. Likewise, some had crashed and burned in a game that is as ruthless on the photographer as it is as stressful on the celebrity. I would also learn that these two creatures of fame, the paparazzi and the celebrity, need each other. Indeed, most of the time they feed off each other. Should a celebrity want to improve their popularity, their management would often tip off the paps as to where they might be drinking or eating and how the celebrity might take their time getting in or out of a taxi, or, in the case of female celebs, they might wear a revealing outfit, should the paps take a few pictures that could find their way into the magazines. Popularity: a toil for those that ache for it, and those that create it!

Within a couple of days I had a line of paps ready, willing, and able to assist. Each of them would talk openly about their unusual careers, snapping pictures of the most interesting people on the planet. None were in awe of the celebrities they chased or worked with. In fact, they often thought the celebrities were boring, self-obsessed starlets, or wannabe movie icons that would go out of their way to play the paparazzi game. In no time I had the home address of Le Van Thanh and what car he drove and his daily movements. Amazing! I know good detectives that aren't that efficient.

I headed out of Paris to a quiet little suburb with a number of houses tucked away in a back laneway. One house, a very big house, undergoing renovations, belonged to Le Van Thanh. A new Mercedes was parked on the driveway. I took with me a United Nations–accredited French translator to help my attempts to talk to the onetime security guard. Then I pressed the buzzer at his gate. And pressed it again. And again. Fifteen minutes later a man walked out of the front door and down the long driveway, strewn with weeds. It was Le Van Thanh. All of a sudden my translator started to fidget, so I guessed a chat was imminent.

The first thing I noticed about Le Van was that he was tiny, maybe only five foot four inches, or 160 cm in the metric scale. Plus, he never looked obviously Asian, even though he was from Vietnamese parentage. The next obvious thing was his body shape: he was pumped. Obviously a bodybuilder, he looked super fit for a man who would have been forty years of age. And he smiled, all the time.

My translator got to work and explained who I was and my previous career path and how I had investigated the Princess Diana death since a few days after it happened, having flown to Paris from Australia. Le Van and I shook hands. He then opened a pair of big steel gates that barred access to the property and the three of us stood on the driveway and I threw a few questions at the man—mostly as to whether he would allow me to tape-record the interview or film it. He kept smiling and shook his head; there would be no formal interview. This cat-and-mouse conversation went on for a few minutes until it was obvious Le Van was not going to entertain a formal chat. All that was left was my attempt to ask about his whereabouts on the night of the accident and his car.

Le Van went on to say, over and over, that he had had legal advice to not speak of that night to anyone. However, as we persevered he let it slip that he signed a police statement back in November 1997, saying that he was at work on the night Diana died. But he had since changed his statement that he was (in fact) driving around Paris streets on that same night. And that he was about to sign his new statement—a revelation—when his own sister stepped forward and told him not to sign the fresh statement as he could be prosecuted and sent to jail for five years as he "refused to stop and help injured people at the scene of an accident."

This extraordinary thirteen words almost got lost in translation, as my UN translator tried keeping up with Le Van. Once I fully comprehended the statement by the now-confirmed driver of the Fiat Uno, I tried desperately to get him to reiterate his comment on tape. All without success. At least I had the UN translator that could prove his comment. Le Van then became anxious to close off our chat and started ushering myself and my translator away from his driveway. His body intruded into my personal space and I was slowly backpedaling, and, in time, I was standing outside Le Van Thanh's property line. The bodybuilder had cleverly used his bulk to move an unwanted sticky-nose from his driveway! He kept smiling as he pressed the button on his remote control and the big steel gates closed on me.

Then, he was gone.

The one takeaway I gained from my twenty-minute attempt to talk to Le Van was that not once did he ever say that he wasn't at the accident scene. Not once did he say that he was innocent of any involvement in the accident. Not once did he say, "Hey, you've got it wrong, I have nothing to do with this," even though I believe him to be innocent of any wrongdoing. In my view he was just the wrong man at the wrong place that night when a juggernaut came hurtling down the roadway. Instead, Le Van just smiled his faint, yet supremely confident smile and stood his ground. I wanted to know why he remained silent when the evidence that points to him was so compelling.

***

It was Le Van Thanh's final comment to me, about not helping injured people at the scene of an accident, that really annoyed me. I had long suspected he and his Fiat Uno were at the merge lane, ever since I tried unraveling the accident with Vincent Messina, back in 1997. Then it dawned on me. If I knew, the French cops must absolutely know.

I immediately requested an interview with the French forensic science division, and in time was granted a tour of their facility and a chat with its head of forensic paint analysis section. It was imperative that I didn't let my cat out of the bag, and to not mention a lot about Princess Diana. More so, I would tell them I was doing a documentary on forensic science and the fascination of being able to detect and identify from paint samples. This was my cover story. I needed to stick with it.

In time, I went out to the forensic facility and spent an afternoon with the head of the unit, a policeman who had been in the allied science field for over twenty years. I got lucky again and discovered through small talk that he conducted analysis on the Fiat Uno sedans that were being confiscated by police back then, in an attempt to identify which Fiat Uno collided with the Mercedes-Benz. Surprisingly, the policemen was happy to talk about it and we focused a lot of my interview time on Princess Diana.

As we sat opposite each other and the camera rolled I was eventually able to ask a question, "Did you analyze the Fiat Uno of Le Van Thanh?" The officer stated that he did, and explained that he focused his analysis on the rear of the car only. This shocked me. Because I knew that there was damage along the driver's side of the same Fiat Uno, if you believe Sabine and her husband. I was then in a precarious position. What to ask next, bearing in mind as a general interview on motor vehicle paint identification I would be unlikely to know too much about the finer points of Le Van Thanh's car? I went for broke and asked:

"Did you make an analysis or examination of the left-hand side of the red car?"

What happened next disturbed me.

The otherwise confident policemen had a fit of nervousness the likes that I cannot recall seeing from such a qualified person before. He set about fidgeting, stuttering, and scratching himself underneath his nose, on his top lip—a classic sign of my question hitting a fragile point in the policeman's memory. The policeman's eyes dropped and he then composed himself and returned his answer: that he only examined the rear area of the car. He finished off by saying that the Le Van Thanh Fiat was "not compatible with the accident of the Mercedes."

Yet, if all things are to be believed, Le Van Thanh's car was *exactly* compatible with the accident of the Mercedes. I left the forensic facility pleased that I wasn't asked to leave, or told to leave the country as I was certainly asking way too many questions. In leaving I was even more determined to keep pushing the subject of Le Van Thanh's Fiat Uno. I instantly tapped into my paparazzi friends and sat around workshopping the problem. It was then that the most senior of all paps asked if I would like to read a copy of the police report into the investigation into the death of Princess Diana.

Again, my chair started to wobble as I nearly fell off it.

It turned out that the sister of my friendly pap was having an affair with one of the key police involved in the original investigation and for a sum of only two thousand Euros I could get a copy of the paperwork. It was this off-the-wall comment that made me realize that as far as the French way of doing things, nothing surprised me anymore. I simply grabbed at the opportunity, paid over the euros, and waited. The next day I was delivered a large canvas bag, the sort of bag you could stash a million dollars into. Instead this time there were two thousand pages—a Euro a page—of official police- and lawyer-stamped documents all related to the Princess Diana investigation. *Funny place, Paris*, I thought as I instantly pulled up my chair and started reading. All day and all night.

By the next day I had an assortment of useful and useless information. Bearing in mind that I know what a police file is supposed to look like, this mess was just as expected: an unindexed, nonchronological, slapped-together mess. But there was no doubt to its veracity. There were official stamps on every page. I was shocked at the realization that the French investigative section leaked like a sieve, and such sensitive files were openly offered for reading—at a price.

In short, most of what I read was pointless in getting to the truth of how Princess Diana's Mercedes collided with a Fiat Uno. But what I did glean was that the police had been barking up the wrong tree all along. They believed the collision between the Mercedes and the Fiat was inside the tunnel, just meters from where the Mercedes slammed into the thirteenth pillar. This assumption was without any forensic or factual basis. It seems it was just a hunch by a surveying engineer who presented copious drawings to show the (wrong) point of impact. All a crazy and very wrong hunch. While the drawings were very impressive, they were pointless.

It was clear from the file that the crime scene never received any real attention. This was exactly as I suspected. The police had no idea of the importance and the relevance of the merge lane versus the speeding Mercedes. No idea of the dynamics between the two cars and the exchange of force from the Mercedes onto the tiny Fiat. Nor did they have the slightest idea that the Mercedes was airborne. Worst of all, the police missed all the forensic marks, scrapes, and skids, and their entire theory was propagated on the Fiat and Mercedes impacting in the tunnel. All nonsense.

As I read the file, I was able to find a set of signed and stamped forensic laboratory statements. Most bore two or more signatures, authenticating the information contained on the report. One such report contained four signatures, one of which was that of the senior forensic policeman I had interviewed in the paint unit days earlier. The report dealt with the damage between the Mercedes and the unknown Fiat. In actuality, it was a definitive document outlining the facts of the crash. In part it read, "The contact between the two vehicles would have been on the front right wing of the Mercedes and the rear left panel of the Fiat Uno . . . the rear left-hand panel of the Fiat would have been damaged in the collision."

As I read formal explanation of where the damage would have been on the Fiat, I couldn't help recall what Sabine said to me, as she undertook a sketch of the damage on the Fiat, "(on the panel) behind the driver on the left toward the back."

Here were four forensic men stating on a forensic certificate that the Fiat that collided with the Mercedes would have been damaged where Sabine said it was.

Yet, the senior policeman who signed the certificate told me, nervously, and in a stuttered voice as he fidgeted, that he never checked Le Van Thanh's car for damage to the left panel on the driver's side. He only examined the rear of the car for damage. So, who's telling fibs, and why? If we believe Sabine (and I do, categorically), then Le Van Thanh's car was riddled with scratches and dents along the driver's side for a thorough examination by forensic police. Scratches and dents that Le Van Thanh's panel-beater brother may have filled in, and corrected, using automotive body adhesive.

The forensic reports make it abundantly clear that each Fiat Uno would have been checked for damage on the left driver's side of the car. So, again, why the fibs?

By the time I got to the end of reading my misappropriated documents it dawned on me: there was not one single, lone, solitary document or report on Le Van Thanh. Not one. Yet, the world media were told—by the French police—that Le Van Thanh was arrested in November 1997, and his car confiscated and analyzed. This defies logic. I have a copy of Le Van Thanh's own police statement, as do, probably, hundreds of journalists. Yet, there was no Le Van Thanh file in the two thousand pages I digested. Again, why was he not part of the public record? Police record? Who removed his file from the file I was reading?

This opens the door to a greater concern. Someone, or perhaps an entire police task force, in France and (perhaps) later in England was openly removing, omitting anything to do with Le Van Than or his Fiat Uno car. Why? There can be no mistake on this proposition, it appears to be so blatantly obvious.

The more I think of it, the more I realize that perhaps my suspicions could be taken one giant step further.

Could the Ministry of Justice in France be covertly involved in such an omission?

Could the French government have ordered the omission? On the grounds that they didn't want it to be known, in history, that a French national was partly responsible—even though innocently—for the killing of Princess Diana?

As gigantic a thought as this is, it makes sense. Is the whole sordid affair, the death of three people in a tunnel, that bad, or that serious, to warrant such shenanigans?

Or is there another reason for constantly and persistently expunging the name and car details of the Fiat driver from the public and police records? I long ago wondered what lays between the lines of this intriguing story that we don't know, yet? Or are not allowed to know.

CHAPTER FIFTEEN

As a journalist, I had been investigating Diana's story—in one way or another—for years. So much of what I had discovered would sync up perfectly with what Colin McLaren had discovered that had been overlooked.

So, we did what we had to do. We went back to Paris. We went back to confront the one man who had the answers. The one man who has never spoken publicly: Le Van Thanh. The French police had dismissed him as a player in the tragedy owing to an intact taillight (but if he could respray his car, he could surely replace a taillight). Operation Paget barely mentioned the Fiat, and Metropolitan Police Commissioner Lord Stevens claimed the driver would be impossible to track down. Yet that was precisely what we did.

Colin and I went to Paris to find answers to the one of the most elusive questions in modern-day history: why, how, and by whom Princess Diana was killed. We were supported by Aaron Tinney, a top-notch reporter from *The National Enquirer* who had been doggedly attempting to get answers to this elusive mystery for the previous two years and had broken ground in uncovering new information. We were also joined by local photojournalist Pierre Sue.

Together, we journeyed to where Le Van Thanh lived, about an hour outside of Paris.

By this point, we had no doubt whatsoever forensically that Princess Diana's car was hit by another car, seconds—a millisecond or two—before it went out of control . . . or was caused to go out of control. The other car has been proven through paint sampling to be a Fiat Uno. A huge search for Fiat Unos all around Europe, particularly in and around Paris, was able to identify that the car in question was owned by Le Van Thanh—the French national of Vietnamese ethnicity. He and his family were living in Paris; he was a security guard working in Paris.

His father was approached by the media back in 1997, and he admitted that his son came home that night panicking and decided to change the color of his car from white to red.

The painting was done sloppily and hastily. What happened for Le Van Thanh to cause him to do such a shoddy job on his little Fiat Uno, and to do it immediately after the night Diana was killed?

In the twenty-two years since Diana's death, no private investigator or journalist in the world had spoken to Le Van Thanh—except for Colin, albeit not on tape.

Colin had forced a conversation with him in the driveway of his home. We were going back to that driveway now—the same home Colin had previously visited. Was there a reason for his reticence, other than not wanting to be known to history? Was he as innocent to the whole thing as Princess Diana herself was? She was just driving along in a car; her car of course was in the hands of professionals who had made all the errors.

Colin heartily agreed with me that this trip to see Le Van Thanh needed to be made.

What has been initially frustrating to McLaren is the comparatively quick and cursory way the scene of the accident was cleaned up. Then they swept up and hosed down the crime scene and opened it back up to traffic within four hours. None of this made any sense according to crime-scene principles and procedures.

When Colin first analyzed the crime scene, he cast his net much wider to include a large part of the approach road. The Alma underpass is a dangerous construction. Just before the tunnel, an on-ramp merges from the right. Then the road drops sharply down a hill that veers 15 degrees to the left. The French police focused their investigation on a 60-yard section of the road inside the tunnel.

Colin's work paid off. He found new compelling evidence the police had missed in their hurry to reopen the tunnel. When Colin tried to share his findings with the French police, they were unreceptive. Now, he shares them with us.

The dominant theory at the time—the one upon which the French police operated—is that the paparazzi harassed the Mercedes all the way to the Alma tunnel, three-quarters of a mile away. That their camera flashes blinded the driver and made him crash.

Witnesses said they saw motorbikes pursuing the Mercedes on the chase. And yet when the police arrested the paparazzi after the crash, they found no photographs of the speeding Mercedes in their cameras. How is that possible?

"On the roadway, I found two parallel skid marks, just over seven meters long," Colin mused to me. "They looked very fresh and, of course, my first question was were they from a Mercedes-Benz? So, I measured them. I photographed them. And then I looked for somebody that could help me."

To find out how the paparazzi actually behaved, Colin next tracked down the first police officer to arrive at the crash site.

He found that there were perhaps ten photographers who arrived shortly after the crash. There is no evidence that they got in the way of the EMTs, and no evidence they caused the crash.

This then points Colin to consider the lone motorcyclist with the flash. . . and the white Fiat.

Colin knows that the Mercedes outran the paparazzi long before it reached the Alma underpass. Yet just outside the tunnel it is forced to brake hard. But none of the investigations so far have explained why. His review of witness statements taken during the French investigation shows him that one saw what made the Mercedes brake so suddenly.

As Colin shared with me, "What's interesting about [the witness observations] is that they hear the screeching of tires before the Mercedes enters the tunnel. That must be the braking that certain witnesses talked about in this area. And also it must be related to the seven-yard-long skid marks that I found. None of these witnesses saw what made the Mercedes brake so suddenly or what made it crash. None of them saw a small white car entering the tunnel, though two people did see it racing out of the underpass just after the crash."

The skid marks now look very sinister. Colin reviewed statements from witnesses who say they saw things in the tunnel that could be seen as a deliberate attack. Another witness in a vehicle some way behind the Mercedes sees something very similar.

This other witness found by Colin, who wishes to remain anonymous, told him, "There was an intense flash of light followed by something hitting something, a bang. And then screeching."

Colin does not believe that the car carrying Diana had had its brakes tampered with. He believes they were depressed on purpose by the driver.

A motorcycle was in proximity, and there was a flash.

Does this finally explain the mysterious skid marks at the top of the hill?

Colin thinks it does, telling me, "I believe the Mercedes and the Fiat collided 60 yards before the tunnel—where I found the skid marks. From here, using the forensic principle that every contact leaves its trace, I've plotted step-by-step what happened to the car that was carrying Diana."

Colin has worked out what the Mercedes did in those missing seconds between leaving the paparazzi behind and its fatal end in the Alma tunnel. But what made Henri Paul lose control of the car outside the tunnel?

A light vehicle like the Fiat Uno. This is where the elusive white car enters the frame once more. From the on-ramp on the right. Diana's driver Henri Paul slams on the brakes. But at over 100 mph after seven yards, the ABS system unlocks them. He tries to avoid the Fiat but clips its rear left taillight and scrapes along its side.

Paul misses the bend in the road and rockets straight ahead. Directly in front of him is a wall. What happens next is incredible. Traveling at 104 mph, the car went over the ridge of the hill. Even if it is airborne for a second, at that speed, that car will cover over seventy feet. And the wall is closer than that. At the bottom on the road surface, Colin finds east-west gouges and also scallop marks, semicircular marks, indicating a wheel rim had hit it. This right-end tire, it was the only tire that had a tear or a cut in it, probably three or four inches long.

The Mercedes hits the thirteenth pillar, then ricochets across the road and slams into the tunnel wall where it comes to rest facing the way it came. The motorcycle disappears. Likewise, the white Fiat Uno disappears from the tunnel, leaving a host of unanswered questions and prompting a massive search for it.

Then, something very telling happens. After eliminating Le Van Thanh, the French authorities stop searching for the car and its driver. And no reason is given.

Initially, Colin wondered whether the reason they stopped searching is because they found the white Fiat they were looking for. This, however, has been revealed not to be the case. But if this is the situation, then why is the Fiat quickly eliminated from the investigation?

This now becomes the toughest question of all. More suddenly than seemed possible, we were ready for our confrontation in Van Tranh.

***

DETECTIVE'S NOTEBOOK.

DATELINE: 2019. Revisiting the Crime Scene

It would be almost four years before I returned to the scene of the crime, or, to be more correct, the Alma tunnel. Despite the time lag, I still thought of the sad motorcar accident often, and all its twists and turns. Even though I obsessed over it at times, my biggest problem was that I held no official office, I had no authority to investigate the incident or demand documents or facts. I had long been an ex-cop, having resigned from my own police department, and was now busy making documentaries in the field of true crime and cold cases. My current work commitments saw me head back to Paris again in June 2019. A media executive in America, Dylan Howard, had read my books and was highly complementary on my thoroughness, my eye for investigative detail. He was picking his own way through the death of Princess Diana, and I was impressed with his investigative know-how and desire to cast aside the crap and find the truth to one of the world's great mysteries. He was also producing a podcast on the death of Princess Diana and asked if I could play a role. He got me at "play a role." I was on an aircraft in double-quick time. Any reason to have another dip at trying to unravel this enigma of a puzzle. And, besides, gumshoeing Paris with Dylan Howard seemed like an earnest thing to do!

Upon arriving in Paris, Dylan and I were introduced to our fixer, which is the name of a production assistant that runs around attending to our needs, like finding equipment, chasing down a person that might help us, or driving us to a location. We were blessed with a fixer who was born in and lived in Paris: Pierre.

Not only did he know Paris like the back of his hand, but we would also learn that he was once a fast-moving paparazzi photographer. More so, he was one of the paps that lay in wait, out front of the Ritz Hotel, trying to second-guess what time Princess Diana and Dodi were going to leave the Ritz, and by what route.

Pierre had an added bonus to his background: he was part Vietnamese, by ancestry. Although he had never been to Vietnam, his ethnicity niggled away at me, as one of the things Dylan and I wanted to do was try and force another chat with the part-Vietnamese Le Van Thanh.

I would learn that Pierre was part of the chase to follow Princess Diana once she left the Ritz. Trouble was he fell for the two-card trick and followed the decoy car from the hotel that took he and his paps colleague (we'll call Alain) to Dodi's plush apartment at the high end of the Champ Elyssa, just near the Arc de Triomphe. Most security details run decoys, to throw the paps off their scent, and this time half of the paps fell for the trick. As we know, the other half chased the Mercedes from the back door of the Ritz and along the Cours Albert to the tunnel, and the rest is history.

But, with Pierre and Alain, they were oblivious to the tunnel accident as they arrived at Dodi's apartment and tried to work out what had happened. Then, as they milled around, out the front of the apartment building, they noticed the building security guards were acting oddly, and taking urgent calls on their mobile phones. Pierre had the cunning to get in close to them and hear what was being discussed. He heard that there had been an accident in the Alma tunnel, a short distance away, but no one was sure if it involved Dodi and Princess Diana. The uncertainty grew as time ticked over, mainly because Dodi was supposed to arrive at his apartment with Princess Diana some thirty minutes earlier. Pierre had been a pap a long time and didn't hold much store for coincidences. A missing princess and an accident nearby? The pap answer was clear. He grabbed hold of Alain and they jumped back onto their motorcycle and headed toward the Alma tunnel, the supposed site of the supposed accident.

It would be forty minutes since the accident that Pierre and his colleague parked their motorcycle at the crash scene and observed hell breaking loose in the world of billionaires and royalty.

The approach road was a sea of confused people and emergency workers trying to act unconfused. Pierre instantly set his eyes on the photographic potential and with camera in hand ran down the approach road and to the tunnel entrance, in search of a front-page picture. What he saw would be indelibly etched into his mind: the mangled Mercedes, twisted beyond recognition and swarming with medics as heat and stream seeped from a ruined engine. There was a lone uniform cop at the entrance of the tunnel who barred access to Pierre, who could just stand and watch the end result of mayhem. Against the far tunnel wall stood seven fellow paps, lined up in an unruly way, a cop was taking their details. Within minutes Pierre had decided to retire his camera for the night; it was obvious death had come to pay a visit to the paparazzi and Princess Diana show.

Little did Pierre register but Alain—who he last saw parking his motorcycle—was having more of an active time back at the approach road to the tunnel. As Pierre and Alain got off their motorbike, they observed a police speed camera on a tripod, mounted on the center median strip that divides the Cours Albert fast moving roadway with the slower-moving merge lane. The camera was pointing at the cars approaching the tunnel. Both paps recall the flash of the speed camera light, going off as cars approached and were (obviously) caught on film speeding. There were two uniform cops standing at the tripod as Pierre raced down to the tunnel. Alain, unsure what tragedy lay ahead, decided to take out his camera and photograph the two uniform cops at the speed camera. They appeared to be dismantling the tripod, however the pap saw the camera flash a couple more times. Then something extraordinary happened. Upon seeing Alain taking pictures, both uniform cops ran toward the innocent paparazzi, who reacted by fleeing. The fitter cops pounced upon him after a short chase. They then, without any justification, set about punching him around the face and head, as they grabbed at his camera and film bag. What happened next defies logic. The cops them confiscated the film footage and all Alain's other film rolls and camera and told the photographer to move on, which he did, thankful to be free of the violence. At this point Pierre had returned to the area and saw his colleague's bloodied face and clear signs of a beating and the cops walking away with the speed camera and tripod, as well as Alain's films and camera. Alain was too fearful to challenge the cops. After all, it was Paris, and cops are not lightweights.

What fascinates with this vivid account is twofold. Firstly, in the days that followed the accident there were many conspiracy theorists stating international spies were responsible for the killing of Princess Diana. To prove their wild propositions they used an alleged—and innocuous—sighting of a strange and bright flash. Suggesting a flash was used to blind the eyes of the Henri Paul, the drunken driver of the Mercedes. Obviously, here was the flash. On a tripod, catching speeding motorists.

The second and more worrying aspect of the flash of light relates to speed. The speed the Mercedes was doing. My automotive engineer went to great lengths using his state-of-the-art computer equipment to "prove" the exact speed of the Mercedes, seconds before it smashed into the thirteenth pillar. Yet, it appears the French cops had their own proof of speed, on the camera film inside the speed camera, pointed at the Mercedes-Benz as it hurtled adown Cours Albert, heading for death. There could be no doubt, from what the paparazzi twins told me, that the speed camera was working and captured at least one or more images of a crazed Henri Paul racing along the roadway.

So, what happened to those images? And, why did the French cops want to dismantle the speed camera at that exact moment? But, more troublesome, why did they set upon Pierre's colleague and brutally assault him before seizing all his pictures? Possibly pictures proving the existence of a working speed camera?

From an evidentiary point of view, the speed camera would corroborate Vincent Messina's assessment of speed. And my own assessment was in line with Vincent's. It would also make a mockery of the official police estimate that the Mercedes was traveling at a speed of only 60 mph, or 100 kph. (This speed estimate was given to the media some months after the accident.) All nonsense when you look at the damage suffered by the Mercedes. A car with such horrendous damage must have been traveling at a ridiculously fast speed. So why the absurdity of 100 kph? Especially when there was photographic evidence to the contrary.

The images in the speed camera never formed any part of the official investigation or outcome. Why not?

It was Pierre's recollection of the speed camera calamity that made me wonder if some of the madcap conspiracy theorists were correct. Insofar as, did the French cops play some underhanded role in the causation of death of Princess Diana and her companions? While I am not a conspiracy theorist in any shape or form, I couldn't help but wonder about the rationale of the two cops being caught dismantling an active speed camera at the scene where the world's most popular woman had lost her life at the hands of a imbecilic Frenchman riddled with booze and drugs. As I have said before: odd place, Paris.

Another reason why the speed camera images would be telling, and help understand the accident, must be mentioned. As the speed camera undoubtedly took image(s) of the speeding Mercedes, it would have certainly taken many images of the speeding paparazzi on motorcycles as they too raced toward the tunnel in pursuit of their prey. They were only a short distance behind. It would have been interesting to view these paparazzi images and see how many motorcycles were in chase and what the paps were really up to.

Were they too close to the Mercedes?

Were they doing anything illegal?

Were there others—unknown motorcycles or cars—in the pack of paps chasing Princess Diana?

More importantly for me, was it possible to see the slow-moving white Fiat Uno approaching the Cours Albert merge lane. And, as police know, speed cameras are a great source for catching a good photograph of the driver of a car. We will never know!

My luck in catching Le Van Thanh for a chat was still working as Dylan and I headed out to his house in an outer suburb of Paris. He lived in the same big house, with the same long driveway, and as it turns out the same weeds and renovation materials that were scattered about. Clearly a busy man. After a touch of uncertainty, after pressing the same gate buzzer, Le Van drove up in a gorgeous late model Mercedes-Benz and parked on his driveway, gates now open.

As he stepped from his car I immediately noticed how much more muscular he had gotten since we talked four years earlier. He and I shook hands again as we recalled our past chat. Pierre acted as translator this time and set about asking Le Van if we could talk. Le Van was disinterested. But not disinterested enough to refrain from smiling constantly.

Dylan and I tried to win over Le Van by explaining that we were not filming and had no cameras, we just wanted to talk. Of course, I was wearing a microphone and Le Van looked at my microphone lead and smiled. By way of softening the scene, Pierre told Le Van that I had a personal viewpoint that he (Le Van) was innocent, another victim in the accident that claimed many lives. Le Van Thanh said, “You don’t listen . . . there’s nothing to worry about.” He seemed mighty confident. We persevered.

I asked him why he needed to paint his car from white to red so quickly, to which he replied, “The police report, they know why I repainted it.”

When asked for an actual reason all he would say was, “When you have no money and you have a damaged old car, what do you do?”

We knew that his bother helped him repaint the car, just after the Diana accident, so I figured that he was referring to his brother helping him, presumably at no cost. This dovetailed with what his father was reported to have stated, that Le Van came home and seemed worried and immediately set about repainting his car, from white to red.

I knew Le Van would only give me a few minutes, so I shifted the subject to his lack of assistance with the police from England, who opened their own task force inquiry and tried to get Le Van Thanh to assist. Le Van then dropped a bombshell, as he once did previously, talking to me, four years earlier. He said, “You know what the French police told me? Not the same law as in France, don’t go there . . . don’t go there [to England]. It’s the police, which means they don’t agree with each other.”

It was this comment that shone a light on Le Van Thanh. He seemed supremely confident as he told us that the French police instructed him to not assist the English police into their probe into the death of Princess Diana. The French police telling a crucial witness to not assist a lawfully constructed investigation? I was gobsmacked. And of course Le Van, in an act of déjà vu, from four years earlier, never bothered to claim his innocence in the car accident that killed Princess Diana. Not once did he say that we were barking up the wrong tree.

And with that the smiling Le Van Thanh pressed his remote-control button, and the big steel gates shut us out. Just as Le Van had shut out the world from any knowledge he might have had, to unravel one of the great mysteries of the twentieth century.

Within minutes Pierre was driving back to Paris with a silent Dylan and myself back into the city of lovers. Not a sound was heard for at least the first fifteen minutes as we rolled over the comments of Le Van Thanh, coupled with what happened to Alain at the speed camera, and the saga of the flashing light. Then, as if on que, Dylan and I turned to each other and said the exact same words: *"What the fuck are the French trying to cover up?"*

Collectively, we were at a loss. A loss as to why the French cops seemed to go all out to stymie any attempt to identify who was involved in an accident that killed Princess Diana and her companions.

Or was it no accident, after all?

I knew well the historical animosity that festered between the English and the French, pettiness that went back much further than the dark days of the swashbuckling battle of Waterloo. But, in modern times, when the world and billions of eyes were on Paris, with newshounds picking over every facet, would the French want to upend any genuine attempt to discover what happened in a dirty, poorly designed, underlit tunnel that ran along the Seine, past medieval footings, all the way out to the cheese country of Normandy?

Only the French would know. I don't. Or at least I can't prove it.

***

Here is the full transcript of the exchange between Le Van Than, Colin, and Dylan:

Translator: They're doing a podcast and writing a book, actually, on the show, and they want to exonerate you.
Le Van Thanh: Oh no, that's okay.

Translator: The idea was to exonerate you, and show that you are a victim in all this.
Le Van Thanh: But I am exonerated; I don't care, to be honest.

Translator: They were just trying to exonerate you in this story. That you didn't do anything; you're really a victim (of circumstances).
Le Van Thanh: Yes, but I know I didn't do

anything. That's why I don't need to be exonerated, sir.

Translator: Well, let me explain—they came from far away; they took the plane from Australia to come here.
Le Van Thanh: Yes, I know. Yes, but they shouldn't have bothered.

Translator: Couldn't you just talk for a couple of minutes?
Le Van Thanh: No.

Translator: You have nothing to say?
Le Van Thanh: Yes, I have nothing to say.

Translator: No one is accusing you here, pay attention. That's what I'm telling you.
Le Van Thanh: No, but you don't listen. I know, there's nothing to worry about.

Translator: It was just to exonerate you through new evidence. They just have a question or two to ask you. Don't you want to answer them?
Le Van Thanh: No, no.

Translator: Definitely not?
Le Van Thanh: Definitely not.

Translator: He (Colin) says he has read all the police reports and that you are innocent.
Le Van Thanh: But people say otherwise, but that's okay.

Translator: Yes, he talked to witnesses who you saw that night; and you are completely innocent, and you have nothing to worry about.

Le Van Thanh: I know that, sir. That's why I don't even need to talk to them, if they know. I know that. We're all happy; we all know it. But then again, I don't mind at all. People can think what they want.

Translator: Yes, no, that's right. But . . .

Le Van Thanh: Because you know, you are Vietnamese, I am a Buddhist.

Translator: Yes, I know.

Le Van Thanh: That's why I let them think what they want.

Translator: Oh, yes.

Le Van Thanh: They imagine everything they can imagine, it's not my problem.

Translator: Okay. There's just one thing on his mind, you're completely innocent, but you repainted your car. That's what he doesn't understand. It's the only thing.

Le Van Thanh: Yes, it is. That was mentioned in the newspaper and so on. You can read it everywhere.

Translator: But what was the story then?

Le Van Thanh: I said it from the beginning.

Translator: And why did you repaint it?

Le Van Thanh: I will not repeat the same thing.

Translator: If you have already said it, you can say it. I don't know anything about it.

Le Van Thanh: Last time—the people they were filming me and everything—

Translator: But now you're not being filmed, you can clearly see, you're not being filmed.
Le Van Thanh: No, I don't know. I'm not looking. Everyone knows that. The police report, they know why I repainted it.

Translator: But then, why was that, what was the reason? That's right, actually what messed things up. I don't know if . . .
Le Van Thanh: When you have no money and you have a damaged old car, what do you do?

Translator: Okay. He just has one last thing to say to you. He's a really great cop. It's not a . . .
Translator: No, there is no problem. There were lots of things that were said to me again.
Translator: We are friends, I would like to tell you something. Are you listening? The English police is coming to see you soon. Because he, there is an English policeman who told him, they want to question you. They will come to see you, because when they asked you to come you didn't go.
Le Van Thanh: No, but I know they will come. Several times they told me they would come back. Because eventually they told me, "Yes, they will come." They wanted me to go to England.

Translator: Yes, that's right.
Le Van Thanh: You know what the French police told me?

Translator: No.
Le Van Thanh: "It's not the same law as in France; don't go there."

Translator: Oh, it was the French cops who suggested that you shouldn't go?
Le Van Thanh: Don't go there. He told me: "Not the same law as in France, don't go there . . . don't go there (to England) it's the police, which means they don't agree with each other. It's the police, which means they don't agree with each other, in other words."

Translator: They will come to you. He says, "If you need him, he can testify that you are innocent. Because he's a former police officer with a proven track record."
Le Van Thanh: Don't worry, I will receive them well.

Translator: Are you going to receive them well? [laughs]
Le Van Thanh: Yes, I will receive them well.

Translator: Yes, yes, they are in France, of course. No, no, they can't do anything anyway.
Le Van Thanh: I will tell them the same thing I told you.

CHAPTER SIXTEEN

"That's why I let them think what they want."

Of all the words spoken by Le Van Thanh during our confrontation with him, these are the ones that most haunt me personally.

Van Thanh knows he is a pawn. He knows that there are powerful forces capable of destroying his life. And he is not insane.

In this simple line quoted above, Le Van Thanh is telling us that he cannot do other than what he has done. He must allow the public to believe what they will, because the alternative is unthinkably dangerous.

Will he be killed for speaking the truth? Will his family? Will he find himself the victim of an "accident" just like Diana's?

All of these are clear possibilities.

It is also outrageous that a man should be telling us—pleading with us, really—to understand his situation in a certain way. . . and to have the institutions of the world turn a deaf ear.

Even if Le Van Thanh wished to tell us the truth, he feels that he cannot.

Surely this fuel demands for a new inquest to be opened on the tragic death of Princess Diana.

That is exactly the feelings of Mohamed Al-Fayed, who through his lawyer, Michael Mansfield QC, told our investigation that if it can now be shown Le Van Thanh was driving the white Fiat Uno, there is a genuine case to be made to reopen the inquest:

> There is a real question mark here because the French authorities were particularly anxious to ensure that it was blamed to the paparazzi.

> That's why they were all arrested to begin with. He (Le Van Thanh) had the car resprayed. It is very suspicious.
>
> If it's him in the tunnel—if it's his Fiat—whether it was an accident or whether he was trying to get in the way. I have no idea.
>
> The Mercedes obviously did hit the Fiat. Whether that was an accident by the driver driving too fast into the tunnel or whether the Fiat Uno was in the wrong lane, I can't take it beyond that. I don't know what part the Fiat Uno played other than it obviously had a role as a vehicle that was there. But whether the driver did this deliberately or not obviously, and what his background is, and why, all the rest of these other questions are in the same league as the [James] Andanson story.
>
> Witnesses have said it. It's not contrived. That's the concrete evidence. . . . What I'm more interested in is the sandwiching of the car. There are other drivers out there that have not been traced.

Likewise, former BBC royal correspondent Michael D. Cole (who after leaving the BBC, worked as director of public affairs for Harrods, and thus also as a spokesman for its owner Mohamed Al-Fayed) suggests our remarkable interview with Le Van Than should be passed to British and French authorities as part of a formal request to reopen the Diana inquest as a cold case inquiry.

> As a matter of urgency, this information should be conveyed to an officer of the court. If it is reported to the French police or the British police, then there will be the temptation, or the possibility anyway, that somehow the information will be buried.
>
> But first of all, Mohamed Al-Fayed needs to know about it, and then the proper authorities need to know about it, and then, given the possibility that this gentleman will actually make an affidavit, make a sworn statement, as to what happened to him twenty-one years ago, nearly twenty-two years ago, then other people than me can make a judgment about what to do.

> But it certainly is prima facie cause for a new thoroughgoing look at what went on, because if this was going on, what else was going on?

Mohamed himself declined to be interviewed but through another spokesperson wrote a letter stating:

> First, he [Mohamed] thanks you for giving him this opportunity to speak again on this subject and for couching your invitation in such pleasant and sympathetic terms. Second, he hopes he may decline your invitation in a similarly polite way without causing offence. The fact of the matter is that Mr. Al-Fayed spends his precious time with his family and therefore is not minded to submit to further interviews upon this very difficult subject for him and his whole family.

Yet there will always be those who simply wish the matter were closed. Many feel that opening an inquiry will do more harm than good. Those who take this position usually do so on the grounds that those involved have "suffered enough."

Take for example, the words of Tiggy Legge-Bourke, nanny and companion to Prince William and his brother Prince Harry and a personal assistant to Prince Charles between 1993 and 1999: "I think it's extremely hard on both the dukes. I wish everybody would just be quiet and let it all go to sleep," she reluctantly said when contacted for this book.

One can, perhaps, not entirely fault Leggy-Bourke. After all, it is very human to wish for unpleasant truths and disruptive secrets to simply "go away."

But that is what we cannot do.

***

Diana is frozen in the embers of our imaginations.

She is an iconic, tormented, long-legged blonde.

Like Marilyn Monroe, Diana never got to age beyond thirty-six. But twenty-one years after she became immortalized as a tender-faced English rose, those who loved the princess still can't help wondering how life would have played out for her if she had not died.

In closing, it is appropriate tribute to Diana—and also an important way of emphasizing precisely what was lost when she passed away—that we offer an account of what might have been. If we take things from her surviving the horrific wreck and disregard all the negative possibilities surrounding her untimely death, what could her life look like today? We imagine a future for Diana . . . one as a global human rights campaigner, lover, wife, mother of a future king, and doting grandmother.

Firstly, and to be quite abrupt about it, Diana would now bear a series of pink scars on her body and face after surviving the wreckage in Paris' Pont de l'Alma underpass. Her face—perhaps the most famous in the world—would have a bright mark ribboning from the side of her left cheek to her jawline to remind her, and the world, of how she could have been killed when she smashed her head into the front seats of her Mercedes S280 on August 31, 1997.

The gowns she wears in public would not show her cleavage, as Diana would want to cover up the thick scar tissue stretching from the top of her neck to close to her navel where surgeons at the Pitié-Salpêtrière hospital caved open her chest to massage her torn heart back to life.

Her scars are a reminder of something she never wanted to dwell on: the death of her Egyptian playboy lover Dodi. She would have spent years after the crash that claimed the lives of Dodi and their driver Henri Paul dwelling on what-ifs.

What if they had decided not to leave the Ritz and stayed at the hotel as Diana wanted?

What if she had extended her humanitarian visit to Bosnia to highlight the horror of land mines instead of going to Paris to see Dodi?

What if she had worn a seat belt in the back of the Mercedes that plunged into the thirteenth pillar of the Pont de l'Alma tunnel?

But despite spending years blaming herself for the heir's death, Diana has by now regained the twinkle in her eye. Much of her happiness stems from having found love again—and from seeing her two boys married, with her eldest William giving her three grandchildren. And as she moved into the modern era, Diana would have pared down and simplified her look—becoming a style icon like her idol Jackie Kennedy.

Her makeup would be simpler—aside from the foundation she used every day to cover her facial scar—and her beautiful hair would by now be straighter, longer, and blonder.

She would have reunited briefly with the heart surgeon lover who dumped her before she got together with Dodi. Being treated for follow-ups and consultations after her crash with Hasnat Khan would have provided her with the perfect opportunity to see the cardiac surgeon again.

But, despite Diana's dreams, she would have realized he was right about their romance having no future—as he wanted to remain anonymous, while she was still the planet's most photographed and followed woman.

By now, Diana would also have kept up a cordial relationship with Mohamed Al-Fayed, after weeping with the Harrods tycoon following Dodi's burial on August 31, 1997. While Mohamed continues to harp on about how the British establishment killed his son, Diana has moved on and is using her fame as a force for global change.

She would still be fighting for peace in war zones and acceptance for the diseased and homeless. She would ramp up her work with children's charities, continue to crusade for the homeless and attack difficult issues including HIV/AIDS. She would continue those unforgettable face-to-face visits and embrace those ailing and in need, the people to whom she dedicated her life. Organizations concerned with AIDS, leprosy, land mines, homelessness, drug addiction, and terminal illness all continue to receive huge boosts from her involvement.

Her work for the International Campaign to Ban Landmines was posthumously rewarded when the campaign won the Nobel Peace Prize in 1997—but had she lived, it's a prize Diana herself could conceivably have won had time allowed her to fully mature into the force for good she so clearly was capable of being.

And Diana would have found new charitable causes to help and promote. She would have campaigned against Britain leaving the EU—and the referendum may have gone against Brexit if she had been alive to share her opinions on the matter with the public who adored her. She would have joined #MeToo—sharing her opinions on her Instagram, Twitter, and Facebook pages.

Diana would have given high-profile interviews to tell how she had been a

#MeToo victim at the hands of cruel Prince Charles, who cheated on her while driving her to bulimia and suicide attempts by berating her over her weight.

And she certainly would have despised Donald Trump—joining marches against his visit in London.

Closer to home, she could initially have found both her sons' choices of wives formidable. Both Kate and Meghan were nothing like her when she joined "the firm"—whimperingly humble and scared behind her fringe and long lashes. Yet it was Diana's mission to modernize the royal family that led her boys to choose modern women as wives. And Diana would soon have reveled in their choices, seeing how dramatically her influence had altered the stuffy firm she despised.

Quickly, Diana would take Kate and then Meghan under her wing—advising them on how to play the media at their own game and ignore criticism against them. She would have supported Harry in his plea for the press to leave Meghan alone. She would have told trolls not to focus on Kate's post-baby body. And she would have loved sitting on the floor of her apartments at Kensington Palace, with William and Kate's three children crawling over her.

On the other hand, if Diana had lived, William and Harry may not have felt the need to choose Kate and Meghan as wives. Had she lived, William might have married someone with a showier pedigree, and with whom he had far less of a bond. After all, without the ache caused by missing his mother, he would not have needed the calm good sense and discreet loyalty of Kate quite so much.

Harry is more likely to have ended up marrying an actress. He would still have been the "Party Prince"—scolded harshly but lovingly by his mother for dressing as a Nazi in 2005, and calling one of his Asian Army chums a "Paki" four years later—and being photographed partying naked in Las Vegas in 2012.

Diana's own personal life would be far from empty.

Realizing she needed someone stable, it's likely she would have got together with a Silicon Valley–type tech entrepreneur due to her admiration of using media for her own ends. The couple would have had children—Diana always wanted more than two children, and yearned for a daughter.

But the world's most famous grandmother wouldn't be perfect. After leaving the royal family, she had already fallen into a lifestyle followed by Hollywood celebrities—full of hangers-on, beauticians, psychics, life coaches, and spiritualists. It's an obsession she would have carried on.

She would have had Botox and followed a beauty regime as extensive as Gwyneth Paltrow's to stay looking young—but would never have gone overboard as "elegance" was always the cornerstone of her look. For a woman with a history of bulimia, vanity was something she would never have shaken off.

Surviving the 1997 crash would also have given her the philosophical outlook to forgive Camilla for stealing Charles. She would also have made up with her estranged mother Frances, before she died from brain cancer in 2004. But Diana would have remained largely estranged from her former in-laws, Prince Philip and Queen Elizabeth, only nodding politely at them and exchanging pleasantries at social events and dinners.

At the point of her death, Diana was said to have been ready to launch herself, fully, as her own person on the world stage. She was loved, and she knew the power of being loved. She was inspired to use that love for good ends. Diana would have made her own place on the world stage, to the benefit of the unfortunate people she championed.

She would have adored Barack Obama, mistrusted David Cameron, giggled at Nicolas Sarkozy, and despised Vladimir Putin and Kim Jong-un.

An international style icon and humanitarian ambassador, she would split her time between homes in California, New York, and London.

By 2018, the memory of Dodi would be long faded and rarely asked about in interviews. Their summer romance of 1997 would have been as long gone as the tan she picked up sitting lonely and reflective on the diving board of Dodi's dad's yacht. And she would never have been spotted shopping at Harrods.

Yet there is much about which we do not need to conjecture, for Diana's impact can still be seen as a living testament today. Diana's missions to modernize the monarchy and improve the lives of society's outcasts lives on through her sons—and their wives. Meghan and Kate's new habit of shutting their own car doors on public engagements stems from Diana's vow to shake the stiffness out of the firm.

As Diana once declared, "I would like a monarchy that has more contact with its people." Her charity work that continues through her sons was the main way she became a queen of hearts.

Even though she found the media's intrusion into her personal life "intolerable," Diana knew she could use it as a force for good to shine a light on the causes and people who needed the attention most. She became a patron of more than a hundred charities, and, during her nonstop visits to hospitals, schools, and fund-raising galas, became renowned for spending hours talking to people and listening to their stories.

* * *

Even though that fairy-tale ending is not something we can enjoy in the real world, Diana's legacy is still living on in our present world.

Prince Harry continues to champion his mother's cause for a worldwide ban on land mines and is now a patron of The HALO Trust—an organization dedicated to protecting the livelihoods of those affected by war. In 2017, the British government pledged $131 million to Prince Harry's campaign against land mines, two decades after Diana helped bring the issue to global attention after wandering through a live minefield in Angola in 1997.

It was January 13, 1997, wearing blue jeans and a blazer, when Diana stepped into the throbbing heat of Luanda, the capital of Angola, after an eleven-hour flight to southern Africa from the UK. The country was reeling from a twenty-year civil war that had left at least nine million mines scattered on land amid a population of ten million. Angola's streets were populated with men, women, and children without legs, few of whom had wheelchairs or even crutches. Some 70,000 people had stepped on land mines and every 333rd citizen was an amputee—yet only a few hundred false limbs were fitted every month.

Diana met sixteen-year-old Rosaline, who had lost her right leg and the baby in her womb after being blasted by a mine. Then there was seven-year-old Helena, who had gone out to get water and stepped on a mine that blew out her guts. As a saline drip kept her alive while flies buzzed around her body, Diana came to the child and covered her with a blanket before talking softly to the child and stroking her hand.

Helena, who died shortly after the visit, asked afterward about Diana, "Is she an angel?"

Diana said at the time, "I'd read the statistics that Angola has the highest percentage of amputees anywhere in the world. That one person in every 333 had lost a limb, most of them through land mine explosions. But that hadn't prepared me for reality."

Just after Diana's walk through the minefield in Angola, 122 governments gathered in Canada to agree on a treaty banning the use of antipersonnel land mines. The Nobel committee awarded the campaign the Nobel Peace Prize, coupled with the name of the leading American campaigner, Jody Williams.

In the House of Commons, during the second reading of the Landmines Bill, in 1998, the British foreign secretary, Robin Cook, paid handsome tribute to Diana, Princess of Wales, for her "immense contribution to bringing home to many of our constituents the human costs of land mines."

Diana was not there to hear it. She was in her grave.

Harry's HALO Trust recently called for the world to become free of the weapons by 2025.

In 2016, the British sexual health charity Terrence Higgins Trust thanked Prince Harry when his live HIV test had a huge impact on public testing for the disease. It was similar to the moment in April 1987, when speculation around the virus was rife, and Diana was invited to open Britain's first AIDS ward at Middlesex hospital. A photograph, which made front-page news around the world, showed her shaking hands with HIV-positive patients without wearing gloves.

The move publicly challenged the notion HIV/AIDS was passed from person to person by touch and highlighted Diana's affection and compassion for people living with the disease. Gavin Hart of the National AIDS Trust said, "In our opinion, Diana was the foremost ambassador for AIDS awareness on the planet and no one can fill her shoes in terms of the work she did."

Harry took his 2016 HIV test live on Facebook to demonstrate how easy it is. Since the test, the Terrence Higgins Trust has reported a fivefold increase in orders of the self-testing kit to 150 orders a day.

Harry also created his own charity, Sentebale, founded in 2006 to help children living with HIV and AIDS in Lesotho. It means "forget me not"—named in honor of Diana.

To mark the tenth anniversary of Sentebale, Harry said, "My mother died when I was very, very young, and I didn't want to be in this position. Now I'm so energized, fired up, to be lucky enough to be in a position to make a difference."

Both William and Harry were taken by the princess to see the help offered at the homeless charity Centrepoint's shelters and, at the age of twenty-three, William followed in his mother's footsteps when he became patron of the good cause. He has also slept rough for nights with the homeless to promote the good cause and said, "My mother introduced that sort of area to me a long time ago. It was a real eye-opener and I am very glad she did. It has been something I have held close to me for a long time."

Despite relinquishing most of her charitable causes after her divorce from Prince Charles in 1996, Diana became patron of Centrepoint in 1992 and remained in the role until her death in 1997.

Prince Harry has promoted the mental health charity Heads Together that he founded with brother William and sister-in-law Kate by disclosing he sought counseling after enduring two years of "total chaos" while still struggling in his late twenties to come to terms with the death of his mother.

In a bid to help slash the stigma around talking about mental health and stop the scourge of young male suicides, the prince—aged twelve when his mum died—confessed he "shut down all his emotions" for almost two decades after losing his mother, despite his brother trying to persuade him to seek help.

Harry said, "I can safely say that losing my mum at the age of twelve, and therefore shutting down all of my emotions for the last twenty years, has had a quite serious effect on not only my personal life but my work as well."

Diana's impact—even from beyond her grave—has been incredibly powerful.

According to the Princess Diana Memorial Fund, set up in response to the donations that poured in at the time of her death, the general public and community groups donated some $44 million. By the time the Fund closed in 2012, it had awarded 727 grants to 471 organizations, and spent over $145 million on charitable causes.

In March 2013, The Royal Foundation of the Duke and Duchess of Cambridge and Prince Harry took over the legal ownership of the fund, ensuring any future income would be donated to charities.

Like Diana, and using Diana as her model, Meghan has declared her passion for humanitarian causes, and before her marriage to serve as a UN Women's Advocate for Women's Political Participation and Leadership and volunteered with the organization, One Young World. Her biography on the royal family website reads, "These early experiences helped to shape her lifelong commitment to causes such as social justice and women's empowerment."

The duchess is regularly seen with Harry at charity events, and the pair was recently spotted in London attending a gala performance of the musical *Hamilton* for the benefit of Sentebale.

It echoed Diana's constant support for the arts and charity. Her final public appearance before her death was on June 3, 1997, when she attended the English National Ballet's performance of Swan Lake at the Royal Albert Hall—the story of Odette, a tormented princess turned into a swan by an evil sorcerer's curse.

Diana also continues to be carved into a new generation's consciousness.

She will be immortalized next year with a statue, a musical, the Princess Diana Legacy Award ceremony and the Princess Diana Lecture on HIV. A statue of the princess is being created by a sculptor whose portrait of the queen appears on UK coins.

Princes William and Harry commissioned the statue of their mother in January 2017. They said in a joint statement about choosing artist Ian Rank-Broadley to produce the tribute for the grounds of Kensington Palace:

> It is clear the significance of her work is still felt by many in the UK and across the world, even twenty years after her death.
>
> Ian is an extremely gifted sculptor and we know that he will create a fitting and lasting tribute to our mother. We look forward to unveiling the statue, which will allow all those who visit Kensington Palace to remember and celebrate her life and legacy.

Rank-Broadley's most recognized work is his depiction of the monarch, which has been on all coins in the UK and Commonwealth since 1998. More recently, his bronze work depicting the realities of war became the focal point of the Armed

Forces Memorial at the National Memorial Arboretum, Staffordshire, when it opened in 2007.

A 2019 musical cowritten by Bon Jovi keyboardist David Bryan—simply titled *Diana*—has explored her life to rave reviews.

Shortly before her death in 1997, Diana was said to be considering a move to California, to start a new life with her sons. It's fitting, then, the show is being staged in Orange County. It is being held at the Mandell Weiss Theatre, which houses La Jolla Playhouse events and is located on the campus of the University of California San Diego.

Set in 1981, the year Diana married Charles, the majority of the musical will focus on Diana in her twenties, and explore her relationship with Prince Charles, his affair with Camilla Parker Bowles and Diana's relationship with the press.

The synopsis on La Jolla Playhouse's website reads:

> It's 1981 and the world is hungry for a royal wedding—but is the twenty-year-old bride prepared for what comes after? Following her fairytale union, Princess Diana faces a distant husband, an unmovable monarchy and overwhelming media scrutiny. But her modern perspective and remarkable compassion galvanizes a nation, even as it threatens the royal family's hold on England.

Diana's Tony Award–winning director Christopher Ashley said about the writers of the musical, "Among my favorite longtime collaborators are Joe DiPietro and David Bryan. Their new musical brings to the stage one of the greatest cultural icons in modern history, and I can't wait to share it with Playhouse audiences next season."

Three more major Diana events focused on her humanitarian work will also happen next year.

Created in the wake of the royal feeling hounded by the press, the Diana Award Anti-Bullying National Conference will focus on the princess's belief in young people's potential to change the world and take place during Britain's anti-bullying week in November.

The Diana Legacy Award ceremony recognized young people in May 2019 for their "extraordinary work in their local communities." Founded in 1999 in her memory, it is now an independent charity that offers mentoring services to young people and campaigns against bullying.

And in June 2020, the Princess Diana Lecture on HIV will be delivered in conjunction with the National AIDS Trust and the Elton John AIDS Foundation. Elton last year delivered the lecture at the Institut Français.

We know that Diana leaves behind a living legacy of hope. There is copious evidence of this fact. But one comes away, still, with a feeling of what has been lost, and of what might have been.

The media, the government, and—sometimes—even the royal family itself glorifies Diana. Every biography is a hagiography. Every remembrance is flattering.

But there was another Diana. A real and true person. Her power and magnetism was such that her vicissitudes moved governments and brought out the worst in nations. Like Helen of Troy, the power of her radiance had a darker side. It moved men to murder. And, in the end, they killed even her.

In the days and months ahead, as the McLaren investigation continues, an even fuller, more complete portrait of Diana will—for the first time—be possible. We will know the full truth behind the how and why. The granular details on the facts we know now will come even more sharply into focus.

We will see her as more fully human. More touchable and relatable. More like us.

We will also comprehend the horror of what it meant to have the crown figuratively hovering above her head, like a Sword of Damocles. (A sword that would go from hypothetical to very real.) Diana wanted the things that most women in her place would want. She wanted freedom to make her own choices. She wanted love and excitement. And she wanted to help others whenever she could.

And for this, she was killed.

The glamorous circumstances that thrust her into the light and made her probably the most famous woman in the world also became her prison. And as she fought against the press of the bars, the prison grew tighter and tighter around her. Even divorce could not save her. Perhaps, in the end, nothing could have. By the time Diana knew what was happening—and what the stakes were—run though she did, she could not outrun the world's most powerful forces.

And when we do know more, we will finally be able to appreciate her as a woman in full. To know the full truth of her story. We will understand the length and breadth of what we done to her, and what it means for the institutions we supposedly trust and revere.

And then everything will change.

To honor the memory of Diana, it has to.